Metacognition in Young Children

Metacognition is known to be an important factor in academic achievement but it is also important in a wider life context. The ability to reflect upon how we are thinking can help us to make wiser decisions in all aspects of our life.

This book addresses how metacognition might be fostered in young children. Examining theories of particular relevance to primary school age children, the author combines her empirical work over the last 8 years with the work of other researchers to show that children of all ages display metacognitive processing, given the right kind of environment. Drawing on evidence from psychology and education, *Metacognition in Young Children* brings together international research from different curriculum areas. As well as the traditional areas of science, mathematics and literacy, the author considers metacognition in physical education, information and communications technology, art, drama and music. The book argues for a development of metacognition theory which takes account of wider contextual and political factors. This book includes:

- real classroom examples, taking account of the whole child, socio-cultural context and the curriculum;
- practical examples of developing metacognition across the curriculum;
- advice on building metacognitive environments in the classroom;
- development of metacognition theory.

Essential reading for educational psychology and research students, this book will also appeal to trainee and practising teachers with an interest in facilitating young children's development into wise and thoughtful adults. It offers practical advice supported by theory and evidence, and presents new ideas for the future direction of metacognition research.

Shirley Larkin is a lecturer at the Graduate School of Education, University of Exeter.

Metacognition in Young Children

Shirley Larkin

Routledge
Taylor & Francis Group

LONDON AND NEW YORK

First published 2010
by Routledge
2 Park Square, Milton Park, Abingdon, Oxon OX14 4RN

Simultaneously published in the USA and Canada
by Routledge 270 Madison Avenue, New York, NY 10016

Routledge is an imprint of the Taylor & Francis Group, an informa business

Typeset in Bembo by Pindar NZ, Auckland, New Zealand
Printed and bound in Great Britain by TJ International Ltd.,
Padstow, Cornwall

British Library Cataloguing in Publication Data
A catalogue record for this book is available from the British
Library

Library of Congress Cataloging-in-Publication Data
Larkin, Shirley.
    Metacognition in young children / Shirley Larkin.
        p. cm.
    Includes bibliographical references.
    1. Critical thinking in children. 2. Metacognition in children.
    3. Cognitive learning theory. 4. Learning, Psychology of. I. Title.
    BF723.C5L38 2009 2010
    155.42'43—dc22   2009004476

ISBN13: 978-0-415-46357-7 (hbk)
ISBN13: 978-0-415-46358-4 (pbk)
ISBN13: 978-0-203-87337-3 (ebk)

ISBN10: 0-415-46357-2 (hbk)
ISBN10: 0-415-46358-0 (pbk)
ISBN10: 0-203-87337-8 (ebk)

For Henry, who changed my life, brought me
joy and inspired my thinking.

Contents

PART IV
New thinking

153

Acknowledgements

Many people have helped in the creation of this book, some more overtly than others. Sometimes the short conversations, the chance meetings, the brief exchange of ideas have provided me with new and different ways of thinking. So thank you to all colleagues and friends both inside and outside of education who have taken the time to listen, to challenge and to discuss ideas about thinking. In particular, I wish to thank the teachers and children I have worked with over the years for their valuable advice, patience and enthusiasm. Special thanks to the research teams from CASE@KS1 and Talk to Text for giving me the opportunity to investigate metacognition. Thanks also to Philip Adey, who took a chance and who has provided me with honest and critical support over the years. This book would not have been written without the work of John Flavell and Ann Brown whose ground breaking research has inspired many researchers and teachers. I have also drawn on research from a wide variety of sources and my thanks go to all the researchers working in this area, especially members of the EARLI SIG on metacognition, for continuing to inspire me. Finally, a big thank you to all those who have supported me through the writing process, the editorial team at Routledge and especially colleagues at Exeter University who have made space for me to write. I could not have completed this book without the support and love of special friends, so thank you to Bill, Trish, Sr. Stella and friends at Blessed Sacrament parish.

Part I

Metacognition in children and adults

Chapter 1

What is metacognition?

> It is at least conceivable that the ideas currently brewing in this area could someday be parlayed into a method of teaching children (and adults) to make wise and thoughtful life decisions as well as to comprehend and learn better in formal educational settings.
>
> (Flavell, 1979, p. 910)

What is this area? This area which can help people to understand better, to learn better, to achieve better academic results and for me, the most important part – to make "wise and thoughtful life decisions"? When John Flavell wrote this in 1979 he was giving a name to a process of thinking which we all engage in at sometime, but which we rarely sustain long enough to gain the benefits from. Flavell was referring to the process of reflecting on our own thinking and keeping track of how our thinking is getting us closer to or further away from our goal. The term "metacognition", which Flavell and his colleague Ann Brown gave to this type of reflection has led to a whole new area of research and the fruits of these studies are now being seen in classrooms across the world. At the same time though, the word metacognition has sent some people running for the hills. When I ordered a book recently with the "M" word in the title, the book shop assistant checked the title with me at least half a dozen times as she tried to track down my order. Every time she asked a colleague, she would turn to me again and say "What was it called again?" When I proposed the title for this book some colleagues suggested that using the "M" word in the title would put readers off all together and I should make it more reader friendly by using phrases such as "higher order thinking" or "reflective thinking". Why did I stick to my guns about the title? Well, the term metacognition, while a bit unwieldy, is specific and identifies a particular process of a shift in thinking. "Meta" refers to a change of position, a sense of going beyond or to a second order or higher level, and "cognition" refers to our faculty of knowing or thinking. So the "M" word describes a higher order of thinking, one that is reflective and goes beyond the ordinary level to reflect on thinking itself.

An example will clarify the distinction between the different levels of thinking. I may think "I will stop for a cup of tea now", an ordinary level thought, but if instead of immediately acting on that thought, I stop and take a little time to reflect, I might think about why I had that thought in the first place. Is my body telling me that I am dehydrated? Or do I have an internal body clock which is tuned into sending me certain signals at certain times of the day? Perhaps the reason for my thought was not related to thirst but to feeling tired or bored or stuck or even in need of a reward for having done some work today. From any one of these thoughts I could follow where my own thinking leads. I may become interested in any one of a number of areas from philosophy to neuroscience and biology. I might choose to pursue one of these areas and start an internet search, or I might choose to ignore all these thoughts and return to writing this chapter. On the other hand I might act on this thought and make a conscious decision to stop and make tea. Becoming aware of all the different thoughts which might lie behind my initial thought means that I have shifted my position from the ordinary level of thinking to thinking about the thought itself; why I had that thought, how it was linked to my biology, emotional state or psychology, and then to make a conscious decision about what to do about the thought. At the same time, while writing this, I have been partially monitoring that initial thought and occasionally checking back in to see if I still really want a cup of tea or if the moment has passed. From the initial fairly ordinary thought, I have been on a thinking journey about the thought itself and have brought my past knowledge about myself, about what a cup of tea would do for me and about whether I want to stop what I am doing to make one to bear on my decision to wait a little while longer and then have a proper break.

All of this second order thinking, or thinking about the thought itself, is metacognition. I hope you can see that from one very simple thought I could shift my thinking position in order to reflect on the thought and make a good decision, at least a decision that is right for me at this time. So, if one thought as simple as "I want a cup of tea" can lead to thoughts which might fire my curiosity about many subjects that I don't know about, might motivate me to learn something new or as in my case keep me centred on the task I'm engaged in, then you can see that the power of using metacognition in educational settings is vast.

In everyday life, particularly in social situations, we may make this shift in thinking quite often; for instance how many times have you reflected on why you said something to somebody, or why they seem to think that about you, or whether they know that you know that they know etc. In general, however, in our educational settings we are not encouraged to reflect in this way. The aim of many teachers is to keep children on task, solving the maths problem, writing the story or practising one of the several very necessary skills children need to acquire for life outside of school. The aim of many children is to complete the work as quickly and as successfully as possible. The rewards for this may be a chance to play, or at least not to have to do the work again, or some form of praise from the teacher. It is not only children who think this way, many adults too aim to complete their work as quickly and efficiently as possible so that they can go and do something more enjoyable or so that they can gain their hard earned reward more quickly. Unfortunately, metacognition doesn't fit into this way of working very well. It can lead to more efficient and thus quicker ways of working, but it also entails a slowing down of the process of thinking. However, the rewards can be increased motivation and interest, maintaining on task behaviour and developing skills and strategies, which enable us to transfer knowledge from one domain to another. Becoming more metacognitive is about slowing down and taking time to enjoy the thinking process, even to marvel at the ability we have to think about so many different things and to allow ourselves to follow our thoughts.

Time

> Sweet childish days, that were as long
> As twenty days are now.
> > William Wordsworth,
> > "To a butterfly" (1801)

It seems a common experience that we remember our childhood days as being long and slow; there was lots of time to play and do the things we liked. Yet if you sit in any primary school classroom these days you will find a day governed by time. Teachers are under pressure to cover the content of the different curriculum areas; to ensure that the children in their class learn the skills necessary to progress in our highly literate and numerate culture; to ensure that children develop a sense of themselves as citizens of a wider world; to instruct children about healthy ways of living and the value of exercise; to provide opportunities for children to develop their social skills and to provide knowledge and awareness of spiritual matters or religious faiths. All of this has also to be differentiated for different ability levels, to take account of individual needs and to be accomplished efficiently and within time allocated slots. Teachers and support staff can be forgiven for thinking that trying to facilitate metacognitive development among all of this is not feasible – there just isn't the time to do it.

Our schools and classrooms are microcosms of our world and the Western world is obsessed by time and efficiency. Adults are always busy. If they are not busy working, they are busy planning to go on holiday to get away from being busy. We pack so much into a week away, seeing sites, meeting new people, planning days out that it is not uncommon for us to come back from holiday and say that we need a holiday to recover from the holiday. This need to use time well and efficiently pervades our culture. In education, assessed outcomes can be the driver of how time is spent. It is not only children who are assessed on performance; teachers, schools and countries are also subjected to the same outcome led assessments in the form of national tests and league tables. The problem with facilitating the development of children's metacognition is that it takes time and it has no obvious assessed outcome. It is difficult to measure progress and there may be nothing tangible to show for the work you have put in.

Metacognition is often seen as the reflective part of a teaching session. If practised at all, it is usually in the final section of a lesson, where children are asked to reflect on what they have learned; to verbalise how they solved the problem; to evaluate how difficult or easy they found the work and to think about how they might tackle such a problem in the future. The time constraints of the curriculum can mean that it is particularly difficult to fit this reflective element into a lesson. Furthermore children are often reluctant to engage in meaningful reflection when the playground beckons.

Asking young children to reflect on their thinking after the event, without any training in how to do this, is unlikely to produce a metacognitive experience. It is difficult for any of us to recall what we were thinking about some time ago. In the case of small children, the ability to verbalise thinking is also an issue. This latter point is linked to an important debate in metacognition theory, the need for metacognition to be conscious.

Consciousness

Whether metacognition is by definition a conscious act or whether some forms of automatic processing can also be deemed metacognition is an issue still debated by metacognition theorists. Automatic processing has been defined as fast, requiring little effort and control by the subject and operating at a level below consciousness. Theory suggests it takes two forms. One that is not age reliant and which does not require any cognitive effort and a secondary form where some conscious behaviours become automated over time, with age and with practice (Brown, 1987). This second form is problematic for theories of metacognition because a cognitive act which was once included in the metacognitive repertoire may become automated and unavailable to consciousness. A good example of this would be in learning to read, where a good deal of conscious effort is initially employed in linking sounds together and understanding the connection between written symbols and sound. However, as this process becomes more automatic, there is less need for conscious reflection or conscious monitoring of the reading process, unless the reader hits a problem word. Then the reader has to stop or slow down and make a conscious decision on whether to re-read, use a dictionary or bypass the difficulty. So the cognitive skill of reading is subject to metacognitive monitoring but theorists differ in the extent to which they include this unconscious monitoring within metacognitive theories.

Automatic processing is unavailable to consciousness and so it cannot be voluntarily controlled. This is obviously beneficial, since we would get nowhere if we had to be consciously aware of all of our thinking, all of the time. Fast, automatic processing frees up working memory capacity as information is processed more quickly and transferred to long term memory, for future conscious retrieval. A slower processing of initial information, it has been argued, clogs up the system and information is lost before it ever reaches storage (Anderson, 1989, 1992). Some theorists suggest that metacognition can include processing which is "available to consciousness" rather than wholly conscious (Baker, 1994; Veenman *et al.*, 2002), however it is unclear what this would mean. Thoughts are either conscious or not; the fact that we can reflect on our thinking and perhaps bring automated cognition back into consciousness is not the same as being consciously aware of our thinking as it proceeds.

When we reflect, we are engaging our memory and our attempts to remember how we thought about something are likely to be an interpretation of what we actually thought at the time. I would argue that in order to develop metacognition, we must become aware of our thinking as it goes on, rather than relying on reflecting on our thinking after the event. Thus for me, metacognition has to be about conscious thinking about thinking, conscious monitoring and control of our thinking. It may be that when these cognitive skills are practised over time and in many different situations, aspects of metacognition may become automated, but in working with children or students with little or no apparent metacognitive processing, there is a need to be explicit and to model conscious metacognitive behaviour. It is certainly true that people may make decisions and reach conclusions about people or events unconsciously. However, if we are to take onboard Flavell's call for metacognition to help us to make "wise and thoughtful life decisions" it is necessary for us to be more conscious of *how* we are making decisions or reaching conclusions. This may not alter our decision but in becoming aware of how we came to make the decision we may learn something about ourselves and our decision making skills, which may benefit us in the future.

Language

In order to model metacognition we need a language which involves what are called mental state words, e.g. "know", "think", "believe", "guess", "remember". A good deal of research with children about their understanding of different mental state words has concluded that young children are not consistent in their use of these words and that understanding of them is a long process which continues throughout childhood. An important study by Wellman and Johnson (1979) investigated children's understanding of "remember" and "forget". They report that previous research suggests that "remember" is one of the earliest mental state verbs that children use. In their study, children of 3, 4, 5 and 7 years old were told short stories about a child character, an object and two hiding places for the object. The child was then asked a series of questions about the character in the story, including why he had looked in a specific place for the object and whether or not he had remembered where the object was. The researchers varied the stories so that in some, the character had no previous knowledge of where the object was, so could not remember or forget its location, only guess. This enabled the investigators to find out whether the children in their study actually understood the words or were just differentiating the words depending on whether the object was found or not. The results showed the words were first differentiated by the 4-year-olds but their use of the words was dependent on whether the object was found or not and not on whether the character had previous knowledge of where the object was. Only the 5 and 7-year-olds understood the link with previous knowledge and this understanding was more advanced for "remember" than for "forget". Wellman and Johnson conclude that understanding of these mental state verbs is a progression from relying on performance to make the distinction to an understanding of the cognitive states that the verbs relate to. More recent work by Lockl and Schneider has confirmed the developmental trajectory of understanding mental state words but has also concluded that while comprehension of mental state words is necessary for the development of understanding cognitive states, development of knowledge about cognition, specifically about memory, can also aid understanding of mental state verbs (Lockl & Schneider, 2006).

Studies such as these have important implications for helping children to develop metacognition. Developing children's understanding of the mental state words is important for developing metacognition, but this does not mean that we should restrict facilitating metacognitive development until this linguistic understanding has developed. Instead, use of different modes of communication such as visual and aural stimuli can be used to develop understanding of cognitive states and mental state words. I will return to these ideas in Part III.

Models and theories of metacognition

Arguably the most important theory of metacognition to date is Flavell's original conceptualisation. Growing out of his work on memory; the Piagetian legacy of the link between memory and intelligence (Piaget *et al.*, 1968); the work of Brown (1978); and studies such as Markman's on comprehension monitoring (1977), Flavell developed a model of metacognition which includes: metacognitive knowledge, metacognitive experience, goals (or tasks), and actions (or strategies) (Flavell, 1971, 1979).

Metacognitive knowledge is described as the stored knowledge about one's own cognitive states, about others' cognitive states or about the nature of cognition in general. Metacognitive knowledge also refers to an understanding of how different factors may interact to influence our own thinking. The Flavell model categorises these different factors into person, task and strategy groups. In the person group is our knowledge of ourselves and others as thinking beings, including that people think differently; that different people have different beliefs about thinking; that different people may be better at some tasks than others; and an understanding of how cognitive processes such as attention, concentration and remembering affect performance. The person category of metacognitive knowledge interacts and is linked with the task category.

The task category includes our knowledge about the task, e.g. is it similar to any other task we have done? do we have all the information we need about the task? and, given this knowledge, can we reliably predict our success or failure on the task? The strategy category of metacognitive knowledge includes knowledge about which strategies are useful to achieve our goals. A distinction is made between cognitive strategies which are directly related to doing the task itself and metacognitive strategies which are geared towards monitoring progress on the task and providing new strategies or new ways of thinking about the task in order to make progress. Flavell gives the example of studying for an exam, where you may monitor your progress by testing yourself; this he says is a metacognitive strategy aimed at assessing your own knowledge and monitoring your learning, but it may lead to a cognitive strategy of writing your revision notes in a different way. It can be difficult in real situations to differentiate between these two kinds of strategy use and it is clear from Flavell's model that all the categories are linked and interact with each other. It is this metacognitive knowledge which we can consciously retrieve from memory in order to perform a cognitive task. However, Flavell also acknowledges that this metacognitive knowledge which we build up over time, through experience and practice on different tasks, can also unconsciously affect cognition.

Flavell describes how the metacognitive knowledge base is developed from experience, in particular through metacognitive experiences. These may be conscious and arise from already stored metacognitive knowledge, e.g. remembering a strategy you used to solve a similar problem or they may be more emotional, for instance a feeling that you are stuck on a part of the problem. In order for these metacognitive experiences to be fruitful in developing the metacognitive knowledge base they must be worked through and not shied away from as too time consuming or too psychologically difficult. Only by providing children with opportunities to practise working through metacognitive experiences are they likely to develop a sound metacognitive knowledge base. Luckily, Flavell (1979, p. 908) described for us the conditions under which metacognitive experiences are most likely to occur

> in situations that stimulate a lot of careful, highly conscious thinking: in a job or school task that expressly demands that kind of thinking; in novel roles or situations, where every major step you take requires planning beforehand and evaluation afterwards, where decisions and actions are at once weighty and risky; where high affective arousal or other inhibitors of reflective thinking are absent.

While Flavell's work provided the basis for the theory of metacognition, the 1980s and 1990s saw a burgeoning of research on different aspects of metacognition and a development of more detailed theoretical models. Kluwe's work in the early 1980s was important in stressing self agency and executive control, i.e. that our thinking is under our own control (Kluwe, 1987). Borkowski's work throughout the 1990s showed how metacognitive knowledge could impact on motivation and self esteem. His detailed model defined the characteristics of successful learners and linked metacognition to self regulated learning. It describes how a child might first develop knowledge of learning strategies and through practice in multiple settings learn when and how to best use these strategies. Then the child begins to understand the link between the use of the strategies and successful outcomes and this begins to build their metacognitive knowledge of themselves as a learner. The model includes self beliefs, self worth and knowledge of possible selves as well as personal motivational states. Borkowski shows a reciprocal relationship between the use of strategies and a sense of self efficacy; thus making an important link between strategies, which can be taught, successful learning and self esteem (Borkowski, 1996).

Metacognition has also been included in larger theories of intelligence. In particular Sternberg's triarchic theory of intelligence describes three basic components of intelligent systems: metacomponents, performance components and knowledge and acquisition components (Sternberg, 1985). While the performance components execute the plans of the metacomponents, the metacomponents also feed back information, i.e. provide the monitoring and control function of the system and make decisions on the use of strategies to achieve success. In doing this, the metacomponents are also acquiring information about what works for particular tasks and this can be stored in memory for future use. Thus metacognitive knowledge about self, tasks and strategies is developed. A similar notion is used by Sanchez in a model of metacognition which involves not only consciousness and control but a third component called "self-poesis" (Sanchez, 1998). This component means that metacognition is not only conscious and exerting control over cognition, but is also creating itself through a kind of spiralling loop of feedback.

Metacognitive knowledge has been differentiated by a number of researchers into declarative, procedural and conditional knowledge (Brown, 1987; Schraw, 1998; Schraw & Moshman, 1995). This links metacognitive knowledge with theories of knowledge acquisition in general. Declarative knowledge is the knowledge that we can state about ourselves, about others and about the world. In terms of metacognition, this would equate with knowledge about ourselves and others as cognitive beings and our knowledge of how the mind works. Procedural knowledge is knowledge about how to do things. This may be our knowledge of different strategies or our knowledge of different skills. In terms of metacognition, this would include our reflections on particular tasks and how they relate to other tasks and to our knowledge and use of monitoring strategies. Research into how experts and novices solve problems has shown that experts do not only rely on superior knowledge about the subject to solve a problem, but also use different ways of framing the problem in the first instance. The researchers named these "surface" and "deep" strategies and suggested that it was experts' ability to reflect on themselves, the task and the strategies available that made a qualitative difference in their ability to solve the problem (Chi *et al.*, 1980).

Conditional knowledge is understanding when and how to use what we know, e.g. when to use different strategies such as committing facts to memory, making mind maps or writing notes, and when to draw on our past knowledge of similar situations. In terms of metacognition, conditional knowledge is linked to monitoring and control of our thinking. It enables us to use the feedback from monitoring our progress on a task to alter the way we are thinking about the task. Skilled problem solvers use metacognitive processes to monitor and modify their image of the problem as they go about solving it (Hayes, 1981).

One common experience that we all encounter when faced with a problem or a question is what researchers have called "feeling of knowing". It is thought that we are cued by aspects of the question to decide whether or not to search our own memory for an answer. This process may be completely automatic and while it is a form of monitoring, it is one that is not normally conscious. However, these feelings may exert particular influence on how we tackle a problem. For instance, experimental studies on students have found that when the researchers presented them with maths problems which contained information similar to earlier problems they had encountered, the students often believed they knew the answer to the new problem even though the new problem was of an entirely different kind. Thus, rather than analysing the problem properly and deciding on the best strategies to use to solve it, their rush to answer the problem was based on a mistaken belief that they had already met the problem before and simply had to use their memory to provide an answer. The similarity with the earlier problem had given them a feeling of knowing the answer (Reder & Ritter, 1992).

Research such as this shows us that while we may monitor our thinking, our monitoring may not be accurate. We can be confident that we are right about something, e.g. a feeling that we know someone's name if only we could retrieve it from our memory – what is called a "tip of the tongue" experience – when in fact we don't know their name, but something about them has cued us into thinking that we have met before. As well as these feeling of knowing states, researchers have also investigated what are called "ease of learning judgements" and "judgements of learning". Ease of learning judgements are predictions of how well we will be able to learn something, solve a problem or remember a list of facts, whereas judgements of learning are measures taken after completing a task and relate to how accurately someone can judge their performance. In both cases, young children have been found to be less accurate than older children and this ability increases over the elementary school years (Schneider, 1998). I will return to age related differences in Chapter 3.

Feelings and emotions play an important part in learning, but until fairly recently the research on metacognition has concentrated on the cognitive aspects rather than what is called the "affective aspect", i.e. how our feelings and emotions relate to our thinking about our own thinking. However, these feelings of confidence or doubt, interest or boredom, affect how we are likely to approach a task. Thus, they impinge on the metacognitive regulatory aspect of monitoring ourselves in relation to the task and informing how we proceed, or whether we just give up altogether. Our past experience with a particular task or situation can lead us to form judgements about ourselves under such conditions. So, presented with a similar situation we may have a metacognitive experience, i.e. we are conscious of experiencing particular feelings triggered by the task in front of us. Flavell (1979) suggested that metacognitive experiences may be fleeting, e.g. feeling puzzled for a moment or may be longer lasting, e.g. when you think hard about whether or not you really understand something. Metacognitive experiences can occur at any time and may be related to your progress towards a goal or may be more related to metacognitive knowledge, for instance when you suddenly remember how you solved a similar problem before. Metacognitive experiences are full of emotion and feelings and thus can be influenced by a person's mood. Recent work on the link between mood and metacognitive experiences has shown that a negative mood before starting a task is linked to feelings of difficulty during the task (Efklides & Petkaki, 2005). However, this may not be a bad thing as feelings of difficulty may result in investment of more effort and more high level thinking about the task. Also a positive mood may not have immediate effects on how a task is approached or progressed, although it tends to become clearer as problem solving continues. Thus a positive mood is linked to resilience and to maintaining interest.

While a great deal of research on metacognition since the 1970s has been based on information processing models and cognitive psychology, there is another strand of research which is particularly important for a wider understanding of how metacognition can help us to make "wise and thoughtful life decisions". This strand of research comes from social psychology.

Social psychologists have always been concerned with the self and how people develop self awareness. In addition there is concern with social relationships and how people understand each other, how social environments and cultures impact on our beliefs about ourselves and others. Agency, the idea of a self regulating person who acts intentionally in the world through planning, monitoring and evaluating her own behaviour is an important concept for social psychologists. In a seminal article at the end of the 1990s, three theorists made explicit the links between the field of metacognition research and social psychology: Jost, Kruglanski and Nelson (1998). They stated that metacognition is not only important for academic life, but that people are using metacognitive processing to make social judgements all the time and this is necessary for successful communication. However, as well as knowledge of others, they highlighted the role of metacognition in forming our own understanding of how our mind works. It is not a huge jump to see how a theory of ourselves as learners, which was formed in early childhood, can endure throughout our life with positive or negative effect. Thus we can form damaging and erroneous metacognition, which can be very difficult to alter. Similarly, people can form theories about themselves and others in terms of social competence or work, which may have more to do with their own thinking about such things as intelligence and cognitive skills than about the situation as it presents itself.

The social psychology dimension of metacognition research is particularly important because it addresses the situation – the social and cultural context of our metacognitive judgements. It acknowledges that how we think about our own thinking and how we develop metacognition about ourselves, others, tasks and strategies is dependent on the social and cultural context. Moreover, social psychologists argue that academic attainment is at least partially a result of the thoughts and beliefs we hold about our own and others' cognition. Most parents and teachers know that it can be very difficult to change someone's perception of themselves as "not good at …" or "not capable of …" We can get locked into perceptions of ourselves or others which constrain our relationships, whether that is in the intellectual arena or in the social world. Social psychology has provided an opening to an expansion of metacognition research which is important for the larger view of metacognition as important for life, as well as for educational purposes.

The development of work on metacognition from a social constructionist perspective has been particularly important for educational practice. Drawing on Vygotsky, the notion of metacognition developing from social interactions has linked metacognition to the broader issue of self regulated learning. So, in education, we are aiming not simply to teach curriculum subjects, but also to ensure that our students understand how to learn and to take responsibility for their own learning. Metacognition, both in terms of knowledge of self, task and strategies and in terms of monitoring and controlling our own thinking is crucial to the development of self regulated learning. The social constructionist perspective has highlighted the complex system of interactions between individuals and the environment which construct the metacognitive knowledge base.

Boekaerts (2002) likened the complexity of learning environments to a rainforest ecosystem. She showed how the interdependence of the plants in this dynamic ecosystem constructs an environment in which each individual is able to flourish and grow. The analogy leads to a call for a greater understanding of the structure of the learning system and how students interact and compete with each other, including an understanding of the self regulating processes that occur. Although the majority of thinking skills programmes which aim to facilitate the development of metacognition or self regulated learning take account of the socially constructed nature of knowledge, there is less systematic research on the complex interactions which specifically impact on metacognitive development. Some socio-cultural models of learning which take account of the different levels of contextual influence, such as the classroom environment, wider school issues and national educational policies have begun to make a mark on metacognition research, e.g. Thomas has contributed a number of studies to this area of work (Thomas, 2002; Thomas & Mee, 2005), but metacognition is still largely studied by psychologists rather than by educational theorists. Many studies of classroom interventions which either focus on metacognition or have metacognition as a part of their programme are concerned with the impact of metacognitive training on academic attainment.

While a growing number of studies consider social interactions and the impact of the learning environment on the success of the programme, few try to deconstruct the complex web of factors impacting on an individual's development of metacognition. A number of different approaches to metacognition research may need to be developed in order to come to a greater understanding of its nature and purpose. One strong contender for a new perspective on metacognition is the approach of critical social theory. A critical theory of education would include a deconstruction of current educational practices, a focus on existing ideologies and a move towards a pedagogy of social transformation and empowerment (Kellner, 2003). A theory of metacognition which encourages a process of reflection and self criticism, enables people to engage in dialogues about education, takes account of the needs of specific groups in specific situations and enables reflection on issues such as the relationship between learner and teacher is one that can be used in the service of constructing a more socially just and democratic education system.

A second approach to metacognition which is compatible with the first is a focus on the individual's experience of metacognitive processing. A research strand linking cognitive psychology and phenomenology has a long history in terms of understanding consciousness. More recently this interdisciplinary perspective has developed within qualitative research in psychology and education. A phenomenological approach to metacognition would focus on how the individual experiences her own thinking. Using phenomenological analysis can provide a detailed and contextualised picture of an individual's experience of such cognitive processes as remembering or a map of how an individual's awareness of her thinking changes throughout a task. These and other ways of thinking about how the study of metacognition may develop will be discussed in Part IV.

The aims of this book are to consider the factors which contribute and constrain the development of metacognition in young children; to relate the development of metacognition to life-long learning and to open up some new areas for the future of research into metacognition. Young children are defined as children from infanthood to age 11. In the UK this covers pre-school and primary school education. As a teacher, education theorist and mother I believe that by engaging in practices which facilitate young children in developing metacognition, we are encouraging empowered learners who are able to: take responsibility for their own learning; engage with others in meaningful ways; and make wise decisions for themselves and society. In Part II I consider the different projects that aim to facilitate children's metacognition across a range of curriculum areas.

While this book will focus on metacognition for learning, this is seen in its widest sense. To date much of the research on metacognition has been based on individuals' metacognitive processes at different ages; the cognitive structures underlying metacognitive processing; and, more recently, on the social and cultural contexts of developing metacognition. However, I want to broaden the notion of metacognition to include how developing metacognition can serve both individual fulfilment of potential and to argue for the role of metacognition in developing individuals capable of making wise life decisions and thereby fostering more just and democratic education systems. Chapter 2 will consider the reasons for developing metacognition in more detail.

Why develop metacognition?

In Chapter 1 I suggested that developing metacognition is important for life as a whole and not only for academic success. However, in a highly literate culture, where academic qualifications are necessary for simply opening the doors of life's opportunities, academic attainment is important. From the earliest research in this area the link was made between learning and metacognition. For Brown (1987) the purpose of metacognition is in directing and controlling learning. In this early framework it was thought that metacognition would only be possible in later childhood. Even so the effect of the regulatory and controlling mechanism of metacognition on cognition is an important concept for educationalists and psychologists. There are many difficulties in trying to study this link between cognition and metacognition. Theorists have argued about the extent to which metacognition can, in fact, be separated from cognition. For instance when we solve a maths problem we are using cognitive strategies; only when we begin to think about how we are thinking about the maths problem or begin to consider how well we are doing, are we engaging metacognitive processes. While in theoretical models there may be a clear distinction between these types of thinking, in practice we move backwards and forwards between metacognitive and cognitive processes and sometimes these moves are rapid. At one level we can say that we are engaging in metacognition when we are stopped in our tracks by a lack of comprehension, a sudden feeling that something doesn't make sense, however this may be a fleeting experience and if we ignore it, not one that will necessarily improve our performance. At another level we may make a very conscious and strategic decision to plan how we are going to tackle the problem and to draw on our past experience of similar problems. In this case we would be engaging in a much more sustained period of metacognition, which is likely to impact on our performance and to increase our own knowledge about ourselves as thinkers.

In real classroom situations it is very difficult to know whether children are engaging in cognitive or metacognitive processes, unless they are encouraged to talk about and discuss their thinking. Some studies have tried to measure the metacognitive aptitude of children and compared this to their success on various tasks. A study by Swanson (1990) in the USA gave Grade 4 and 5 children a questionnaire to measure their metacognitive aptitude and a cognitive ability test to measure their academic aptitude. The children were then set a series of problem solving tasks. The results showed that the children who scored high on the metacognitive test outperformed the other children on the problem solving tasks regardless of their scores on the academic aptitude test. Thus it appears that metacognition is not the same as general aptitude and that metacognition has a positive effect on cognition in terms of problem solving. A more recent study by Veenman, Wilhelm and Beishuizen (2004) tested elementary school children, secondary school children and some university students on a variety of tasks. These were computer based reasoning tasks, which were designed to show how the students were thinking about the problems. For instance, one task was to discover how different things would affect the growth of a plant. The different elements included the frequency of watering, the use of insecticides, positioning of the plant, the size of the pot, etc. After completing the task the children and students were asked to describe what effect all the different elements would have on the plant. This was a measure of learning, but in order to measure metacognition the researchers collected log files from the computer which showed what the participants had done to solve the task, e.g. had they tried to vary more than one element at a time? Had they looked back at their earlier experiments? The researchers used these data as measures of metacognitive skill. They gained some understanding of the way the participants had thought about the task and reflected on their own knowledge. The results showed that metacognitive skills were at least partly independent of intelligence and that metacognitive skills have a positive impact on learning.

This area of research, usually undertaken by cognitive or developmental psychologists, is fraught with problems both philosophically and practically. Measuring or assessing constructs such as metacognition and intelligence is a highly contested practice. It is difficult to know exactly what one is measuring at any given time and there are many other variables to take into account such things as mood, emotion, confidence, and motivation which can all affect how well people of all ages perform on a task. So it is difficult to give any definitive answer to the question of how metacognition affects learning. Having said this however, many small studies can build into a knowledge base of the effects of metacognition on academic performance. A picture is emerging of the positive effects of metacognitive knowledge, of monitoring thinking and controlling thinking on a range of academic tasks across all age groups and ability ranges. Some very interesting work has been carried out with "gifted" children.

"Gifted" children and metacognition

The National Association for Gifted Children (NAGC) in the UK states that there is no one simple definition of "gifted". In the UK the Department for Children, Schools and Families prefers to use "gifted" for students who have high intellectual and academic abilities, whereas "talented" is used to refer to students who might be exceptional in sport or the arts. However, in the USA, Pennsylvania State defines giftedness as high performance in "intellectual, creative, artistic, or leadership capacity, or in specific academic fields" (NAGC, 2008). The NAGC is concerned to make clear that "giftedness" cannot be based on IQ scores alone. However, the organisation describes some of the characteristics of giftedness which include:

- Understands and makes abstractions earlier; may ignore details.
- Is quick to recognize relationships, including cause-effect; may have difficulty accepting the illogical.
- Evaluates facts, arguments, and persons critically/may be self critical (edited from NAGC 2008).

These qualities seem to me to be particularly linked to metacognition. For instance, a child who begins to make abstractions is moving away from the cognitive level of processing to a higher level; a level from which to look down upon thought processes and to evaluate, monitor or control them. This notion of metacognition is closely aligned with Piaget's notion of "reflected abstraction" (Piaget & Inhelder, 1976), which he described as unlikely to develop before adolescence. However, it seems that in gifted children this ability may develop much earlier. In recognizing relationships between different elements, gifted children may be using metacognitive processing to go beyond the surface level of seeing a problem in isolation and like the expert problem solvers in the novice/expert studies of Chi, Feltovich and Glaser (1980) discussed in Chapter 1 may instead be tapping into the underlying structure of the problem in order to make connections. Thus gifted children may be using metacognitive processes of retrieving stored metacognitive knowledge about how one problem works in order to solve a new problem. In evaluating facts and arguments the gifted child is not only concentrating on the facts as presented but is considering the source of those facts and is thus engaging in an exploration of epistemology, or knowledge about knowledge including where it comes from. In addition being self critical is an aspect of self monitoring and reflection which is characteristic of metacognition. So the question is, do gifted children have higher levels of metacognition than other children?

In a study of kindergarten and first grade children in the USA, Paula Schwanenflugel and her colleagues compared the metacognitive knowledge of young children identified as gifted by the state and participating in a gifted school programme, with other children not identified as gifted (Schwanenflugel et al., 1997). The children were between 6 and 7 years old. The researchers used a questionnaire which included questions about the children's knowledge of factors affecting memory and remembering and questions about factors which might impact on their attention. There may be difficulties in using a questionnaire method with such young children, but the researchers suggest that the children understood not just the language of the questions, but also the meaning. The results showed that in general the gifted children had much higher metacognitive knowledge than the other children. The researchers suggested that children who consistently make metacognitive comments might be gifted but unidentified as such. However, the authors state that it is not clear whether gifted children simply learn metacognitive skills faster than other children or whether they will maintain their lead in terms of metacognition throughout their lives. An earlier study by Davidson and Sternberg (1984) found that while children not identified as gifted could be taught metacognitive strategies, which brought their problem solving performance up to the level of the gifted students, the gifted students would spontaneously search for and select the information they needed. So the gifted children were using their metacognitive knowledge to help themselves in terms of using strategies in new situations.

In a review of the literature on metacognition and giftedness Steiner and Carr (2003) acknowledge studies that show metacognition as one factor in the performance of gifted children, but they also describe studies where gifted children performed less well and were unaware of their own mistakes. The authors conclude that while there are some components of metacognition in which gifted children excel, e.g. in knowledge of what factors might affect their own performance, in other areas such as monitoring their own thinking, gifted children may not be much further ahead than other children.

Learning disabled children

If metacognition is at least implicated in notions of giftedness in children, what does this mean for children with learning difficulties? Firstly, the two terms are not exclusive. It is quite possible to have a gifted child with a specific learning difficulty, e.g. in terms of reading print. In addition, children with learning difficulties on the autistic spectrum are also sometimes gifted in specific domains.

In the UK the Disability and Discrimination Act (DDA, 1995) has a broad definition for a disabled person, which includes people with learning disabilities, dyspraxia, dyslexia, as well as physical difficulties and conditions such as epilepsy and diabetes. The DDA defines disability as "a physical or mental impairment which has a substantial and long-term adverse effect on his or her ability to carry out normal day-to-day activities" (DDA 1995, p. 2, 1:1).

In addition, the Education Act (1996) defines special educational need as "a child has special educational needs if he or she has a learning difficulty which calls for special educational provision to be made for him or her" (Education Act 1996, p. 20). The definition is very broad and includes for instance a child with a visual impairment which can be ameliorated through provision of material in a different font size or colour, as well as children with severe learning difficulties.

It can be difficult to compare studies of metacognition and learning difficulties or disabilities as different studies use different definitions of these terms. This is often compounded by different cultural uses of the terms. In addition, in the

UK there are few studies on metacognition in young children, as the concept tends to be subsumed into educational projects on developing thinking skills or developing self regulated learning. However, in other countries a good deal of research has covered the areas of learning disabilities and metacognition in both specific subject areas and in terms of global learning difficulties. Learning disabled children tend to be identified by their performance on a series of cognitive tests including IQ and tend to be at least one year behind the average for their age in reading and maths attainment. One aspect of metacognition in which learning disabled children have been found to differ from non identified children is in the use of strategies. A study by Gaultney (1998) in the USA sought to investigate how learning disabled children in Grades 3, 4 and 5 compared to non disabled children in their awareness of memory and the strategies that might help someone remember. The researchers found the answers to be much more complex than a simple comparison study might suggest. The non learning disabled children recalled more items than the learning disabled children and the older children recalled more than the younger children. However, in terms of strategy use the picture was less clear. The learning disabled children did use strategies to help them to remember the items but these were not always as effective as the strategies used by the non learning disabled children, particularly for the younger children. The learning disabled children also used a less varied repertoire of strategies both in order to commit the items to memory and to recall them. It seems that the learning disabled children had less knowledge of which strategies would be most useful at which point in the task and were less able to use strategies efficiently. The study complements earlier work by Togerson and Houck (1980) which showed that learning disabled children may not have less knowledge of strategies, but that the strategies they use may not be the most efficient ones for the task. They tend to stick to using strategies they are familiar with and are less flexible in the way they use them.

Having taught children of different ages from pre-school to further education and now in higher education, I have often come across children for whom learning within a school context is a difficult and painful process. Learning across all subjects at school depends upon our abilities in a range of cognitive processes such as memory, attention, comprehension, concentration. Finding difficulties with these processes or with more physical problems of co-ordination, sight or hearing can make the classroom a very daunting place. So much of our education is based on understanding instructions, remembering how to do something, using tools such as pencils, pens and rulers, and paying attention to teachers and peers. Learning disabled children appear to have less developed or a lack of metacognitive awareness and while this will impact on performance in different curriculum areas, it can also lead to a more general negative self image, as someone who is not capable of learning or "not good at" specific subjects. This can all too easily become a self fulfilling prophecy. However, most children, whether learning disabled or not, are capable of developing some metacognitive awareness. It is this awareness which gives us some control over our own learning, including an understanding of how we can play to our strengths, compensate for our weaknesses and understand the relationship between what we do and the successes we have.

A study of children who are categorised as learning disabled in the specific area of maths education, carried out by Garrett and colleagues, found that these children were less good at evaluating their own answers to maths problems. They found it more difficult than other children to recognise when their answers were correct or incorrect. The authors suggest that teaching children strategies and the metacognitive elements of when and how to use the strategies is not enough to help children with these specific difficulties. Instead children need to be shown how to recognise correct and incorrect answers and to develop their awareness of the metacognitive skill of evaluation (Garrett et al., 2006).

The work with children of special educational needs, gifted children and those with learning disabilities highlights one of the major theoretical debates in metacognition. This is whether metacognition is specific to a subject area or domain or whether there is such a thing as a global or general metacognitive facility. I will return to this point in Part II.

Metacognition outside the classroom

While a great deal of research has concentrated on metacognition in terms of skills useful for academic life, developing metacognitive awareness is also important for social life. Much of the research in this area has been around the development of children's understanding of themselves and others, otherwise known as the development of "theory of mind". I will consider this research strand in more detail in the next chapter, but here I am going to concentrate on how metacognition is useful in social situations and the implications of a lack of metacognition for making life decisions.

The history of metacognition research is rooted in developmental and cognitive psychology. However, as I outlined in Chapter 1, social psychologists have a long history of research into how we understand ourselves and each other and how we share theories about the mind and how it works. In terms of communication, we know that the way we communicate with others is dependent on our perception of the particular situation, including our beliefs about our self, the other person and how our message might be received. Social psychologists have shown us how our beliefs, while impacting on how we act in social situations, are very often incorrect. We tend to base our judgements of other people on our perceptions of ourselves in comparison. Jost, Kruglanski and Nelson (1998) argue that the basis for these social judgements is metacognitive because the processes underlying our judgements and beliefs about others are the same as the processes underlying our judgements and beliefs about ourselves. In addition, we all spend a great deal of time considering how other people are thinking, whether that is in relation to ourselves or in relation to their own motivations. They suggest that we are all "amateur psychologists" trying to work out each other's behaviour and that social situations are full of metacognitive judgements about how other people are thinking.

However, more than this, metacognition research has now extended into the clinical and psychotherapeutic arena. It is thought that personality disorders arise from a complex network of emotions and meanings often including a lack of metacognitive awareness in terms of metacognitive knowledge and self regulation (Dimaggio *et al.*, 2007). Much of the work in social psychology has been concerned with how adults attribute meaning to social events. The link to metacognition is made when we reflect on how we are thinking about the events. So, when reflecting on negative social events, people may begin to attribute the cause to something fixed about their own personality and thus begin to develop a negative self image. Our ability to monitor our own thinking in this area is obviously important for self esteem and even for good mental health.

In terms of children, much of the work has been based upon children's confidence in understanding social situations and whether their answers to social recall tasks can be manipulated by the social situation. For instance, 8- and 10-year-old children were found to be similar to adults in giving higher confidence ratings after giving correct answers compared to when they had given incorrect answers. They demonstrated that they had some awareness of their own ability to accurately remember details of a social event. However, this was only the case when they were able to provide answers to a neutral question. When the researchers asked them questions designed to mislead them, the children were unable to judge whether their answers were correct or not and this lack of monitoring of their own recall was even more pronounced when the researchers continuously tried to mislead them. Thus while the children were able to monitor their thinking and reflect on their answers when not under social pressure, once the pressure was there their ability to monitor correctly was compromised (Roebers & Howie, 2003). This has obvious implications for children as witnesses to criminal events and indicates the power of social influence on metacognition.

Another area in which metacognition has been investigated is in terms of marketing and persuasion techniques. There is now a whole area of research on what is called "market place metacognition". This is described as research which focuses on the social factors of interactions within the market place and is specifically interested in the metacognitive elements of people's beliefs about their own mental states and their beliefs about the intentions and mental states of others with whom they are engaging in business (Wright, 2002).

We can see that it is important to understand how people might try to persuade us to buy one product over another and we need to have some idea of how to evaluate the claims they are making. In addition, it is important for business people to understand how their messages may be received and how customers make decisions based on their understanding of what the seller is up to. Investigations of how we are persuaded to take action in response to an advertising message have shown that it is not just the thoughts we have, but our level of confidence in those thoughts which influences our behaviour. This notion of confidence requires a reflection on the thought itself and a reflection in terms of an evaluation of self in relation to the thought. So I may think that the free computer with every mobile phone contract offer I am being shown represents a good deal, but unless I can reflect on that thought, evaluate it and feel confident about my own evaluation I am unlikely to act on the thought.

Research in this area has also shown the importance of emotion for feelings of confidence. Tiedens and Linton (2001) found that feeling certain and confident was related to feeling happy and that when people felt sad they were less confident about their evaluation of a persuasive message. This kind of research does not only have relevance for advertisers and people trying to persuade us to buy products, it also shines a light on how our thoughts and emotions are linked and has relevance for our understanding of how we can gain some control over our own thinking and influence our own actions in a self regulating manner.

One way in which children may be encouraged to develop metacognition outside of the classroom is through engaging in conversations about advertising and messages of persuasion. For instance, we might ask children how the messages make them feel; whether or not they think the product will be worth the money and how they think the advertisers are trying to persuade us to choose this product. In this way developing metacognition goes far beyond the classroom and is not only tied to gaining better academic results but also to developing knowledge about self and others in relation to the world.

Of course some of these skills develop naturally through age and experience and some people may able to make wise life decisions without necessarily understanding the process or reflecting in a metacognitive manner. However, if we can make metacognition more visible, if we can consciously reflect on our thoughts and communicate those reflections to others then we may be able to make wise life decisions consistently. But what is wisdom?

Wisdom

In a post modern world the idea of wisdom is a difficult one. There are many competing definitions, drawing on different sources, ancient and modern. So whenever we use words like this it is expected that we will produce a definition and describe the limits of our concept, what we consider to be included in wisdom and what is not. Yet at the same time we each have an intuitive idea of what constitutes a wise decision. Arguably when communities were more cohesive and bounded a shared understanding of what constitutes wisdom would have been more easily communicated. In the Old Testament Book of Wisdom, Solomon describes how he has come to know Wisdom as "an inexhaustible treasure" (Wisdom 7:14). It is Wisdom (personified as a female spirit), who enables man to know God's will, since man's own reasoning is inadequate, bonded as it is to a mortal body and weighed down with the cares of the world. It is Wisdom who consistently saves man from his own foolish decisions. Solomon prays for God to send Wisdom to dwell with him to guide him in governing his people justly so that all of his actions will be acceptable to God. "She is a breath of the power of God" (Wisdom 7:25). While Solomon is concerned with ruling in accordance with God's will he is also concerned with the earthly decisions he will have to make as a ruler and it is Wisdom who will enable him to make these decisions because it is she who has given him knowledge of what exists and of how the world works: "And now I understand everything, hidden or visible for Wisdom, the designer of all things, has instructed me" (Wisdom 7:21).

This Old Testament notion of wisdom has knowledge at its heart. Without knowledge of the world and knowledge of God's will people are unable to make wise decisions. Without this knowledge we may be making decisions based on feelings, or intuitively, and how then could we be sure that our decisions would be pleasing to God and in accordance with his will? This notion of wisdom also includes the idea of knowing that we know. Solomon knows that God has sent Wisdom to help him, he knows that he is being guided in all of his earthly decisions and he prizes Wisdom above all else. He says that at first he didn't realise that it was Wisdom who was responsible for all the good things that had come to him, but he comes to this realisation and begins to know Wisdom herself, so that he can pass on to others knowledge of Wisdom, her source and her actions.

In Aristotelian terms wisdom is distinct from other forms of knowledge. "Phronesis", often described as practical wisdom, is different from "episteme", the ability to reason abstractly and from "techne", the ability to make an artefact or to perform a skill. Phronesis is about how we should live and how we should act in order to create a just world. However, phronesis is not only a skill in terms of solving problems and making good judgements, but also an ability to reflect on how we are making those judgements and what the outcomes are likely to be. Aristotelian philosophy is based on the notion that all things have a natural growth through a series of stages to completion or "telos". Knowledge of this system and why it is so, is distinguished in Aristotle's writings as "sophia" and is distinguished from phronesis in its concern with the fundamental nature of things. Practical wisdom cannot therefore be taught as if it is theoretical, nor is it just the outcome or end product of abstract philosophising about the world. Practical wisdom is much more than this. It is an activity in itself which seeks goodness and is born out of human goodness and is thus related to moral virtue. The virtuous person is one who lives in obedience to external rules but also exercises reason in order to choose just and wise actions. Thus practical wisdom is a process as well as knowledge of what constitutes good actions.

In the secular cultures of the West it can be difficult to understand the moral aspect of wisdom in terms of external laws. Miller (2007) has suggested that decisions about human life rely on individual personal decisions, which are uncertain and based on experience, events and predictions. Our understanding of the situated nature of the decisions we need to make in life means that we cannot rely just on our knowledge of how the world works or on our reflections, however rational, of universal laws. Making wise and thoughtful life decisions is the responsibility of each individual and involves self awareness as well as awareness of the world. Perhaps the most notable project on wisdom today is that by the Berlin Wisdom project at the Max Planck Institute. In an article with Jacqui Smith, Baltes, one of the founding members of the Wisdom project, describes wisdom as "excellence in mind and virtue" and "an expert knowledge system dealing with the conduct and understanding of life". This latter knowledge domain they call "fundamental pragmatics of life" (Baltes & Smith, 2008). It is this knowledge which is used in planning and deciding on life goals, in managing life's problems and in making sense of our own history and experience. Baltes and colleagues argue that this is how individuals construct their own lives and how people contribute to the construction of other lives.

For over two decades the researchers in the Berlin Wisdom project have married philosophical understandings of wisdom with psychological theories of how people make life decisions. The model of wisdom they describe includes Aristotelian notions of knowledge as both *factual* knowledge about life, human nature, relationships and identity and *procedural* knowledge, which is akin to phronesis and is knowledge of when and how to apply theoretical knowledge to life's decision making. In addition, the Berlin model includes what Baltes and Smith term "metacriteria" (ibid.) which include knowledge of the larger external influences on life including history, society and culture. This knowledge is termed "lifespan contextualism". The second metacriterion in the model is "value relativism" and this is described as knowledge about different value systems and goals which would lead to tolerance and respect for the beliefs of others. The third metacriterion, and one I find most interesting as a component of wisdom, is described as knowledge about "fundamental uncertainty of life" and how to manage this. While not directly concerned with metacognition, as it is explained by cognitive psychology, the work of the Berlin group seems to parallel many of the more philosophical aspects of a broad concept of metacognition, which encompasses declarative knowledge about the self and the world; procedural knowledge about how to make good decisions or solve problems; and conditional knowledge about when and where to use this knowledge.

It is perhaps Robert Sternberg who, since the 1990s, has made the connection between metacognition and wisdom more apparent. Sternberg's definition of wisdom is as a balance between different factors and involves the application of both experience and intelligence for the common good. It is interesting that his more psychological definition of wisdom should still include the goal of the common good, rather than only individual fulfilment or individual enlightenment. He dismisses problems of understanding whose version of the common good we should be working towards and what values it should be based on as side issues which detract from the common understanding of universal values. However, the means to achieve these values may not be universally shared and thus, for me, the need for individuals to work towards making wise and thoughtful life decisions and understanding their own thinking in relation to these decisions is fundamental to the bigger goal of wisdom in service to the common good. To borrow from the environmental lobby, when we begin to think about wisdom we should be concerned with "acting locally and thinking globally".

Sternberg describes 16 ways of promoting wisdom in the classroom. The fundamental basis for this is "that one teaches children not what to think, but rather, how to think" (Sternberg, 2004, p. 169). Sternberg is careful to separate wisdom from intelligence and says that we should encourage children to see beyond the narrow confines of academic achievement, pointing out that high IQ scores do not necessarily equate with making good and wise life decisions. In his 16 principles for developing wisdom in children, Sternberg makes a number of suggestions which can be described as facilitating metacognition. These include: understanding how wise people think and make decisions; encouraging critical thinking and incorporating values; seeing things from multiple viewpoints; and understanding and monitoring one's own thinking.

Of course teaching children how to think about their own thinking and how to achieve an understanding of the balance of factors which can lead to making wise and thoughtful life decisions is necessary, but this does not take account of the individual's will to want to do this and to desire wisdom. Solomon spoke directly to his fellow kings in other lands when he beseeched them to listen and to learn about wisdom, but he acknowledged that they must listen with will, in order to be instructed (Solomon 6:11). These days we might think more about motivation than will. What are the links between motivation, metacognition and making wise life decisions?

Motivation

We all know what it means to feel de-motivated towards a task. We may ascribe these feelings to any number of causes from physical causes such as tiredness or illness to emotional causes such as anxiety or depressive mood to psychological causes such as attitude or lack of interest. Some of these causes may be fleeting; we may know that we will feel better and more motivated towards the task in a relatively short time. However, we may also feel de-motivated because of more enduring thoughts about ourselves including our ability in a specific area or more global feelings of unworthiness.

Theories of motivation suggest that our beliefs about ability, as either fixed or as an outcome of effort and learning, influence our approach to a task (Dweck, 1999). If these attributions are lasting they affect our motivational style or the way in which we approach and respond to tasks and whether we begin with a sense of possible success or probable failure. There is a vast field of research on motivation, much of which is outside the remit of this book, but theories of motivational style are particularly important for their connection to learning and to metacognition. How we ascribe our successes and failures will have an impact on how we approach new challenges. Three types of motivational style which are relevant to children's learning are: learned helplessness, self worth motivation and mastery oriented.

   The notion of learned helplessness came from research with animals during the 1960s. Seligman and Maier (1967) found that when control over their environment was taken away, dogs lapsed into a state of helplessness, were unresponsive and lacked any motivation to respond. School children who see failure as inevitable and feel no sense of personal power over their ability were also termed "learned helpless" by Diener and Dweck (1978). This style of motivation is said to be independent of ability, so that children may be perfectly able in a subject but their own perception of their ability and their view of ability as fixed, negatively impacts on their performance. This can lead to a cycle of failure followed by avoidance of future challenges and more failure, so that a self concept of "I'm no good at X" is created and perpetuated. Children exhibiting this motivational style are also likely to give up easily, especially when they hit an obstacle or "get stuck" on a part of the task. In addition to this having a negative impact on academic performance, the feelings of inadequacy associated with this motivational style are likely to impact on self concept and self esteem, and thereby transfer to other areas of life.

   Covington (1984) described another motivational style as self worth motivation. Children demonstrating this motivational style are often concerned with their success on a task in terms of their own self esteem rather than with successful completion of the task itself. These children are likely to ascribe to a fixed view of ability and believe that if they do badly on a task this is because they are of low ability. For children exhibiting this style of motivation, tasks perceived as difficult are likely to cause a high degree of anxiety and stress, because as the chance of failure is heightened so is a threat to their self concept and self esteem. It is likely that they will try to avoid these threats by suggesting that the task is not worth doing or does not interest them. The third motivational style described in this model is that of mastery oriented. Children exhibiting this style are likely to focus on task oriented strategies and effort. They understand that ability is not fixed, that learning involves failure and mistakes and consequently they are more likely to think about how they have solved a task. Thus they build a base of metacognitive knowledge about themselves in relation to tasks, which has the benefit of enabling them to transfer their learning from one situation to another.

   These broad categories of motivational style can serve as reminders to teachers and others to guide children's thinking about the bigger issues of intelligence and ability and to guard against perpetuating ideas about ability which may impact negatively on developing metacognition. However, motivation is no more a fixed trait than ability. It is a complex and dynamic mixture of external and internal influences. Self determination theories such as those by Deci and Ryan (2003) focus on self reflection and the extent to which we choose to act in certain ways. These motivational orientations are seen as part of a continuum of self awareness and responsibility. At one end of this continuum are amotivational orientations. Children and learners who display this type of motivation see little connection between their own actions and the outcomes of their performance on a task. They tend to be turned off by a subject because they cannot see its relevance for themselves and their world view. There may be some legitimacy in this stance but more often it is a result of some negative association between self and task that has been created and is kept in creation by a lack of positive associations and feelings of lack of power. The second orientation on the continuum is termed extrinsic motivation and is determined by the extent to which the focus is on the outcome of the performance, whether this is in terms of academic success, utility or social approval. The third orientation is intrinsic motivation, where people place the emphasis on self knowledge factors such as wanting to study a subject because of personal interest, curiosity or in a sense of self development. The focus here may be on the feelings of excitement or self worth that the learning provides rather than on any extrinsic reward. Displaying this type of motivation is clearly linked to feelings of autonomy and empowerment. If learning is being driven by feelings of desire to learn or enjoyment of the process of learning, then there must be some sense of reflection on oneself; and knowledge about oneself as a learner. This is the metacognitive knowledge aspect of developing metacognition. In addition, if enjoyment and excitement is being felt from the process of learning then there is more likelihood that the learner will be aware of or be actively seeking out different ways of learning. So children who have a sense of excitement about learning, as most do in the early years, are already primed for developing metacognition.

The difficulty for those in charge of structuring the learning is in providing an environment which will nurture this seedling and allow it to mature. Some children are likely to be more resilient than others in their self determined motivation to learn and so we often see a few children in every class who have metacognitive awareness, regardless of the classroom environment. However, the aim is to facilitate the metacognitive development of all children and this I believe can only be done alongside a facilitation of empowerment and self oriented learning.

While motivational orientation or style may determine approach to learning and impact on development of metacognition, it seems just as likely that development of metacognition will impact on motivational orientation and approach to learning. As we develop metacognitive awareness of different tasks, such as how they differ from or are similar to other tasks, and whether they are complete or require further information, we begin to seek out strategies which will help us to work through them. As our knowledge of useful strategies grows through experimentation in different situations, we develop metacognitive awareness of how we are approaching a task and when to use these strategies. This leads us to monitoring how well we are doing in pursuit of our own goals and to making decisions about whether to change strategy, continue or seek out a new way of approaching the task. All of this leads to feelings of empowerment – that we have the power to change the way we think about something, to alter our course in midstream if it isn't working and to explore other options. Research on expert and novice problem solvers has shown that this type of self determined learning is what experts engage in, whereas novices in a particular field tend to stick with strategies they already know regardless of whether they are working or not.

Theories from motivational research have much to offer us in understanding the complexity of metacognition and enable us to take account of emotional response as well as cognitive processing. Through these links we are better able to see how our environments may facilitate metacognitive development and autonomous learning.

Chapter 3

Ages and stages

If we want children to grow up to make wise and thoughtful life decisions and we believe, as John Flavell does, that developing metacognitive awareness will have a positive impact on this goal, then we must try to facilitate the development of this awareness. In order to do this an understanding of the origins of metacognition and the likely factors mediating its development is necessary. This chapter considers metacognition from a developmental perspective. However, there are criticisms of the whole field of developmental psychology and its tendency to work with deficit models. Feminist critics such as Erica Burman have highlighted some of the deficiencies inherent in the developmental perspective and it is worth being aware of these limitations when considering the development of metacognition.

Burman (1994) argues that developmental psychology is not simply a benign scientific approach and that its findings lead to norms against which children are compared and women (as mothers) often scrutinised. In addition, findings from this branch of psychology can lead to interventions which perpetuate a cycle of measuring and standardising children's development. Burman argues that much of the research in developmental psychology is divorced from the real complex world in which we live and provides a simplified view of the social world as another set of variables to be controlled or accounted for. Developmental psychology tends also to be based on Western and, Burman argues, middle class norms. Because the theory of metacognition was constructed from research by developmental psychologists, there is a tension between what the theory of metacognition tells us and the way in which that theory was developed. I do not believe that there is necessarily a resolution to this difficulty, but it is important that we acknowledge how our understanding of metacognition and its development has been formed. It was not so long ago that the consensus among psychologists was that metacognition was only possible with the onset of formal operational thinking in early adolescence. Some researchers still maintain that this is the case and that evidence of earlier metacognition is really a pre-cursor to the real thing, sometimes called "proto-metacognition". However, one area which has a cohesive history of research and where there is some consensus about children understanding mental processes is the area commonly called "theory of mind".

Theory of mind

Theory of mind refers to our ability to reflect on ourselves, i.e. become self conscious and our ability to reflect on others and become conscious of the way others may see us. It involves thinking about how information is represented to us in terms of beliefs, desires or goals. Theory of mind is necessary for understanding the social world and our part in it. A less developed theory of mind makes social interactions more difficult as we fail to see things from another's perspective or fail to interpret social cues.

One of the main differences between theory of mind and metacognition is that most children develop a theory of mind quite easily and without direct instruction, although it is obviously a development facilitated by social interaction and children with very limited social interaction, such as those found living in neglected or "wild" conditions, do not have a developed theory of mind. However, in most ordinary settings children come to understand some things about their own mental life and that of others. There are a number of tests which psychologists have used to find out if children have developed a theory of mind. These are often known as "false belief tests" and are based on the idea of children understanding that other people have minds of their own and can think different thoughts – the development of what Piaget called "de-centering", where the child is no longer only focused on herself but can see things from another perspective (Piaget & Inhelder, 1969). It was commonly thought that children with difficulties on the autistic spectrum would have a limited theory of mind and metacognition. However, a study by Farrant, Boucher and Blades (1999) found that autistic children were less likely to make use of memory strategies but were not significantly different from other children in terms of performance on metamemory tasks (see below) or false belief tasks.

One theory of mind test I have used with children is often called the "Smartie tube test" (Wimmer & Perner, 1983). In this test a child is shown a tube of Smarties and asked what they think is in the tube. The child usually replies Smarties or sweets. The researcher opens the tube and shows that in fact it contains crayons and not sweets. The tube is closed and then the researcher asks the child to imagine that her friend has just come into the room and has been asked what is in the tube. Will the friend reply Smarties or crayons? If the child says Smarties then she is displaying a theory of mind which acknowledges that other people may not know the same things as she does and she can put herself in the position of the friend seeing the Smartie tube for the first time. If, however, she says that the friend will answer crayons, then she is endowing the friend with the same thoughts and knowledge that she has. There are various versions of this test and others like it based on children understanding that other people do not have access to each other's thoughts. Results from numerous tests such as these have indicated that children develop this ability around the age of 3–4 years old and that before that age they rarely answer these tests correctly.

However, for a more detailed consideration of what performance on these tests might mean at different ages see Fabricus and Imbens-Bailey (2000). They argue that children's success on these tests at 3 or 4 years old does not indicate that children understand the mind as representational. Rather passing these tests only shows that children have some knowledge about their own thinking and can project that knowledge onto others to explain how others think and know things. Thus Fabricus and Imbens-Bailey argue for a later and slower development of understanding the mind as representational than success on these types of theory of mind tests might suggest.

Carpendale and Chandler (1996) similarly argued that what has developed by the age of four is a "copy theory of mind" in which children mentally represent behaviour in the world in a straightforward copying sense. They suggest that this is only the beginning of developing a theory of mind and that it is not until much later (middle childhood) that children consciously construct representations and are conscious of doing so. They call this an "interpretative theory of mind" and describe this as the ability to understand that given the same information, two people can have different but valid interpretations. Thus this interpretative theory of mind is a much more sophisticated ability involving grasping that understanding is not a simple copying process but involves interpretation and construction of meaning. Chandler and Helm (1984) devised a test which involved showing children an obscure section of a drawing and asking them what they think the drawing is called and then asking them to say what their friend might say the drawing was called if they saw the same section. Finally the full drawing is revealed to the children. The children are asked a series of questions to determine whether the children could hold in their mind perspectives that were different from their own, whether they could invent other perspectives and ascribe them to others, and finally whether they felt it was alright for different people to hold different interpretations of the same object. When I conducted a similar test with 5–6-year-old children, only 43 per cent passed this test well, although many more partially passed the test. This suggests that, as Carpendale and Chandler said, this interpretative theory of mind is much more complex, develops later and involves more metacognitive awareness. An illustration from what the children in my study said in response to the questions will make this qualitative difference clearer.

In my version of the test I used two small dolls, Bob and Sam. The child was first shown a small portion of a drawing and asked to name the drawing, then Bob came along and the child was asked what Bob would call the drawing. Sam then came along and the same question was asked. Amy, who was 5 years and 8 months old at the time of the test, gave original thoughts to the two dolls. I then asked her:

ME: So Bob and Sam say it's different things, is that OK?
AMY: Yeah because different people have different sorts of seeing and she might not know these are called triangles [pointing to the drawing] and so she

calls them pointy shapes and he [Bob] might know they are triangles and so he calls them triangles.

ME: So again all three of you now have seen exactly the same thing, but you all call it something different, is that OK?

AMY: Yeah, cos people see different things and we all know different things because if God made us all the same it would be really really boring, say like we had seven Shirleys and seven Amys.

This is fairly obvious to an adult but not to most 5-year-olds. Other children in this category expressed similar views that different people would give different interpretations of the picture because "they have their own imaginations" or "different people know different things" or "different people think in different ways even if they are brother and sister". A comparison with another child of a similar age shows just how sophisticated these children's understanding was. The same test with Denise, who was 5 years and 6 months old at the time, provided different results. While she ascribed different ideas to the different dolls and to herself, her explanation of why is quite different:

ME: Why is it OK for them to say different things?

DENISE: Cos one is this side and one is that side [in fact both dolls are in front of the drawing and an equal distance from it. I try to persuade Denise that this is the case].

ME: Why will they both say it's different things if they are looking at it from exactly the same place?

DENISE: Cos one is a bit back and one is in front.

No matter how much I tried to persuade her that there was little difference in the position of the tiny dolls in relation to the picture, Denise could only offer this physical explanation for why they might give different interpretations.

Other children, also stuck in this physical explanation, suggested that one doll must be older or taller than the other, although they were the same size and similarly dressed, or that one doll had looked more closely at the picture.

A third category of children did not ascribe different thoughts to the dolls, but had the dolls and themselves all giving the same answer. Among the reasons for the similarity was that the dolls were friends and so would have the same thoughts. Some children maintained that it was impossible for two people looking at the same drawing to give it a different title, even though it was not clear what the drawing was. These children tended to argue that if different people gave different titles to the drawing, one of them would be wrong. They maintained the idea that the drawing has a physical reality that is fixed and only one title can be correct.

Results of tests like these show just how complex theory of mind is and how it may develop in terms of levels of sophistication throughout childhood and into adulthood. We all know some adults who are particularly perceptive about other people and can empathise readily with others – it seems likely that this skill begins to develop in early childhood with the onset of understanding that other people have different thoughts.

Understanding mental processes such as thinking and believing; what they are and how they influence actions, is crucial to understanding the social world, whether that is in terms of business relationships or personal relationships. Without the understanding that different people believe different things and that the context can alter beliefs, we would find it very difficult to function.

In terms of research, the work on theory of mind was often separated from work on metacognition. The metacognition research has developed out of earlier work on memory and metamemory and this work has provided us with a great deal of information about at what ages and stages children's understanding of mental phenomena develops.

Metamemory

Metamemory was one of the first components of metacognition to be studied. It was from the study of metamemory that Flavell constructed his model of metacognition. As described by Flavell and Wellman, metamemory involves knowledge of one's own memory, how it works, what factors may influence it, what strategies may be useful in helping us to remember things as well as ongoing control and monitoring of our memory (Flavell, 1971; Flavell & Wellman, 1977). A great deal of work on metamemory was carried out in the 1970s and 80s. Some of this work focused on children's knowledge, and use, of strategies to aid memory performance on tasks of recall.

In a seminal study of children's memory, children from kindergarten to Grade 5 were interviewed in an attempt to find out what children of different ages know about their own memories (Kreutzer et al., 1975). The children were presented with real life memory tasks such as remembering a telephone number or advising another child on how best to remember a list or a story. The study found a number of interesting things about these children's understanding of memory and memory processes. Firstly, it was found that the youngest children, those in kindergarten and in first grade, seemed to understand words such as "remember", "forget" and "learn" and they had some understanding of different types of memory, that things that happened long ago might be harder to remember, but also that short term remembering of facts or numbers is also prone to forgetting. These young children also had some idea of strategies which might help them to remember something, including using other people or other external processes such as writing it down. So even very young children are aware of how others can help them with internal processes such as memory. The study went on to find that while the kindergarten and Grade 1 children knew some things about memory, middle school children knew more things and were more aware of the impact of context, type of information and individual differences on memory performance. The older children were found to be more aware of the actual experience of remembering and understood that different experiences could impact on how well they remembered something. The researchers concluded that by the end of the elementary school years, children had come to understand a great deal about memory.

My own research with 5 to 6-year-old children found a good deal of individual difference in terms of metamemory and also some sophisticated understanding of memory processes (Larkin, 2007a). I undertook a small scale study with forty 5- to 6-year-old children randomly selected from 6 Year 1 classes in one London borough. The test was a version of Kim's Game. Sixteen objects – some small plastic toys, e.g. a fish, a frog, a parrot, and some natural items, e.g. a shell, a stone, a leaf were shown to each child. The child was then asked to do anything they wanted to help them to remember the items. After 2 minutes the items were covered up and the child was asked to recall as many as possible. Then the child was asked what they had done to help them to remember so many items; whether it was easy or difficult to remember them and why; how it could be made easier; what advice they would give to a friend who wanted to remember them as well as they had and finally which bit of themselves did the remembering and how it did that. All the children used some kind of strategy to remember the items which included naming them, grouping them into categories and telling stories with them. However, there were some differences in the way children accounted for memory performance. For a small proportion of children (less than 10 per cent) remembering was largely a mysterious process; it was linked to "cleverness" but was seen as largely automatic. These children had some understanding that remembering was connected with their brain but they said it was really done by the eyes and could not be explained. They placed a great deal of faith in adults' memory, especially their mothers, who they claimed never forgot anything.

A second group of children (about 20 per cent) had more understanding of the use of external agencies in remembering – they might make use of their mother to remind them of things. Some children in this category linked forgetting to feeling sad and had a view of their brains as a kind of store house which needed to be periodically cleaned out before more information could be stored.

However, the largest percentage of these Year 1 children had a more sophisticated view of memory and remembering. For instance, they mentioned using strategies such as making stories out of the objects, putting them in alphabetical order or grouping them. One child referred to "sorting out" and "sorting in" – by this he meant firstly putting the objects one at a time into a circle made from the necklace (he called this "sorting in") and then removing them one at a time, while saying their names again (he called this "sorting out"). He claimed that this helped him to remember the objects and he did indeed get all 16 objects correct. Some children referred to the importance of touching the objects as the feel of the object could then be stored in your memory and would help you to recall it. The children in this category also had some ideas about where their memory was located and how it functioned. They distinguished between remembering and learning and between remembering and thinking. One child said that we can learn by watching others but we cannot remember that way. This is quite a sophisticated understanding from a 5-year-old. Other children linked remembering to concentration and the need to work hard at it. They also understood that their memory is fallible and is linked to emotional experiences.

It seems clear that young children know and can verbalise a good deal about memory and memory functioning. However, this knowledge does not always equate with performance and young children have been found to over-estimate their memory capacity and claim that they can remember more than they do and are unaware of the discrepancy between their prediction and performance (Cavanaugh & Perlmutter, 1982; Schneider, 1998). So while even pre-school children can use memory strategies and talk about them (DeLoache *et al.*, 1985), there is a rapid development in knowledge about memory, memory strategies and using strategies appropriately between the ages of 6 and 11 (Schneider, 1985). However, both children and adults display inaccurate metamemory at times. We may believe that we remember an event which has not occurred or we may believe that we have forgotten the details of an event that we are sure did occur. So not only is our memory fallible but our thoughts about our memory can also be doubted, regardless of our age. What is often missing from the developmental perspective on metamemory is the influence of the social context on the performance of children on metamemory tasks.

Bless and Strack (1998) have highlighted the social influences which impact on confidence beliefs about memory. Their argument is based on the understanding that when we are not confident about our own answers or judgements we seek cues to the correct response from other people. Thus the way interview questions are asked may cue us to respond in certain ways. This is often the case with interview studies with children, where the power dynamics between adult interviewer and child respondent leads the child to want to provide a correct or acceptable answer. Both adults and children can find it difficult to admit that they don't remember something because this appears to be a deficit. Similarly, children may claim that they use particular ways of remembering things because they know that using strategies is supposed to be a good thing and something which they are encouraged to do. It is likely that this knowledge of what is expected grows through the school years as teachers reinforce these good study habits. Thus results showing children's development of metamemory may be partially due to them answering questions in a more appropriate way as they get older. This is not a bad thing by any means – school learning is of course about developing good habits for learning and developing good metamemory is likely to aid academic performance in the long term.

A longitudinal study by Lockl and Schneider (2006) sought to find links between theory of mind, language and metamemory. Through a series of tests and interviews with children 4–5 years old over two years, they found that metamemory improves over the pre- and early school years, as does understanding of mental state language. This confirmed previous studies but this new study also found a good deal of individual variation in the results so that children who were advanced in these areas at age 4 and a half maintained that advantage and children who were behind at the start remained behind the group at the end of the study. This has obvious implications for education. In addition, the study found that children's ability on theory of mind tests, such as the false belief tests, predicted their ability on metamemory tests and that children who passed these tests had a better understanding of metacognitive vocabulary. However, the relationship between language, theory of mind and metamemory is complex and reciprocal. The study found that while children need to understand meta-cognitive vocabulary to develop metamemory, developing metamemory aids development of metacognitive language.

While metamemory is the pre-cursor of theories of metacognition, and in the early days the term was used interchangeably with metacognition, another branch of developmental research has been concerned with how children come to know about knowledge and the sources of knowledge. The study of develop-ing epistemology has also been linked to developing theory of mind.

Meta-knowing

Deanna Kuhn (2000) includes metacognitive, meta-strategic and epistemo-logical features in her theory of meta-knowing. She traces the development of meta-knowing from the development of theory of mind in young children to the later development of critical and scientific thinking. Meta-knowing is defined as awareness and understanding of one's own cognitive functions and those of others. Kuhn differentiates between "knowing that", which is the knowledge we have and build up about our own and others' cognition, and "knowing how", which is referred to as meta-strategic knowledge and is concerned with knowing about mental processes. While some declarative aspect of meta-knowing and theory of mind develops early in childhood, Kuhn argues that meta-strategic knowledge develops much later and while young children might be taught some memory or other cognitive strategies they are unlikely to use these spontaneously. The conscious use of strategies is a metacognitive act which involves monitoring performance and deciding when to use a strategy, selecting the appropriate strategy and evaluating the effect of its use through more monitoring processes. This is a process which is only likely to develop over time through experience, practice and support.

Kuhn's research on scientific reasoning, including how people understand knowledge, leads her to state that in this area, adolescents and adults display meta-cognitive deficits which are similar to those of young children. For instance, her findings show that many people fail to evaluate the sources of their knowledge claims or make a clear distinction between theory and evidence. In addition, she found that people can become more confident in their beliefs simply through an increase in quantity of information, regardless of the validity of its source. Moreover, this increase in confidence can further obscure understanding of the source of the information. People also use strategies to evaluate evidence incon-sistently. It seems that we often use a good strategy when the evidence presented supports a theory but are not so good at using a valid strategy when the evidence is counter to the theory. Kuhn's work has shown us that many adults lack the metacognitive awareness necessary to really understand the source of their own beliefs and the poor utilisation of meta-strategic knowledge may reinforce this inadequate metacognitive knowledge base. This suggests that in many cases our education processes are not equipping us with the skills necessary to develop more sophisticated understanding of knowledge and knowledge claims.

Kuhn argues that between 4 and 6 years old children begin to change in their understanding of knowledge and begin to differentiate beliefs from evidence which may or may not support the belief. Very young children, those who fail the false belief tests, do not differentiate between belief and knowledge but by the age of 4 children come to understand that knowing is related to a knower and that different people can know different things. However, there is evidence that children, adolescents and even some adults maintain a view of knowledge as existing out in the world and that the job of the individual is to look for and find this knowledge. Kuhn describes this as the "absolutist epistemological stance" (2000, p. 317). The absolutist stance involves being able to evaluate knowledge, to make the distinction between knowledge and belief and to evaluate beliefs as either truthful or not. However, the absolutist looks outwards from the self to concentrate on the external world and knowledge is often evaluated in reference to direct observation or experience.

A further shift in the development of knowing about knowing tends to occur in adolescence. This involves people coming to understand that knowledge is constructed by the knower and that there is no simple external truth to be found. According to Kuhn, many adults remain at this stage of development in terms of their understanding of knowledge. She points out this view can lead to a claim for knowledge for something which is really opinion. Thus, if I believe it to be true, then it is true for me and I have a right to hold that view, just as you have a right to hold your view. The focus of this stage of development is on internal knowing, so that people look inwards to their own beliefs, values and opinions to evaluate knowledge. This is described as a "multiplist" stance.

However, Kuhn goes on to describe another level of development beyond this stage which she terms the "evaluative" (2000, p. 318). It is clear that not everyone reaches this stage of understanding about knowledge, but Kuhn sees this stage as crucial for intellectual life. The "evaluative" stage is one in which the individual understands that people have their own opinions but that it is important to use judgement, to weigh up the claims of conflicting opinions and to use reason to argue for a particular standpoint. While this understanding of knowledge is obviously important for academic life, it is also important for making wise and thoughtful life decisions. If we maintain an absolutist or multiplist view of knowledge, then we are unable to evaluate situations fully because we either do not see the difference between knowledge and belief or we maintain that competing beliefs are equally justified. This is likely to lead us to a stalemate situation where we find it impossible to decide on a course of action, except through using intuition and what feels right at the time. I do not wish to disparage intuition – many important decisions we make are based on a feeling and it is important to maintain our confidence in our own ability to use our instinct and feelings in this way. However, developing an understanding of knowledge as something that is constructed by people, yet can be evaluated with reference to theories, evidence or reason, would complement and enhance our intuitive decision making, enable us to move forward when we become stuck and allow us to reflect on how we got to where we are. Through practice in using evaluation and argument we may begin to understand more about knowledge itself and how we might use knowledge to make decisions. Developing this kind of metacognition about knowledge may also enable us to consciously draw on our skills in decision making, to enable us to make better decisions in a wider range of contexts and situations.

Self regulation

So far I have focused on the development of metacognitive knowledge in its various forms, but the other parts of metacognition are the monitoring and control aspects. It was a seminal article by Nelson and Narens (1990) which highlighted the role of monitoring and control and delineated a tripartite model of metacognition, which is used most often today. Their model is termed a "framework for metamemory" but the principle is the same for metacognition. They describe metacognition as based on three principles. The first is the idea that cognition is on two interrelated levels. They termed these the "meta-level" and the "object-level". The second is that the meta-level is viewed as having a mental representation of the object level and the third is that two processes named "control" and "monitoring" make the dynamic inter-connection between the two levels. The difference between these two processes is in the direction of their influence. Control is the process by which the meta-level impacts on the object-level, to produce some kind of change at the object-level. This might be to start, stop or change an action. But the control mechanism can only do this if it receives information from the object level and this is the process of monitoring. The monitoring of the object-level changes the representation that the meta-level holds and triggers either a "no action necessary state" or uses the control process to make a change. The model views the object-level as a simple cognitive level which does not hold any representation of the meta-level. The model is therefore hierarchical with the meta-level as an overseer of cognitive activity. Nelson and Narens' model goes on to describe the different processes of monitoring and control. These include monitoring processes in advance of learning something, while learning, maintaining the knowledge and recalling the knowledge. These processes include what are called "judgements of learning". These might take the form of predictions about whether a task will be easy or difficult (ease of learning judgements), predictions of how well the task has been learned (judgements of learning), predictions about whether knowledge learned will be recalled later when it is currently unavailable (feeling of knowing). These different monitoring aspects may work independently of each other and may be influenced by various contextual factors. The control processes are triggered by the monitoring process and may include such things as allocating time to the task, selection of strategies and change of strategies and deciding to end the task. It seems reasonable to suggest that skill in monitoring and subsequent control of learning will lead to more efficient use of time and the development of self awareness in terms of learning. Thus this important model of metacognition relates to another sector of research which is known as self regulated learning.

There is some controversy among metacognition researchers as to the status of self regulated learning in comparison to metacognition. For some, metacognition is the overarching concept and self regulation a feature of it. However, for others self regulation is the bigger concept and metacognition is a part of this. I believe that self regulation is the overarching theory, of which metacognition is a part. Models of self regulation tend to include emotions, motivation and context as well as cognitive monitoring and control processes, so they encompass more than is normally found in models of metacognition. However, it is also difficult to see how one would become a self regulated learner without developing metacognitive awareness of self in relation to various tasks and contextual factors. In addition emotional responses are now being incorporated into theories of metacognition in terms of metacognitive experiences (see the work of Efklides et al., 2006; Efklides & Petkaki, 2005).

It is impossible to do justice to the large amount of work on self regulation in this short section. However, it is important to just highlight a couple of different approaches and make the connections between self regulation and metacognition. Self regulated learning, defined as the ability to inhibit impulsive behaviour and to attend appropriately, has been related to academic progress and success independently of measures of intelligence (Blair & Razza, 2007). In their study of over one hundred 3–5-year-olds from low income homes who were enrolled on a programme for disadvantaged children, Blair and Razza found that the inhibitory control function necessary for planning, goal directed learning and problem solving predicted academic outcomes and was especially associated with ability in mathematics. The researchers say that developmental delay in these self regulatory skills can lead to difficulties in making the transition to school and increase the risk of academic failure. Their study makes a connection between these difficulties and social and economic disadvantage. Theoretical models of self regulation have traditionally included more of these social aspects than the more cognitively based models of metacognition.

In particular, Zimmerman's social cognitive model of self regulation views self regulation as a cyclical process involving three distinct and sequential phases, which are named "Forethought", "Performance" and "Self reflection" (Zimmerman, 2000). Each phase includes a number of sub processes. The Forethought phase, which is preparation for beginning a task, includes task analysis and the self motivational beliefs such as expectation of outcome, interest, goal orientation and self efficacy. The Performance phase is subdivided into self control processes such as self instruction and focusing attention and self observation processes, which includes self monitoring. The third phase, Self reflection, occurs after the performance and involves self evaluation and self reaction. While self regulation is important for academic performance, self efficacy beliefs influence aspirations, commitment, motivation, resilience in the face of difficulty and vulnerability to depression, as well as more cognitive strategic thinking (Zimmerman & Schunk, 1989).

Parents are important in fostering the development of self regulatory skills, which benefit the academic progress of their children. In a study of children's aspirations towards certain career choices researchers found that the socio-economic status of a family and the academic aspirations of parents are only indirectly linked to children's choice of career. These factors are mediated by children's own perceived self regulation in terms of the types of careers they judge themselves to be capable of. However, perceptions may not match academic achievement and it is the perception that is the important and deciding factor. Parental influences may help to raise children's perceptions of themselves as effective self regulators and agents of change. The development of these beliefs is likely to have a huge impact on an individual's life course. Self regulation has also been linked to children's ability to resist peer pressure to engage in risky activities such as drugs and alcohol abuse. For these social cognitive models of self regulation the environment is crucial and current research tends to focus on the differences between cultures and families at different times (Post *et al.*, 2006).

Other models of self regulation have highlighted the role of motivation. In particular, Boekaerts' model of self regulation acknowledges the complex environment of school based learning and the competition between different goals, such as academic goals and self fulfilling or self preservation goals (Boekaerts & Corno, 2005). Similarly Pintrich's (1995) model of self regulation includes behavioural, cognitive and motivational factors in different contexts. Pintrich describes different motivational styles, such as "approach mastery" and "avoidance mastery" students. Approach mastery students he describes as being focused on learning and understanding. These students are likely to be more self regulated and capable of monitoring and controlling their thinking during a task. "Avoidance mastery" students, on the other hand, would be more focused on not losing face and would then avoid learning situations which might lead to this. In this sense then, the students are making decisions given competing goals, based on their perceptions of self efficacy.

When children first enter school, often a new and fearful situation, their home based self regulatory behaviour may not be what is required in this new environment. The bigger the discrepancy between their home based regulatory behaviour and what is expected from school, the more difficult the child is going to find the school experience. This is likely to have an impact on the choices they make when faced with competing goals relating to their perceptions of themselves and to learning. Repeatedly choosing face saving or self preservation strategies in the early days of schooling may form habits that are difficult to break. Perceptions of self efficacy may lead to actions which reinforce the construction of negative metacognitive beliefs and impact on academic performance through school and, if not challenged, into later life.

The development of balanced self regulatory processes should therefore be a priority for early years educators, parents and children. While theories of meta-cognition may look to Piaget as a pre-cursor of how metacognition may develop, theories of self regulated learning have much in common with a Vygotskyan approach. This approach focuses on the role of more experienced others in facilitating the development of self regulatory behaviour. The development of self regulation is viewed by Vygotsky as a movement from an inter-psychological level to an intra-psychological level (Vygotsky, 1978). The older peer or adult guides the child through a task by challenging the child to think for herself, to analyse, plan, monitor her thinking and evaluate the outcome. At first these regulatory skills are performed by the adult and provide a model of self regula-tion. Gradually, the child is encouraged to take on these behaviours and to begin to construct a "virtual adult" or internal guide who will perform the same function as the original adult. Through these processes the skills of self regulation begin to be internalised and form habitual behaviour when presented with similar tasks.

Some of the earliest work on this approach to self regulation was carried out with young children by Wertsch (Wertsch 1978; Wertsch et al., 1980). Their studies were based on observing pre-school children working with adults on problem solving tasks. Since these early studies were carried out, there have been many other attempts to study the self regulation of young children. However, it is very difficult to come to firm conclusions. It is not possible to run such experiments within a classic experimental study, including a control group, and also keep the naturalistic context. There are many different approaches to guiding children and this makes it very difficult to compare one adult and child rela-tionship with another. Much of the work in this area has focused on the mother and child working together, but of course the child is also bringing the whole of her experience from other social relationships to the observed activity. Pursuing some kind of statistically significant result based on an experimental procedure is unlikely to capture the richness and unique quality of supportive adult child interactions in terms of developing self regulation. Instead researchers in this area have turned their attention to in depth qualitative studies of the support given by adults to their children over time.

Work by Nancy Perry and colleagues has provided a very detailed account of young children's self regulatory practices during writing (Perry, 1998; Perry & VandeKamp, 2000; Perry et al., 2003). Perry views self regulation as the overarch-ing concept, which includes metacognition, motivation, strategic behaviour and independent learning. Through a very detailed observational process Perry found that young children were capable of managing their own learning, of displaying awareness of their own thinking processes and staying focused on the task in hand. Crucial to this development was the role of the teachers in facilitating this self regulation through creating a supportive environment, being flexible enough to alter the tasks to meet their students' developmental stage and create the best challenge and providing clear instructions and modelling behaviour.

One of the difficulties with all work on self regulation and metacognition is the extent to which the processes can be transferred across subjects. Much of the research on the development of self regulation and metacognition has been carried out in educational settings and has tended to focus on particular subject areas. The second part of this book will consider some of those specific subject based studies and what they may tell us about the development of metacognition in the first stages of formal education.

Part II

Metacognition across subject domains

Introduction

In this part I will concentrate on metacognition in different subject areas, but still with a focus on young children's development of metacognition. Most of the work in this area has been carried out with children in formal school settings. There is less research on pre-school children and metacognition, but I will consider the work on metacognition in these younger children in Part III.

The notion of subject specific metacognition is complex. From one point of view it is clear that metacognition is related to the type of task and to the skills needed for particular subjects. However, in the UK there is a growing movement towards integration of subjects at primary school level, with topics crossing different subject boundaries. In addition, many of the thinking skills programmes, while embedded within a subject area, are also designed to promote metacognitive habits which the student will bring to bear across different subjects. There is also a philosophical point to consider here about where we place the boundaries of specific subject areas. What does it mean to talk about maths as separate from writing? We will see from some of the data that I have collected from Year 1 and Year 2 classrooms over the years that children do not necessarily see the same subject boundaries as adults. I have grouped some subjects together in rather traditional ways, but this is purely pragmatic and does not indicate that I believe that these subjects really do have more in common with each other than a different grouping might suggest. So I hope that you will make links for yourself across these chapters as well as within them.

Chapter 4

Science and mathematics

In this chapter I am going to focus on the pre-cursors to understanding in these two subject domains by drawing on my own work on a programme called Cognitive Acceleration through Science Education at Key Stage 1 (CASE@KS1). This programme is part of a growing family of cognitive acceleration (CA) programmes developed by Philip Adey and Michael Shayer. The original Cognitive Acceleration through Science Education programme was designed to work with secondary school students and was embedded in the science curriculum. See the book *Really Raising Standards* (Adey & Shayer, 1994) for full details of that programme and the underlying theory to all their CA programmes.

CASE@KS1 began life as a research study at King's College in London in association with the London Borough of Hammersmith and Fulham. The aim was to investigate whether the CA principles, which had worked so well in the earlier secondary school programme, could be used to develop materials for use in early primary school. Before I can show you how metacognition is developed through the CASE@KS1 programme it is necessary to have some understanding of the theoretical background to CA.

It is Shayer and Adey's contention that there is a general intelligence factor which underpins more specialist and specific aptitudes. This is a theory which is counter to the popular (among many teachers) view that there are multiple intelligences, each developing separately and at different rates – the theory delineated by Gardner (1993), and often linked to learning styles. Adey and colleagues provide evidence for the hypothesis that specific aptitudes or talents are built upon a general intelligence and that while a child may seem to be talented in one area but less so in another, this is more likely to be for social and motivational reasons, rather than cognitive ones (Adey *et al.*, 2007). The second premise on which all CA programmes are built is that this general intelligence is "plastic" or modifiable. While acknowledging a hereditary factor in general intelligence, Adey's view is that it is the environment which provides the intellectual stimulation for brain and cognitive development. Thus it is possible to intervene in this development and by providing an enriched environment children's thinking can be facilitated and developed. All CA programmes are based on the cognitive developmental theories of Piaget and the social construction theories of Vygotksy.

In Piagetian terms primary age children will develop cognitively from a pre-operational level to early and later concrete operational levels. There are a number of Piagetian tests that can determine at which level children are operating. Perhaps the best known of these are the tests of conservation of number, mass and liquid. An example of the conservation of liquid is the task where a child is shown two beakers. One is tall and thin and one is short and fat. The child watches while the same amount of liquid is poured into each beaker. Of course the level of the liquid will be much higher in the tall thin beaker. The child is asked if the two beakers contain the same amount of liquid or not. A child working at the pre-operational level of cognitive development will maintain that the tall thin beaker has more liquid even when the original measure is highlighted. In my experience of administering this task to young children, a pre-operational level child will be so convinced of her view that the tall beaker has more liquid that she will not change this view no matter how many times the question is asked. However, a child working at the concrete level of operations will equally maintain that of course the two beakers have the same amount of liquid and to suggest otherwise is simply silly. There are similar tests of conservation of number and mass. During the primary school years it is concrete and later concrete operational thinking which develops. CASE@KS1 activities are based on the development of a number of schemata which underpin the development of concrete operational thinking. The schemata are based on Piagetian notions of general thinking which underlie all domain specific thinking. The CASE@KS1 tasks are based on the following schemata: seriation (putting things in order according to length, weight etc.), classification, perspective taking, cause and effect, spatial perception.

The CASE@KS1 programme

While the CASE@KS1 tasks are based on the above schemata, these schemata are crucial to the development of understanding in science and maths. For instance, one task involves children investigating and coming to a shared understanding of shadows and what causes them. Other tasks involve children working together to categorise a set of buttons in different ways, and dealing with the notion of overlapping sets, or describing a scene from another person's point of view. There are 28 activities in the full programme designed for working with collaborative mixed ability and mixed gender groups of six Year 1 children, i.e. aged 5 to 6 years old. After working through some initial activities on working together and collaborating, the teacher is encouraged to form fixed groups of six children who will work on a CA activity once a week. The activities are now published as *Let's Think* (Adey *et al.*, 2001), but Adey is quick to point out that activities alone will not facilitate the development of thinking. The process of working through each activity is crucial to the programme. Thus the professional development of the teachers involved and the need for all classroom workers to understand some of the theory behind CA is crucial to the success of all CA interventions.

The method advocated by Adey and Shayer for all CA programmes is based on a great deal of theoretical work, practical experience and evidence from evaluation of the programmes over 25 years. Fundamental to all these programmes, including the Year 1 programme, are five precepts or "pillars" of cognitive acceleration. These are: concrete preparation, cognitive conflict, social construction, metacognition and bridging. It is through these pillars that children's general thinking is facilitated and enhanced. I will give a brief definition of each of these before concentrating on metacognition. My view is that it is not possible to see metacognition as a separate and distinct stage of the process – as some of the other pillars are – and I will illustrate this with the data from Year 1 classrooms.

The first pillar of concrete preparation is simply the introduction of the task by the teacher to the children in the group. However, even at this stage the children are encouraged to touch, comment on, ask questions about the materials and to listen to each other. The teacher will present the task in such a way as to emphasise its open ended nature. While there may be a solution to some CASE@ KS1 tasks, the emphasis is always on working through the task collaboratively, with a group of peers and teacher support, rather than being the first one to get the "answer". The majority of tasks do not have a simple solution and there can be multiple appropriate responses.

The second pillar of cognitive conflict is at the heart of the Piagetian theory which underpins all CA programmes and the notion of a zone of proximal development, which is in turn based upon Vygotskyan theory. Cognitive conflict is created by providing a challenge which is moderately difficult and which forces the children to stop and think again, perhaps to challenge their intuitive beliefs, or well rehearsed answers.

The third pillar, social construction, draws on the idea that knowledge and understanding is firstly constructed socially and then internalised by the individual. The move from the inter-psychological to the intra-psychological is the basis for Vygotksy's theory of learning and development (Vygotsky, 1978).

Metacognition is the fourth pillar of all CA activities and it is my contention that this should be facilitated from the beginning to the end of the activity, not just left to a reflective section after the task has been completed. Asking very young children to reflect on how they were thinking in an earlier part of the task is more likely to produce stock responses of the "with my brain" variety than any meaningful metacognition. However, the CA materials suggest a sequence which emphasises the facilitation of metacognition at the end of the activity.

The fifth pillar of all CA activities is bridging. This involves making new thought processes useful in different contexts by making clear how the particular schema can be used in a variety of tasks. It is through bridging that CA activities can transfer thinking from a schema to the particular domains of science and maths.

Bottles task

A number of small plastic bottles are filled with different amounts of rice. The task is for the group to predict which bottles will roll down the slope and which will not. Later on the children test their predictions and try to come to some conclusion about cause and effect in relation to the bottles.

The group:

The six children in this group are between 5 and 6 years old. They come from different ethnic backgrounds but all have English as a first language and have no language difficulties. As with all Cognitive Acceleration groups they are of mixed ability in terms of school base line tests of literacy and numeracy. However, the gap between them is not so large. They are of average to above average attainment and all were found to be working at the concrete operational level as defined by Piagetian tasks of conservation. They had also all passed the copy theory of mind tests as defined by the Smartie tube test (described in Chapter 1).

There are three boys: Joseph, Harry and Samuel, and three girls: Naomi, Audrey and Mia.

The task took place within their own classroom whilst other children were working on other projects.

Figure 4.1 Description of the CASE@KS1 Bottles task.

So how does the Let's Think programme facilitate the development of metacognition? In order to demonstrate this I will provide some actual data from the research project from which the Let's Think programme was developed.

In this excerpt the children are trying to predict which bottles will roll:

NAOMI: I think he had a reason for it [referring to Joseph's strategy], but I don't have a reason. I just think the heavy one will roll further.

HARRY: I think the lightest can go fastest and can go further. The heavy can't go so fast because it's heavy, so it won't go as far.

NAOMI: Oh I've changed my mind.

JOSEPH: I've changed my mind too because I think Harry's idea is better than my idea.

TEACHER: And why do you think that?

JOSEPH: Because if it didn't have anything in it would go really fast and then we wouldn't have to pull or push it along.

SAMUEL: If it's lighter it will go faster because it's like a 10-year-old and a grandpa racing. The 10-year-old would probably win because the 10-year-old would be smaller and like the light bottle and he would be younger and have more strength, so the light bottle will go further.

TEACHER: That's an interesting idea. What do you think about Samuel's idea?

JOSEPH: It's a good idea, cos the 10-year-old would be skinnier.

TEACHER: Is the bottle skinnier?

JOSEPH: No, it's quite fat.

TEACHER: How do you know this one is going to go further than this one then?

JOSEPH: Because this one has got more rice in it and this one has got less and the light one goes further up to this end and this one will only go about up to there.

TEACHER: And how do you know that?

JOSEPH: Because this one has less rice.

TEACHER: So what does that mean?

JOSEPH: So it will go further.

TEACHER: Why? Why does having less rice mean it goes further?

NAOMI: I don't understand this.

TEACHER: He's got an idea, he thinks the lighter one is going to go further.

MIA: He's not telling us why.

NAOMI: The light bottle is like a 10-year-old and will run further. I think Samuel's idea is right but it doesn't say why.

AUDREY: Yeah, the light one will go further cos the heavy one is slower.

NAOMI: It's like Molly and me when we rolled down the hill and I was lighter and rolled further.

TEACHER: Naomi has used an example of something she has experienced before and she thinks that the lighter one goes further.

[The children go on to test their predictions and to discuss the results which confound their expectations]

It is clear from this excerpt that the teacher is crucial to facilitating and maintaining the discussion, but if we strip out the teacher's comments we can see her role more clearly. She says:

- And why do you think that?
- That's an interesting idea. What do you think about Samuel's idea?
- Is the bottle skinnier?
- How do you know this one is going to go further than this one then?
- And how do you know that?
- So what does that mean?
- Why? Why does having less rice mean it goes further?
- He's got an idea, he thinks the lighter one is going to go further.
- Naomi has used an example of something she has experienced before and she thinks that the lighter one goes further.

The teacher's role here is to clarify the ideas, to challenge the children's thinking, to act as a memory store for the discussion and to summarise at an appropriate point. The teacher makes it clear that the children should evaluate the evidence given for the claims rather than just the claim itself. Through focusing on "how they know" something and enabling the children to compare different ideas, the teacher has moved the conversation away from the pragmatic level of which bottle will roll further to a more abstract level of explaining and evaluating the ideas about what might happen. I will return to the teacher's role in more detail in Chapter 7.

The children are engaged with and responding to each other. So the question is: to what extent can we say that the children in this excerpt are demonstrating metacognition? If we take Naomi as an example we see that at the beginning Naomi compares her own way of thinking with Joseph's. She realises that while Joseph provided an explanation, she is working on intuition. If we consider this in the light of Flavell's theory of metacognition we can label these statements. Naomi is aware of herself and others as thinkers [SELF category]. She is also aware that different people given the same stimulus may think differently about it [OTHER category]. Following Harry's idea of which bottle will roll further, Naomi changes her mind and demonstrates that she is aware that she has changed her mind [SELF category]. However, later on Naomi displays her confusion again: "I don't understand this." Awareness of understanding or not understanding is sometimes termed "metacomprehension" and Naomi realises that while she thought she had clarified her own ideas, explanations by Joseph and Samuel have only confused her again. This is another example of the SELF category. Mia actually voices the idea that it is a lack of a convincing explanation which is causing the confusion. However, it is Naomi who abstracts from the actual explanation given by Samuel in order to rate it: "I think Samuel's idea is right but it doesn't say why." In terms of labelling responses as metacognitive we have now moved away from a SELF category to a focus on an aspect of the task, i.e. providing an explanation, and we might label this "rating" or RAT. Naomi acknowledges Samuel's idea may be correct but rates it less highly because the explanation is inadequate. Having realized this, Naomi then engages in some quick thinking to provide an explanation from her own experience. Her explanation involves comparing the bottles task to something which she already knows about and so she is consciously drawing on her own experience in another area to provide an explanation for the group. This is also a focus on the task and we might label this "comparison" or COMP.

While we may debate whether each individual statement I have highlighted can truly be viewed as metacognitive, I suggest that it is difficult to decide whether a statement is metacognitive or not, if it is taken out of context. However, by tracking the thinking processes of an individual engaged on a task it is possible to see how conscious awareness of cognitive processes is being used to achieve a goal. Moreover, I suggest that particularly in the case of young children, metacognition is developed through collaboration on a joint task. In the excerpt above, the group discussion and the teacher's careful questioning provide a metacognitive experience for Naomi (and the other children) which enables her to think about herself as a thinker, to compare herself to others and to abstract from simply solving the task to begin engaging in ruminations about the nature of knowledge and evidence. These skills are particularly necessary for scientific thinking. Understanding the need to provide plausible explanations for phenomena and to rate and compare explanations are foundations stones of science.

The CASE@KS1 research programme from which the above excerpt was taken provided a wealth of similar examples of very young children (aged 5 to 6 years) engaging in metacognitive dialogues while working through group tasks. While the programme highlights the five pillars of CASE and tends to see metacognition as the reflection at the end of the task, it is clear from my research within the programme that in these young children metacognition is constructed socially through engagement on the task and not simply through reflection after completion of the task. This is an important point to make, as many of the teachers I have worked with initially view metacognition as something to be facilitated through a plenary session when the whole class can engage in assessing the difficulty of the task and can reflect on the strategies they used to complete it. While there is nothing wrong with engaging children in this discussion at the end of the lesson, my own research has shown that it is during the collaborative process that children begin to work through metacognitive experiences and to construct a metacognitive knowledge base.

One other aspect of the CASE@KS1 research programme which I am often asked about is the extent to which it only works with children who are already adept at working as a group and have well developed language skills. The research programme ran in what was classed as a deprived or disadvantaged part of an inner city area. We worked with children of many nationalities, with varying levels of English language fluency. We also had transient populations in the schools, with asylum seekers and other short stay children moving through the classes. In addition, there were children with a variety of special needs in each class, including hearing loss, behavioural difficulties and autistic spectrum children. In other words we had a population of classes which represented the lower to middle end of the state school primary provision in an inner city area. In all classes the teachers were able to work with the children in collaborative groups on these activities. The data I personally collected from around 70 hours of observations over one year demonstrate the extent to which these young children can engage in metacognition when the environment is supportive.

However, it is not only CASE which has provided evidence of children's metacognition in science education. One important aspect of science education is described by the theory of "conceptual change". This refers to how children's ideas of different phenomena develop over time and with experience. Recent evidence from cognitive neuropsychology has suggested that when naïve ideas are challenged and new concepts are learned, people tend to maintain both their original naïve idea and the new idea, so that rather than changing our concepts we learn to choose the more appropriate idea over and above our naïve idea (Goswami & Bryant, 2007). It is thought that the basis for this choice lies in our ability to inhibit our first response and this develops with age. Inhibitory control is linked to the function of executive control mechanisms in the pre-frontal cortex of the brain and these executive control mechanisms are responsible for metacognition as they control and regulate cognitive functioning. Being able to inhibit our initial response is important in many areas of learning and enables us to plan effectively rather than jumping straight in; to consider whether our answers are appropriate rather than saying the first thing we think of; and to delay gratification, knowing that spending time studying now will pay off later and allow us to think deeply about the sources of knowledge and evidence we are being presented with. For science educators the questions now revolve around how to encourage students to ask appropriate questions about scientific concepts, to develop scientific thinking and to argue based on evidence.

Beeth (1998) described a number of ways in which teachers can create an environment in which scientific concepts can be discussed and negotiated. These include encouraging children to talk about their ideas and why they think what they think, learning about the discourses of science – what kinds of words scientists use and in what ways – and being direct about different epistemologies, for instance saying "Let's think like a biologist". Other metacognitive strategies highlighted by Beeth include using analogies to bridge knowledge of scientific concepts to prior experience; encouraging children to reflect on how they are thinking; discussing the status of a scientific concept and elaborating on why some ideas are better than others; and providing opportunities for children to experience events which counter their naïve understanding of science concepts and to elaborate on the realisation of this discrepancy.

These metacognitive strategies can be seen in classroom based projects such as Project Meta (Hennessey, 1999). This project ran across the primary school phase from Grade 1 to Grade 6 in a US Midwestern elementary school. The teachers used three particular strategies for developing student metacognition in science subjects. First, all the children created posters to describe their initial ideas of specific scientific concepts. Through group discussion some of the underlying thinking behind these concepts was revealed. However, the teacher did not counter these concepts directly – children instead went on to produce models (concept maps, diagrams or actual models) of their theory. Through further group discussion the children made predictions based on their models and this revealed some of the shortcomings of their theories. Children also made audio and video recordings to capture their discussion about the different concepts and models. Hennessey makes the point that rather than teach a check list of metacognitive strategies or ways of regulating behaviour, Project Meta was concerned with more than performance outcomes and encouraged students of all ages to reflect on different strategies, to reflect on why they held certain ideas about specific scientific concepts and to be able to set aside these original concepts in order to consider and evaluate other conceptions. The children were also encouraged to reflect on the links between evidence and their own conceptions; to think about the status of their own conceptions; and to consider the consistency of them and the extent to which they provide an explanatory framework and can be generalised.

The skills that projects such as Project Meta are trying to develop in science education are also relevant to general life skills. Projects such as these eschew the narrow focusing of metacognition into teaching a list of strategies such as planning, checking, evaluating and while including these strategies, they take a much broader definition of metacognition as reflecting on thought, knowledge and beliefs in order to make informed decisions and to understand the basis for those decisions. Thomas and McRobbie (2001) have taken these links one step further to suggest that enhancing metacognition, at least in terms of metacognitive knowledge, can be seen in the same way as conceptual change in science education. Their argument is that children's conceptions of learning, their awareness of themselves as learners and their knowledge of learning processes are constructed over time in much the same way as their conceptions of phenomena in the physical world and that like those naïve scientific concepts, metacognition may be slow and difficult to change. However, by thinking of developing metacognition as akin to conceptual change, we can focus on how children recognise that they have conceptions of learning and the nature of those. We can encourage children to evaluate these conceptions, as they might do scientific concepts, and to consciously adopt new and appropriate conceptions. This new knowledge may not transfer directly to altering the ways in which children approach learning. It is likely that specific links will need to be made between the knowledge base of metacognition and the use of metacognition to aid learning and self awareness. Whether considering conceptual change in science learning or conceptual change in learning about learning, it is necessary to step back from the cognitive level, to abstract and to consider concepts from a more objective position.

Much of the recent work on science learning and metacognition has focused on the socio-cultural models of learning and the construction of knowledge through shared discussion and collaborative group work. In collaborative group work such as that provided by the CASE@KS1 (Let's Think) project, children have to reflect on their own ideas in order to explain them to others and there is a good deal of evidence that even young children are able to think about why they hold certain concepts and what the basis for those beliefs are. The schemata introduced through the early years CASE projects are also relevant for mathematics education and in the next section I will provide some more evidence of young children reasoning and developing metacognition through a CASE task.

Mathematics and metacognition

In common with many other subjects, mathematics has undergone a considerable shift in epistemology over recent times. The once objective, value-free and "true" basis of mathematical knowledge has been replaced by various understandings of mathematical knowledge as being socially and culturally situated, existing in all cultures, in multiple ways and constructed by the learner rather than passed on directly from teacher to student. A further development has been the emphasis on understanding mathematics as a mathematician, thereby highlighting how mathematical knowledge may be similar to, or contrast with, other forms of knowledge. Included in this perspective is an understanding of the discourses of mathematics and how language serves and constructs mathematical knowledge. This shift in perspective from the modernist to the post modernist has also seen a growth in the amount of research on metacognition in mathematics education. There is an understanding now that simply giving children a recipe for working various arithmetic problems is not enough; they need also to understand the language of mathematics, the different ways of reasoning common to mathematics and to be able to monitor their own thinking through self questioning. Lerch (2004) has also suggested that self concept in relation to mathematics is an important aspect of learning. Mathematics seems to cause quite a few problems for learners of all ages and many adults claim to be poor at mathematics, when they have perfectly acceptable skills in other areas. There is often a fear attached to mathematics and this has implications for motivation and self esteem.

In terms of young children, recent research from a cognitive neuroscience perspective has suggested that some aspects of mathematics, in particular knowledge of numbers in the sense of an understanding of magnitude, may be innate, but this does not mean that children are born with a knowledge of the symbolic number system, as these are also culturally bound. Goswami and Bryant (2007) have highlighted this difference and suggest that understanding number is dependent on language, perceptual and spatial development and that learning the count sequence builds upon these cognitive processes to develop a number system.

Carr, Alexander and Bennett (1994) suggested that even young children can and do understand when to use different strategies in solving mathematical problems. Theirs was one of the earliest studies of metacognition and mathematics with young children and included a measure of how the children attributed their success or failure, i.e. whether or not they attributed this to effort or to some external force. So this study linked metacognition in mathematics with an understanding of the role of motivation. The study involved second grade children, aged around 7 years old. Through observation the researchers studied the different kinds of strategies the children used to solve mathematical problems, categorising these as external (such as counting on fingers) or internal, where the behaviour could not be observed, such as counting in the head. The results showed that children of this age were using metacognitive knowledge of strategies and that there was a correlation between the successful use of internal strategies and metacognition. This suggested that correct use of strategies influences and develops metacognitive knowledge which in turn leads to later strategy use. The study also highlighted the link between metacognition, motivation and use of internal strategies. The researchers concluded that both metacognition and attributional beliefs have more effect when children are developing strategies and have less effect on strategies that are already stable, such as many of the external counting strategies. This is probably because by this age these external strategies have become automatic and no longer require metacognitive processing.

In a more recent study of metacognition in third grade children aged 8–9 years, Desoete and colleagues (2001) suggested that in terms of mathematical problem solving, metacognition can be divided into three components. These are labelled "global metacognition", "off-line metacognition" and "attribution". Global metacognition is described as including all metacognitive knowledge, such as declarative, procedural, conditional and metacognitive skills. Metacognitive skills include planning, monitoring and evaluating. Off-line metacognition makes a distinction between metacognition during the task and the off-line metacognition before and after a task. So off-line metacognition includes those skills such as prediction and evaluation which take place before the task begins and once it has ended. The third component they describe is attributions of success and failure, such as whether children attribute failure to lack of effort or to some external source. The study is contextualised by mathematical problem solving, so this three component model of metacognition may or may not hold for other subject domains. However, the study is important in understanding how metacognition impacts on performance in children of this age. The researchers found that children with above average mathematical problem solving had higher scores on global metacognition, but there was no significant difference between average and below average problem solvers on this factor. However, in terms of off-line metacognition a different picture emerged, while above average problem solvers again scored highly on this factor, average and below average problem solvers were also differentiated. The below average problem solvers did less well on scores of off-line metacognition than the average problem solvers. On the third factor of attribution, the above average group had more internal attributions than the average and below average group and there was no difference between the average and below average groups on this measure (Desoete et al., 2001). In a simplistic way then we can say that children who attain well in mathematics also have higher scores on these three components of metacognition. This kind of detailed study in one curriculum domain is also important for our understanding of metacognition in young children and may provide us with a different three component model of metacognition to investigate in other curriculum areas or with younger children.

While metacognitive knowledge is important for mathematics learning, so are the skills of monitoring, reflecting and evaluating. Both young and older children have been found to be particularly poor at this type of monitoring and evaluation, leading to poor performance in mathematics (Carr & Biddlecomb, 1998). Anyone who has taught at higher levels of education, such as college and university level will have seen that these skills do not necessarily develop with age. It may be as Lester and Garofalo (1982) suggested, that children do not view evaluation and monitoring as necessary parts of mathematics, or as Schoenfeld (1987) suggested, that children do mathematics in a step by step way rather than having a global view of what they are trying to achieve. Maybe mathematics teaching has placed too much emphasis on the mechanics of problem solving without teaching children to think as mathematicians. It is also feasible that the classroom environment perpetuates this lack of monitoring. I have often sat in Year 1 and Year 2 classrooms while children are working on mathematics problems. A common occurrence is the children's own peer competition on their group tables to see who will finish first. While teachers, in my experience, repeat mantras about checking answers, there is less emphasis on planning, prediction and evaluation during the problem solving.

One possible way of countering the peer competition is to use more collaborative group tasks in mathematics. In the CA (Adey and Shayer) family of thinking skills programmes, the Cognitive Acceleration through Mathematics Education (CAME) programmes use collaborative group work to enable children to construct knowledge of mathematics from everyday experiences and by using natural language. The early primary school versions of this programme are based within the Piagetian developmental stage characterised by concrete operations. The programme distinguishes between early, middle and mature concrete operations and describes four strands of mathematical thinking which are returned to in progressively more complex ways as children develop through this stage. These strands form the basis for future mathematical thinking and include: sorting and ordering; change and relations; number sense; and representing number. As with all CA activities tasks are designed to engage children in working collaboratively, listening to each other and arguing logically. There is a focus on mathematics learning but also a focus on general reasoning skills and on developing metacognition. Some of the strands used in the primary CAME programme are also common to the primary CASE programme mentioned earlier, e.g. sorting and classifying, seriation and ordering. The following excerpt shows a difference between children's metacognition when working collaboratively and children's metacognition when discussion is left to the end of the class. The first excerpt is from a CASE@KS1 activity and the second from an observation of a Numeracy Hour mathematics lesson for the same children.

This excerpt begins after the teacher has explained the task and the children have quickly jumped in and put the rocks in a line, which some of them believe is the correct order:

TEACHER: So, that was quick, have we done it? Have we solved the problem?
CHORUS: Yeah!
AYESHA: We've put them bigger to smaller.
LEON: I don't think it's right. That one isn't bigger than that one.
POPPY: Well measure them.

Rocks task

There are 12 different sized and differently shaped rocks. The task is for the group to put the rocks in order from biggest to smallest.

The group of six children follows the CASE guidelines for mixed groups as described earlier. The task takes place in the spring term so the group has been working together once a week since September.

The three girls are: Ayesha, Justine and Poppy, and the three boys are: Leon, Edward and Paul.

Figure 4.2 Description of the CASE@KS1 Rocks task.

TEACHER: How could you measure them?
POPPY: With a stick.
[Teacher sends Poppy off to get a stick]
EDWARD: You might not have to measure them if you can just see it.
TEACHER: What do you all think of that idea?
AYESHA: Well, we can see it is bigger, just Leon thinks it isn't.
PAUL: I don't think it is either. Look [he picks up both stones and holds them up next to each other]. This one is shorter than this one.
AYESHA: Yes but this one is fatter.
LEON: [picking up the two stones] I think this one is heavier.
JUSTINE: Oh this is making my head hurt.
TEACHER: Why is that?
JUSTINE: Because no one knows what they think, they keep changing and everyone has a different idea.
[Poppy returns with a ruler]
PAUL: Now we'll know, let's use the ruler.
PAUL: [begins to try to measure the rocks using the ruler] See this one is bigger than that one.
POPPY: But if you measure it across this one is fatter.
LEON: I think this one is heavier.
JUSTINE: This doesn't make sense. This is so hard.
TEACHER: Why do you think it's hard?
AYESHA: We can't agree on it. If we could all just look and see which is the biggest then we could agree and it wouldn't be hard.
TEACHER: Is that a good plan, can we all look and agree?
LEON: No, because we are looking different.
JUSTINE: That's it, that's why it is so hard. We are looking different. Poppy is looking at fattest, but Paul is looking at smallest, I think anyway. I don't know, it's quite puzzling.

TEACHER: What can we do then if it is so puzzling?

AYESHA: We have to agree on it.

POPPY: No we have to agree on measuring it.

TEACHER: What do you mean?

POPPY: We have to decide to measure it across or up and then do them all the same.

PAUL: Yeah I agree, you know we don't even know what big is!

[They all laugh]

This simple task of putting rocks in order of size becomes much more complex when done as a collaborative group task. The children are eager to rush in and complete the task without much discussion. The initial motivation seems to be to get the task done as quickly as possible and if they had all agreed on the order of the rocks, the metacognitive element would probably have consisted of the teacher asking them how easy or difficult they had found the task and why. However, the rocks are very different shapes and once put in an order it becomes quite clear that some rocks could be in other places. This creates the cognitive conflict necessary to provoke higher levels of thinking and metacognition. This group has worked together on CASE tasks since the beginning of the school year and in this second term they are much more confident about expressing their own views within the group. So Leon has no problem in revealing his doubts about the order of the rocks. However, it is Justine who consistently evaluates the task and expresses its difficulty: "Oh this is making my head hurt."

It would have been quite easy for the teacher to ignore this seemingly throwaway remark, but instead she pursues it because she is aware that this is likely to lead to more metacognition than the focus on whether or not to use a ruler. Given this encouragement Justine is able to express her thoughts about the multiple perspectives the group is offering: "Because no one knows what they think, they keep changing and everyone has a different idea." Justine goes on to express her own difficulty in thinking about the task and her feelings of confusion: "This doesn't make sense. This is so hard." And finally: "That's it, that's why it is so hard. We are looking different. Poppy is looking at fattest, but Paul is looking at smallest, I think anyway. I don't know, it's quite puzzling."

In order to obtain this understanding of her own difficulty Justine has had to monitor the task from different perspectives and to weigh these against the goal. Rather than seeking the easy option of agreeing on an order, Justine is more concerned with understanding why she feels so confused and puzzled by the seemingly simple task. By providing a commentary for the group Justine enables other group members to think about possible strategy solutions to the problem of how to approach the task. So it is Poppy rather than Justine herself who has the "Eureka" moment of realising that they need to agree on how to approach the task rather than on the outcome. Paul's final jokey comment actually provides a foundation for an understanding of mathematics. It hints at the idea that language needs to be contextualised and that words such as "big" are of little use in terms of mathematical understanding and require further definition. This task is therefore sowing the seeds of future thinking in mathematics as well as developing children's understanding of collaborative problem solving and the metacognitive skills of planning, monitoring and evaluation.

A further point to make about this excerpt is that it demonstrates how some children are particularly concerned with the group dynamics rather than the task in hand. I saw this over and again in different groups and here it is Ayesha who is keen that the group should reach a consensus rather than exploring the difficulties of doing so. I will return to this aspect of collaborative group work in Chapter 8.

The focus in the excerpt above could be said to be on monitoring and evaluation of the task. Working as a collaborative group facilitates this type of metacognition. However, in many UK classrooms at this time mathematics was taught through the Numeracy Hour. The Numeracy Hour tended to stick to a particular format of whole class introduction to the topic, work in groups on tables and whole class plenary to reflect on learning. In the classrooms I observed, the group work was often individual work but with children sitting in groups. They often asked each other for help on the task. However, in contrast to the collaboration seen on the CASE tasks, co-operative help from peers was often in the form of one or two smart children providing answers for others on the table, when asked, but without any discussion of the process of their thinking. There was also a great deal of social talk in the groups I observed and while this served a social function it was largely unrelated to the task in hand. The metacognition in these types of lessons tended to occur at the end of the lesson when the teacher brought the whole class together and directed

---

Mrs Thomas's class is working on shapes, identifying and naming different shapes and saying what things they have in common and how they differ. The class begins with all 25 children sat on the carpet and Mrs Thomas holds up a variety of shapes and asks individual children to name them. They use the words circle, cuboid, sphere, cylinder, pyramid to describe the shapes. The children have done similar lessons before, so they are revising the names rather than learning them for the first time. After the whole class section, the children go to their group tables. Mrs Thomas comes to work with our table. There are six children, five girls: Katie, Dacia, Kelly, Sabrena and Rosemary, and one boy: Billy.

The children are average to above average in maths attainment according to teacher assessment.

The following excerpt is from the start of the group work. There are sheets of card on the table with a number of different types and sizes of shapes drawn on each card.

Figure 4.3 Mrs Thomas's numeracy lesson.

her questioning to reflecting on learning. The following excerpt is from a Year 1 class not involved in the CASE project, but where the teacher was keen on encouraging group work in mathematics.

TEACHER: What I want you to do is to just look at the shapes in front of you, don't do anything, just look at them.

[Children sit quietly looking at the cards]

TEACHER: I want you to sort these shapes and look very carefully and then put the same shapes together. Sort them out. What shapes can you put together?

[Dacia points to two triangles]

TEACHER: Dacia why do you want to put those together?

DACIA: Because they are the same order.

TEACHER: Order? What do you mean by that?

DACIA: I don't know.

TEACHER: Rosemary has noticed that this shape is similar to that shape. What did you see?

ROSEMARY: They have 4 sides.

KATIE: They are the same, but they are not the same size. That one has 4 sides and that one has 4 sides.

TEACHER: What I want you to do is to think about it and cut the shapes out and put the ones that are the same or have something in common here, and the others that are the same or similar here [pointing to two square hoops on the table]. They must all have something in common, do you understand?

[Children nod]

[Teacher leaves and children begin to cut out shapes]

[Katie puts a rectangle in one hoop]

KATIE TO KELLY: Where does this one go? [holding up a circle]

[Kelly is engrossed in cutting and doesn't answer. Katie leaves the circle and begins to cut out a triangle]

[Billy and Sabrena are working as a pair]

BILLY: Two rectangles they both have 4 sides.

TEACHER: [returning with glue sticks] When you have sorted them you can stick them on these pieces of paper, when you are quite sure.

KATIE TO KELLY: Put the ones together that look the same.

TEACHER: What have you found? What have they got in common?

BILLY: That has the same and that has the same – 4 sides [pointing to two rectangles].

TEACHER: Good. How are you thinking about it?

KELLY: Which one has six sides?

TEACHER: How are we getting on?

BILLY: They've all got 4 sides.

TEACHER: Good. How are you putting your shapes together, in what way? What are you doing to put them in order, what are you thinking about to put them in order?

BILLY: Thinking about these ones.
TEACHER: How do you know they are the right ones?
BILLY: Have the same sides and the same corners.
TEACHER: Good. Now you can stick them on the sheet.

In this excerpt the focus is very much on the cognitive activity of sorting the shapes rather than on any metacognition. The children are working well together, but this is in pairs rather than as a group. The task they have been set has a correct solution, in that the children are encouraged to sort the shapes by type rather than by any other variable such as size or colour. The teacher does not introduce this complication into the task because she is focusing on recognition of different shapes, regardless of colour or size. The children seem to enjoy the task, particularly the cutting out and sticking part. When the teacher asks the children to explain their strategy for sorting and to explain their thinking, Billy's simple answer "they have the same sides and corners" is accepted. The teacher doesn't try to engage the children in thinking more deeply about their approach to the task. This may be because the way the task is initially set up requires little metacognitive skill. There is no obvious cognitive conflict which might challenge the children to think about how they are approaching the task.

Towards the end of the lesson the teacher asks the groups to stop working:

TEACHER: One last thing before we finish off, did you find it easy or difficult?
CHORUS: Easy!
TEACHER: So what did you find easy about it?
CHILD: Counting the sides, we learned the numbers.
TEACHER: What numbers?
CHILD: We learned it more because we knew the numbers.
TEACHER: Did you find it hard Sabrena? What did you find hard in the beginning?
[Sabrena doesn't answer]
TEACHER: What did you find hard Billy? Did you find anything hard about sorting them out?
BILLY: Forgot what shapes go together.

In this section the teacher is trying to elicit some evaluation from the children and asking them to rate the task in terms of ease or difficulty. While this can be metacognitive, in this case the simple chorus of "Easy!" is more of a habitual response than a meaningful thought. When the teacher pursues this line with individual children, she comes up against a block, probably a result of a defence mechanism related to self esteem. There is nothing to be gained by Sabrena and Billy in exposing their difficulty with the task to the rest of the class, so the attempt to facilitate metacognition in this way is bound to fail.

This pattern of asking children to evaluate ease and difficulty at the end of a task is fairly common in the Year 1 classes I have observed over the years.

Sometimes teachers will use different ways of doing this: holding up a thumb for easy, or pointing it downwards for difficulty; or drawing a smiley face on their page for easy, a straight line face for OK or a sad face for difficult, for instance. However, there are three main problems with this approach. First, as I have already said, children are less likely to admit difficulty with a task, especially if their peers are rating the task as easy. Second, asking young children to evaluate a task after they have finished doing it is difficult in itself. It is unlikely that children of this age will remember accurately what they felt or what they thought during the last hour. Third, asking children to reflect on how they solved a problem after the event is fraught with difficulty. Their answers at this stage may well be dependent on other factors, such as wanting to appear knowledgeable about different strategies, suddenly remembering a strategy they have been taught in previous lessons, or wanting to please the teacher with an appropriate answer. The answers may or may not have anything to do with what the children actually did during the task. This is not to say that all attempts at facilitating metacognition at the end of lesson are redundant, but they do need to be carefully structured and to follow on from more meaningful discussion during the task. This can appear difficult to achieve, especially when the focus of the task is on building knowledge about a particular aspect of domain knowledge. However, I believe it is necessary to facilitate metacognitive dialogue while children are working through a task and to provide tasks where both cognitive knowledge of the domain and metacognitive knowledge are equally encouraged.

While CA tasks are based on schemata underlying specific domain knowledge, other programmes focus much more on the particular domain of mathematics. Many of the intervention studies in mathematics have been carried out with high school or college students. For instance, the IMPROVE programme, (Mevarech & Fridkin, 2006), is an instructional programme which trains high school and pre-college students to ask themselves metacognitive questions before, during and after solving a mathematical problem. The questions are grouped into "Comprehension" questions (understanding the task demands), "Connection" questions (bridging the current problem to past, similar problems), "Strategic" questions (focused on the strategies being used) and "Reflection" questions (these include monitoring progress towards the goal and evaluating the solution). The research with college students who elected to take mathematics has shown that students following this programme out-performed other students on mathematical knowledge and mathematical reasoning. These students also developed a higher level of metacognition both in terms of general metacognition and in terms of domain specific metacognition

A recent study carried out with children from 8 to 11 years old considered the connection between self image, cognitive processes, such as working memory and processing speed, and metacognitive processing in mathematics (Panaoura & Philippou, 2007). The study highlights the complexity of the metacognitive and cognitive systems. Children with high processing and high working memory ability also had high self regulatory ability and a positive self image. Self image in mathematics was dependent on processing efficiency and development of a positive self image was connected to working memory capacity and mathematical performance. However, a direct connection between metacognitive processing and performance in mathematics was not found.

One difficulty with studies which seek to investigate the connection between cognitive and metacognitive systems and their connection to performance in specific domains is the problem of how to assess metacognition, and I will return to this in Chapter 9. At present the research on metacognition and mathematics in young children shows a varied picture. Classroom based studies tend to show how metacognition can be directly taught and demonstrate the extent to which primary school children can develop knowledge of when and how to use different strategies, understanding of task demands, and awareness of self in terms of mathematics. Cognitive science studies tend to show the complexity of the metacognitive and cognitive system and there is still much work to be done on the link between metacognition and performance in mathematics, particularly at the earliest stages of learning about number. Language is an important factor in developing metacognition in any domain and in the next chapter I will focus on this in terms of the school based subjects of reading and writing.

Chapter 5

Reading and writing

Learning to read is the fundamental skill necessary for accessing the rest of the curriculum. Children and adults who experience difficulties with reading are disadvantaged in many areas of life. The vast amount of research and academic literature on reading is testament to its importance and it is right that so much effort and energy should be invested in this area. Debates about the best ways to teach children to read proliferate. In the UK the government's backing for a method of synthetic phonics teaching has caused some controversy. The teaching of reading seems particularly prone to new initiatives and some of these are driven more by political and historical factors than by hard evidence. It can be difficult therefore to see the purpose of metacognition in reading. Surely the main purpose is to ensure that children learn to read quickly and process the phonemes into words easily and efficiently. Metacognition can appear to be a distraction from learning the skill of word processing but reading involves much more than just being able to decode the symbols and turn letters into words with meaning. It is here that metacognition has had the most impact on teaching children to read.

Some of the first studies of metacognition in practice involved reading. The reciprocal reading programme of Palinscar and Brown (1984) involved teachers modelling the key principles of reviewing or summarising, questioning, clarifying and predicting in order to aid comprehension of a text. Teachers and students took it in turn to lead dialogues and teachers gave support and gradually gave way to the students as they become more confident. This method viewed reading as a constructive process which involves monitoring and self questioning, as well as control of cognitive processing. Reciprocal Teaching is about making explicit the strategies and skills that competent readers use when they are reading, so that students become aware of reading as a process. The programme was based on Vygotskyan ideas of the social construction of learning and the zone of proximal development. Palinscar and Brown argued that through "guided practice", i.e. the support of another more advanced reader, students would benefit from the modelling of reading strategies by the more expert reader and be helped to use these strategies themselves. Reciprocal Teaching was particularly aimed at readers who could already decode but had problems with comprehension.

Since the 1980s a good deal of research on Reciprocal Teaching has shown that readers do benefit from being explicitly taught the cognitive and metacognitive strategies outlined by Palinscar and Brown. An overview of 16 studies using Reciprocal Teaching concluded that this method of teaching had a significant positive effect on reading comprehension (Rosenshine & Meister, 1994). While I will return to reading comprehension later in this chapter, it would be a mistake to view metacognition as necessary only for comprehension.

Research on poor readers has shown that children who have difficulty with decoding also demonstrate poor self monitoring and control skills (Armbruster & Brown, 1984). Other studies have suggested that these difficulties are compounded by a lack of knowledge of reading strategies, an inability to select strategies and an inability to monitor strategy use. Le Fevre and colleagues have also argued that poor readers are often given inappropriate texts for their age and the reliance on simplistic texts for poor readers does nothing to improve knowledge and use of metacognitive strategies (Le Fevre *et al.*, 2003). This has an obvious effect on motivation. It is very difficult to motivate yourself to persist with an area of learning with which you are already struggling if the materials you are being presented with are also uninteresting.

Many of the early reading programmes for children with below average reading skills for their age concentrated on word level recognition and the decoding of sounds, at the expense of stimulating an interest in the pleasure to be gained from reading. That poor readers read less than good readers has been documented by a number of studies and the effect of this is that poor readers fall further and further behind as their exposure to texts becomes increasingly limited. Stanovich (1986) described this as the Matthew Effect after the parable of the talents in the Gospel according to St Matthew (25:14). In this parable a man entrusts his servants with his property while he goes on a journey. The first servant who had received five talents from the master traded and increased his talents to ten. The second man who had received two talents also traded and increased his talents to four. The third man who had received only one talent decided to hide it in a hole out of fear of his master and so was unable to increase his master's wealth. The parable concludes with the master admonishing the third man and making him hand over his one talent to the first man who has ten. Then he says "For to everyone who has will be given more, and he will have more than enough; but anyone who has not, will be deprived even of what he has." The reason that the third man loses his talent (and for this read literally money and metaphorically gifts from God) is because he hides it in a dark hole rather than thanking God for the gifts he has and using them to good effect. The parable acknowledges that not everyone will be granted the same gifts, but that all can increase their "wealth" by using the gifts they have. If we read the parable in this way then poor readers need to use what skill they have to engage with a wide variety of age appropriate texts, so that by using their "meagre talent" they can increase it. It is therefore the duty of those who are guiding young readers to ensure that the poor readers do not end up like the third servant in the parable. In the next section I will consider the role of metacognition in different aspects of reading, including supporting poor readers.

Decoding and fluency

At its most basic, learning to read involves understanding that printed letters correspond to spoken language. This involves a shift in thinking from concentrating on the content of the spoken message to understanding that language comes in different forms, both spoken and written. This move to a focus on form, characterised by learning the alphabet, has been described as the development of "metalinguistic awareness" (Tunmer & Bowey, 1984). As we gain knowledge about written texts we tend to build our knowledge of how texts are formed. Formal lessons in English language include instruction on the various parts of language: nouns, verbs, adjectives etc. as well as how sentences are constructed and how different forms are used to address different audiences. All of these are examples of metalinguistic knowledge, but at different levels of sophistication. This is a form of stored metacognitive knowledge, something which develops over time, with exposure to more and different texts and through direct instruction. The foundation of this knowledge is knowledge of the alphabet, both knowing letter sounds and knowing that letters have names. Children develop the ability to differentiate between these two through practice. In some languages there is a greater connection between letter names and letter sounds, making spelling words less problematic than in those languages, such as English, where the same letter or groups of letters can sound different simply due to meaning, e.g. words such as "bow" from which an arrow is shot and "bow" to bend or kneel as an act of deference. In addition groups of letters make different sounds depending on the letters which follow and precede them.

While studies of children's phonological awareness and knowledge of the alphabet have dominated investigations into how children learn to read, other aspects of perception such as visual awareness have also been found to be a factor in developing literacy. In particular, studies of children with dyslexia have made a connection between the ability to shift attention in response to visual cues and difficulty with recognising letters within text. Difficulties with both recognising sounds and letters impact on the development of metalinguistic knowledge. Yaden and McGee (1984) showed that poor readers have difficulty with metalinguistic knowledge, including understanding the vocabulary of reading, explaining the conventions of print and understanding the principles of decoding. Difficulty in understanding the skills necessary for reading makes it difficult to apply them in any consistent manner. Thus the metacognitive skills of monitoring and controlling thinking when decoding are less apparent in poor readers. The lack of both metacognitive knowledge about how language works and these metacognitive regulatory skills of monitoring and controlling progress in reading will have an impact on the motivation of poor readers to practise more. The lack of metacognition leads to an inconsistent approach to decoding which provides fewer successful attempts, leading to less desire to try and therefore less opportunity to build a metacognitive knowledge about how written language works, about self in relation to reading and about strategies that can be used to help with decoding. Bryant and Bradley (1985) found that it was the ability to apply appropriate strategies to reading that differentiated between good and poor decoders rather than only phonological ability. It seems that metacognition as both metacognitive knowledge and regulation and control of thinking are crucial elements of successful reading. A great deal of work on metacognition and reading has been conducted on comprehension and the next section will consider how metacognition is instrumental in understanding and making meaning from texts.

Comprehension

> *Polonius:* What do you read, my lord?
> *Hamlet:* Words, words, words.
> William Shakespeare, *Hamlet* (1600)

Reading is about more than decoding written symbols. We read in order to make sense of the world, to learn, to explore new territory and to inspire us to new enterprise. Taking a very cognitive psychological approach to reading can sometimes obscure this bigger picture. So, when we discuss learning to read and the various approaches and strategies we might teach or model, we need to ensure that we don't lose sight of reasons for reading. Reading should be a pleasure, something we indulge in, but we know that for some children who find reading difficult the pleasurable aspects can become buried under check lists of strategies, designed with the best intentions, to increase reading skill and comprehension. While I believe that making visible what skilled readers do in order to understand texts is a valuable activity, this should never be at the expense of encouraging a love for reading. So with that caveat in mind I will go on to discuss the various ways in which reading comprehension has been investigated and taught.

There is no one definition of comprehension. We all bring our own experience, knowledge and background to a text when we begin to read, so the meaning we make of a text is a personal construction. However, texts do not reside in a bubble consisting only of the text and the reader. Texts are constructed by writers who bring their own experiences, knowledge and value systems to the text. Texts are also constructed within larger social, cultural and historical contexts. We cannot divorce reading from this bigger picture. The reader is in dialogue with the writer and with the text. Thus helping children to understand texts requires encouraging them to take an active role as a reader. We can use strategies designed to encourage this active reading, such as asking children to predict what will happen next or to make connections between what they are reading now and some past experience or knowledge. We can focus on imagination and encourage children to put themselves in the place of characters in a fictional story. We can make explicit the links between factual reading about the environment and our everyday lives, or link curriculum subjects through an exploration of one text.

These types of meaning-making strategies tend to come from a transactional view of reading (Rosenblatt, 1969). Rosenblatt viewed reading as an event, something which happens between a reader and a text, situated within a particular, wider context. This event she said is also part of the life of the individual and of the group. The focus is always on the relationship between the text and the reader, rather than on the words and decoding. Rosenblatt's view of texts is one that suggests they do not exist in and of themselves. As they exist, they are simply marks on paper, but they only come into being as texts when a reader responds to these marks and constructs meaning from them. In a similar way the reader only becomes a reader when engaging in this interaction with the marks on paper. This view of reading is about action. The reader brings her own experiences to the text, but only when her focus on the text activates these past experiences. Interpretations are triggered by attention to certain words and images which resonate with our personal experience. As someone experienced in reading, consider these opening lines from Shakespeare's Sonnet 55:

> Not marble, nor the gilded monuments
> Of princes, shall outlive this pow'rful rhyme,
> But you shall shine more bright in these contents
> Than unswept stone, besmeared with sluttish time.
> (Shakespeare, 1593–1600)

The word "marble" may lead us back into any number of experiences of marble. When we touched marble, perhaps in a church or stately home, perhaps we touched something we shouldn't have. We might remember how it felt. We may have tried to carry a piece of marble and therefore might dwell on its weight and solidity. We link our experience of it to a particular time and place and so on. We may choose to linger on these connections or to not consciously acknowledge them but to move on quickly to a different word and set of associations. What we choose to focus on may not always be a conscious choice in the sense of deciding between alternatives – whether to focus on "marble" or on "unswept stone". We can become habitual readers in the sense that we always respond to certain cues in a text which may be linked to our earliest experiences. This also impinges on how we select the texts we decide to read, including the effect of the visual images on a book's cover.

Rosenblatt referred to "aesthetic" and "efferent" reading, which she saw not as opposites but as part of a continuum. Aesthetic reading, or reading for pleasure, would include a focus on the sound of the words, the rhythm of the line, the way the words provide us with the ingredients for creating our own mental images, our own imaginative worlds in response to the text. Efferent reading, or reading in order to do something else, tends to focus on the content of the text – we want to take away some knowledge from the text which we can use in another sphere. Efferent reading suggests that the text is open to miscomprehension, so there is a sense in which meaning is located in the text itself, or at least in the intentions of the writer. In terms of metacognition the reader must become aware of these different possible ways of approaching a text and the teacher's job is to guide the child towards building a knowledge of how texts work at this meta-level. One important strategy is to encourage children to reflect on their response to the text, and to discuss with others how the text connects with their own knowledge about themselves. In this way there is an iterative process between text and reader, with the reader bringing to bear their metacognitive knowledge of themselves to the text and the text helping to construct and develop further metacognitive knowledge of self as a reader.

Monitoring and control

Good readers have automated many of the processes of reading including how they make meaning from the text. We may choose whether to dwell on some beautiful image and allow our thoughts to take us on a journey away from the text, or we may choose to focus hard on meaning because we need to read quickly for a specific purpose. The difficulty for anyone trying to help children to read better is in bringing to conscious awareness what we do as skilled readers. Whether we know it or not, at some level we are constantly monitoring our understanding of a text. We usually only become aware of this monitoring when we are stopped short by an unfamiliar word or phrase, or when we suddenly become conscious of the fact that our attention has wandered away from the text and we are reading words without comprehension. As skilled readers, we are able to use this metacognitive monitoring of our reading to our own advantage. We can choose whether to take a particular action, e.g. re-read, refer to another source, read out loud, or we can choose to take no action, knowing that if we read further we may come to understand and get back on track. Young readers tend not to be aware of this monitoring process nor of the different strategies they may use to understand a text.

One of the simplest ways in which metacognition is instrumental to reading comprehension is in detecting errors in a text; a part of a passage which does not make sense in terms of the whole. Garner (1988) highlighted different types of error which can lead us to become aware of the way in which we are monitoring our reading.

The first type is a simple lexical problem; perhaps we come across an unfamiliar word, sometimes a word written in another language, sometimes an actual printing error. In tests of children's error detection, the passages often contain nonsense words for the children to spot. However, this is problematic since unless told that the passage contains these errors, children (and adults) may believe that they should know the word, and rather than admit to not knowing it they read on. So tests like these may be measuring confidence rather than error detection. The more confident the child is in speaking out and the more amenable the environment is to this, the more chance there is that the child will report on lexical errors. I have a clear memory of reading out loud in my primary class when I was 7 years old and coming across the word "parasol". I had no idea what the word meant, and didn't think I could decode it. However, a picture in the book showed a lady holding what I thought was a fancy umbrella. So when I came to the word "parasol" I simply read umbrella and carried on. At the end of the passage the teacher made me go back to the word and try to sound it out. She explained what it was. Not only had I monitored my reading, I had also taken some remedial action when confronted with the problem. I had used my own knowledge of the world to enable me to come up with a plausible, if incorrect reading.

This relates to Garner's second category of errors, which depend on external inconsistency. Thus readers become aware of their own monitoring processes when something in the text does not conform to their own experience of the world. For instance, if we are reading a factual text on plants and trees and we suddenly come across a claim that spaghetti is the fruit of a particular tree, our internal monitor would put on the brakes and we would most likely read the sentence again.

A similar error, and Garner's third category, is that of internal consistency. An example of this is when something which was described as green in one part of the text is suddenly described as blue in another part. In normal reading any of these errors would stop us in our tracks and we would make a decision of what to do next and whether or not to ignore the error. However, in tests neither children nor adults have been found to be very good at spotting textual errors. Baker (1985) suggested that this is because we expect texts to make sense and so we may not focus our attention on an error and instead skip over it and continue to read for meaning. Sometimes children are told that a text contains errors and are then tested on whether or not they can find them, but this is a different kind of skill to monitoring reading. If we are told that there are errors to be found, which we should report, then we are likely to approach the text as a game or problem to solve, as in those visual games where children are asked to find hidden objects in a picture. Under normal reading conditions we may be making split second, semi-conscious decisions about textual errors. In this sense skilled readers have automated some of the metacognitive aspects of reading, so that monitoring is not a conscious process, but one which is brought to consciousness by a sudden break in reading fluency. Younger and poorer readers, for whom monitoring is not yet automated may continue to read without understanding what they are reading. However, it seems clear that strategies for comprehending and monitoring reading can be taught and a number of different intervention programmes over the past 30 years have provided ample evidence of the role of metacognition in reading.

Metacognitive intervention programmes

Marie Clay's extensive work on reading led to a multi-faceted view of learning to read, but one which has the concept of "inner control" at its heart (Clay, 1991). Children are encouraged to develop awareness of printed forms, as well as skill in monitoring and self correction. Clay describes self correction as working on different levels, from a perceptual level or simple feeling that something is wrong to a more specific conscious awareness which can be verbalised but is less heard as the child becomes more adept. For Clay self correction makes a contribution to reading long before it becomes conscious and truly metacognitive. However, the cumulative effect of using self correction is to construct a metacognitive knowledge base and to develop metacognitive skills of monitoring and control. Clay suggests that self correction is hindered by the use of contrived texts; if there is no room for errors; and if the teacher is too quick to step in and help and if children depend on a single strategy for decoding. Clay makes the case for the complex and multi-faceted nature of reading, which includes both cognitive and metacognitive elements.

Reciprocal Teaching (Palinscar & Brown, 1984; Palinscar, 1982) has been referred to above. The method of an expert other modelling the key activities of summarising, questioning, clarifying and predicting and then providing feedback on the child's attempts to copy these strategies has proved influential in developing metacognitively oriented reading programmes. A more recent version of Reciprocal Teaching is to be found in a study by Le Fevre and colleagues (Le Fevre et al., 2003). In this study a group of 8–10-year-olds in New Zealand took part in a reciprocal tape-assisted teaching programme. The basis of this programme is that children listen to a tape recording of a text while following the printed text. The tape provides a form of support for children who are still working towards becoming independent readers. This support enables children to surmount the difficulties of losing meaning as they focus on decoding. The audio recording of reading also serves as a model for intonation and fluent reading and the researchers argue this has a positive effect on motivation to read.

A great deal of work on reading has been carried out by Pressley and colleagues, with a particular focus on what expert readers do. Constructively Responsive Reading acknowledges that a reader's responses to a text are both triggered by the text and by the reader's prior knowledge which is brought to bear on the text. Good readers are employing strategies at all points of reading, so before actually beginning to read, a good reader has a purpose in mind and will make some strategic decisions based on that purpose and the form of the text. The good reader begins with a plan of how to read the text. During the reading, good readers make strategic decisions about speed of reading, order of reading and re-reading. This also leads to a revision of the initial prediction of what to expect from the text. The reader also brings prior knowledge to bear on making inferences from the text and relates the information to what they already know. During the reading process, good readers also monitor and become aware of the many and varied characteristics of the text. They begin to evaluate the text in relation to their purpose and interest. After reading, good readers reflect on the text and may re-read some sections. They may make strategic decisions about taking notes or using the text in some way. Pressley argues that good readers know about these strategies; where and how to employ them. An intervention study teaching Constructively Responsive Reading across Grades 1–8 emphasised the need for a multi-faceted approach to teaching reading which includes cognitive, metacognitive and motivational factors (Pressley & Gaskins, 2006).

Other interventions include studies which use think-aloud procedures to model good reading strategies for students and to encourage students to verbalise their own thinking when reading (Israel & Massey, 2005). There are interventions which focus on monitoring ongoing reading, while others focus on comprehension strategies. While they may be difficult to implement in some classrooms, the research evidence suggests that where they are used, children learn to read better and are more consciously aware of how they are reading and why.

In their overview of reading and metacognition, Baker & Brown (1984) showed how metacognition was integral to active and constructive reading. They went on to identify metacognitive skills of reading such as: identifying the purpose of reading, clarifying meaning, focusing attention on main aspects, monitoring, self questioning and taking action to remedy problems. More recently, Linda Baker (2005) has suggested that comprehension strategy training and instruction for developing metacognitive awareness in reading should be part of learning to read from the earliest opportunity, but that this type of instruction needs to take account of the difficulties children face with cognitive overload when beginning reading. It is also important that interventions designed to teach or support metacognitive aspects of reading do not become a simple check list of strategies to be employed habitually. They also need to take account of the wider contextual issues of learning to read and what the reader brings to the text.

While a great deal of research has focused on readers and metacognition, fewer studies have focused on writing and metacognition, especially with children learning to write.

Metacognition and writing

Writing is closely allied with reading. Reading provides us with models for writing and writers need to read their work with a regard to audience, genre, meaning, grammatical errors etc. However, writing also includes the difficult motor skills of being able to hold a pencil; to write in the appropriate direction for reading; to be able to stay on the lines or to produce text with some semblance of a straight line; to be able to judge space and how much text will fit on a line. An understanding of the grammatical and punctuation conventions of the language is required too. In a review of young children's metalinguistic awareness, Yaden found that children had different ideas of what reading is (Yaden & McGee, 1984). I have found similarly disparate notions of writing in my research with Year 1 classes. Some of the 5- to 6-year-olds saw no difference in writing and drawing, so while as researchers we were asking questions based on our own notion of writing a text, some of the children would answer in terms of drawing. Similarly, some children made no distinction between writing letters and stories in their literacy lessons and writing numbers in their numeracy lessons. While we may differentiate writing from other similar activities involving a pencil, it is clear that not all young children do so. This suggests that these children are focusing on the motor skills needed to write, to make marks on paper, rather than on content. It was clear from our conversations with children who did focus on writing text that even then there was an emphasis on "being neat", "staying on the lines" and "using finger spaces". These more secretarial skills tended to dominate the answers to our questions about writing and were sometimes suggested as reasons for liking writing. This is probably due to a focus on the finished product – a neat paragraph of well spaced text, with all the words on the lines. Considerably fewer children of this age group talked about meaning. I will return to my own study of young children's writing later in the chapter.

Anecdotally, children appear to confuse writing and drawing and some theories of child development, drawing on Piaget's genetic epistemology, suggest that both drawing and writing develop from a common semiotic function, i.e. an ability to process symbolic information. This ability emerges towards the end of the sensorimotor stage. This view is a domain-general account of the development of symbolic functioning. However, a different view put forward by Karmiloff-Smith (1992) suggests a more specific development of writing, which can be differentiated from the development of drawing or number writing. Karmiloff-Smith describes how very young pre-literate children still make marks on paper and will differentiate those marks in terms of whether they represent a drawing of an object, or stand for letters and represent a name. Her experiments with toddlers, asking them to draw a picture and write a name, showed a clear distinction between the types of scribbles the children made. In addition, she found that the process of producing the scribbles was different, with children lifting their pen much more often when writing the name compared to when drawing the picture. In further studies the researchers found that when asked to sort cards of different types of notational systems, young children differentiated between drawing and writing and between writing letters and number notation. For example, when elements on the card were linked, the card would be accepted as part of the writing group but not accepted as part of the number group. They argue that this is because children are acting within a series of constraints for what can pass as acceptable in these categories. Even when asked to produce a word or number which doesn't exist, young children still worked within these constraints. However, by the age of 4 and upwards some children were able to overcome these constraints to produce pretend words which included drawings or words which repeated the same letter in a string.

There are a number of views as to why this might be, but it seems that different symbolic systems are processed in different parts of the brain. Karmiloff-Smith argues against an innate modularity to the way the brain is structured, suggesting that if these functions are modular in adults, this is due to a process of gradual modularity over time as the different notational systems become more differentiated and thus any modularity is a product of learning. Karmiloff-Smith's research into the development of notational systems is part of a much larger theory which she has developed over many years of empirical research. It is not appropriate to go into detail of this theory here. In summary, though, her theory of Representational Redescription (ibid.) describes how knowledge is represented at different levels. As the child progresses, knowledge becomes more specific. An initial phase of data driven learning leads to a "behavioural mastery" in a particular domain. A second phase, which is internally driven, involves a "redescription" of the initial representations and a third phase is a connection between the internal representations and external data again. The theory is important for metacognition as well as for understanding writing because it postulates that only at the second and third level of representation are the mental representations available to consciousness. A distinction is made between what can be verbally reported, i.e. knowledge at the third level, and knowledge which may be available to consciousness but cannot be verbally stated, i.e. knowledge at the second level. The significance of this for both reading and writing is that young children may have specific knowledge of these different domains and make differentiations between subsets of each domain, such as drawing, number notation and writing, but may be unable to verbalise that knowledge. Only when the knowledge is "redescribed" at the third level are children both conscious of this knowledge and able to describe it. It is this third level that we refer to as metacognitive, but Karmiloff-Smith is also saying that level two representations are available to consciousness so that the reliance on verbal reports for metacognition may be underestimating children's metacognitive awareness.

Studies of writing and metacognition have focused on verbal reports of children's ability to reflect on the writing process, on strategy use or on monitoring. Since the 1980s writing has been seen as a problem solving activity and models of writing have highlighted the cognitive processes involved. One of the best known models of writing is that of Hayes and Flower (1980), which breaks writing down into the three processes of planning, translating and reviewing. Moreover, they showed that writing is a recursive process, so that these three elements occur and reoccur during the writing process. In their model of writing, planning is broken down into goal setting, which establishes the purpose of the writing and sets short term goals; generating, which involves developing ideas and content, and organizing, which focuses on arranging the content and structuring the text. Again these processes interact and reoccur, so that there is a recursive process within the planning phase as well as between this phase and the translating and reviewing phases. Translating is viewed as the process of transforming ideas into written text.

Reviewing is also broken down into sub processes of evaluating, revising and re-writing. Bereiter and Scardamalia (1987) found that young writers become confused about their writing goals during writing and often lose their flow. In addition, through studying expert and novice writers, Bereiter and Scardamalia came to the conclusion that novice writers engage in "knowledge-telling", while expert writers use a "knowledge-transforming" strategy. The difference is evident when viewing children's factual writing. If they plan at all they tend to write a list of the contents of the proposed text and the writing follows the list in a descriptive way. So the emphasis is on telling what is known rather than using writing to communicate thoughts and ideas. In contrast, more experienced writers plan a text with a particular communicative goal in mind and with some understanding of both purpose and audience. The planning strategies of expert writers are often complex and are revised during the text construction. In order for children to develop their writing skills they need to become aware of the different processes involved in writing and develop a more global understanding of writing as knowledge-transforming.

Many studies have used think-aloud methods for studying both expert and novice writers. In these methods writers are encouraged to verbalise their thinking before, during and after writing. In this way expert writers reveal the cognitive processes they are using when constructing a text. Identification of these processes can then lead to instructional methods for teaching younger writers and making explicit some of these hidden and internal strategies. In *The Psychology of Writing*, Kellogg (1994) states that writers develop knowledge about particular writing tasks and their relative difficulty. In addition they must develop knowledge of where and how to collect information for the task. He suggests that writers also reflect on the wider physical, social and cultural environments which may impact on the writing. Writers also develop meta-strategic knowledge, i.e. knowledge of what strategies might be useful for a particular writing task and when and where to make use of them. This involves how best to make use of limited resources such as time. For instance, writers make strategic decisions about whether or not to plan a piece of writing, and in how much detail. As Kellogg points out, this depends on knowledge of the task, of other possible strategies, of the wider contextual factors and knowledge of self as a writer.

In writing, as in reading, children need to develop metalinguistic knowledge, that is, knowledge of how language works; knowledge of sentence structure; grammar, punctuation, spelling; and knowledge of different written forms. As Gombert (1993) suggests, metalinguistic knowledge is different from other kinds of metacognition because its object is not another cognitive activity, such as memory or attention, but language itself. Gombert proposes another category of metacognition which he terms "metapragmatics". Metapragmatics involves a process of going beyond the focus on language itself to focus on the rules for using language. For instance, this might involve knowing that you understand a message or it could relate to the experience of feeling uncomfortable when you do not understand a message. Gombert groups these elements together under a heading of "metapragmatic experience" and suggests that it is this category of metacognition which mediates between metalinguistic knowledge and meta-cognition about communication in its widest form. Young writers are likely to experience many of the feelings which Gombert categorises as metapragmatic, but may not be able to verbalise them, nor to have any insight into what kind of knowledge they lack. In order to develop as writers it seems that we need to develop both cognitive and metacognitive knowledge about writing.

There are different models of the writing process and these focus on the different aspects of metacognition which they highlight as necessary for writing. Fox (2001) draws on Sharples' model of writing as creative design (Sharples, 1999). This model describes writing as a cycle of text generation and reviewing which operates within a set of constraints. These constraints can be both external, such as the topic chosen by a teacher, time allowed etc. or internal, including knowing that you know about the topic, or knowing that you have the strategies necessary for tackling the task etc. The constraints are seen to be different for younger writers and include the ability to form letters, spell and space words appropriately. A further set of constraints relates to emotional responses, in particular to motivation towards the work. There is likely to be, however, a reciprocal relationship between motivation and knowledge of one's own capacity to complete the task.

In order to reflect on writing, writers need to pause and re-read while also reflecting on the goal of the task. Writing is a process of engagement where the writer moves between focusing on putting the words on paper and pausing in order to reflect or to correct errors. Fox suggests that young writers have difficulty with this two stage process, partly because they may only write very small amounts of text at a time and all their resources are focused on forming the letters and words and also because they may have only a vague knowledge of the task. It is difficult to maintain knowledge of the whole and the bigger goal when all of your thinking is focused on how to spell a particular word.

This was clear from my own observations of children's writing during a project called Talk to Text (Fisher et al., 2007). It was a relatively common occurrence to observe Year 1 (5–6-year-old) and Year 2 (6–7-year-old) children stop the flow of their writing to sound out a word or to leave their table to find a spelling guide and then find it very difficult to continue and re-engage with the writing task. In some cases this led to children remaining off task for the remainder of the writing period, while others spent some considerable time before re-engaging. The finished written text sometimes showed where this break had occurred as the text changed narrative direction after this point. A short description of this project and some of the findings from it are presented here.

Talk to Text: using talk to support writing

The project aimed to explore and describe the effects of providing structured opportunities for talk on young children's writing. This was a collaborative project with six teachers of Year 1, Year 2 and one mixed class of both Year 1 and Year 2 children. The teachers were encouraged to design activities around three strategies: idea generation, write aloud and reflection. The reflection strand aimed to develop children's ability to reflect on their writing, to develop the metacognitive skills of monitoring and control and to develop more general metacognitive knowledge about themselves as writers. As a research project, different kinds of data were collected so that as well as the activities aiming to facilitate metacognition, among other things, interviews with children were designed to elicit information about their metacognitive knowledge of writing and of themselves as writers.

In the pilot phase of the study 96 interviews were conducted with children between the ages of 5 and 7 years old. The children were asked such questions as: Are you a good writer? How do you know? They were shown a picture of children writing and asked: Who are the good writers in the picture? How do you know? Followed by: Who are the good writers in your class? How do you know? And finally in this section of the interview: How do people learn to write? The analysis of this set of data showed that the majority of children thought that they were good at writing and 30 per cent of their statements showed that they based this judgement on the appearance of their writing. For instance, they made statements such as: "because I always put finger spaces", "it's neat and really small", "I always can stay on the lines". Nearly 20 per cent of their statements referred to the teacher as the source of their belief, saying such things as "I know because the teacher says well done", or "the teacher gives me stickers for good writing". However, a further 15 per cent of their answers mentioned thinking as a factor in good writing, even though this tended to be rather generalised. Statements such as: "I'm good at writing because I always concentrate on it" or "I think a lot before I start writing" were common in this category. Interestingly, when asked to comment on themselves as writers, only 7 per cent of the children's answers mentioned speed of writing or amount of writing produced as an indicator of a good writer, but when they were asked about how they identified other children as good writers nearly 25 per cent of their statements mentioned speed or amount of writing as the main factor for identifying a classmate as a good writer. It was common to hear them say things such as "Tom is a good writer because he can do three pages without stopping." When asked about how people learn to write, the majority of the answers referred to teachers teaching them how to write. Some children were adamant that it would be impossible to learn to write without a teacher, however about 20 per cent of the responses referred to the need to practise writing. A further 20 per cent mentioned particular strategies for learning to write such as "write down dots and draw round them so that you will be able to learn" and "when you can spell out words then you can write the words". Another 10 per cent of answers could be categorised as more truly metacognitive and showed an understanding of either the self as a writer, or of cognitive strategies for writing, such as planning, checking and revising or an understanding of the link between reading and writing as in this Year 2 girl's comment: "when you can read something it helps you with writing and when you can write something it helps you to read, so they are both like joined in a way".

The interview section of the much larger project demonstrated that while the majority of children focused on cognitive or social aspects of writing, some children were able to demonstrate a shift in thinking from cognitive to metacognitive and to express their knowledge of themselves as writers; their knowledge of strategies for learning to write; and their knowledge of writing as a discipline separate from, but linked to reading.

A study with even younger children by Jacobs (2004) was designed to investigate the metacognitive awareness and development of kindergarten children as they began writing. The study involved only a small number of children, but took place within the normal classroom setting and was conducted by their usual class teacher. After encouraging the children to write, the teacher also conducted short interviews with each child at regular intervals. These interviews asked the children to reflect on their writing, including what they were thinking about while writing, how they had decided what to write and also questions designed to provoke evaluation of their writing. The teacher found that not only could these young children reflect on their writing and identify some strategies for writing, including where to get ideas from, but they also began to ask each other these questions. These types of small scale studies can provide valuable information about how to facilitate metacognition in real classroom situations.

However, writing is not only a cognitive enterprise – it is also a socially constructed one. The Talk to Text project emphasises the social nature of writing by focusing on talk to generate and reflect on writing. Kellogg's explication of writing as a social process draws on the earlier work of social cognitive psychology to describe writing as an act of communication, which depends upon the communicative skills of the writer (Kellogg, 1994). This links to the concept of theory of mind, which develops through early childhood and enables us to take account of another's perspective. However, while a social theory of mind may develop to a functional level by the age of 4, the ability to transfer this skill to written communication develops much later and my own anecdotal evidence from teaching in higher education would suggest that not all adults make conscious use of this ability when writing.

In addition to the need to be able to take another perspective when writing, there is also a need to understand that the nature of the writing process includes the writer being aware of the larger linguistic community of which they are a part. The context in which we sit down to write, along with our perceptions of the task and needs of the audience, influences the ways in which we communicate our written message. Becoming aware of this larger social linguistic context is a type of metacognitive knowledge, which is translated into metacognitive skill when we use it to improve our performance on a written task or to influence our approach to writing.

Developing an understanding of the socially situated nature of writing as a communicative act can be difficult. One way in which children can become more aware of this is to engage them in collaborative writing tasks. In this way, writing can be viewed as not only something that occurs in the head of an individual, which is then transposed onto paper or screen, but also as something which can be constructed socially and performed with others. Authentic collaboration would include more than just the discussion of content and ideas, or acting as editor for another. Collaboration which is likely to facilitate metacognition would also include the negotiation of understandings about the task, maybe discussion about what each individual can bring to the task, some joint decision about the best way to undertake the task, and also some negotiation of how the task will be done.

In my research with 5–7-year-olds I have often been surprised by the ability these young children demonstrate to negotiate and agree on how to tackle collaborative tasks. Children of this age tend to have a very clear view of fairness and go to some length to ensure that no one is left out in a collaborative task. However, this does depend to a large extent on the relationships between individual children. In my observations of high ability boy/girl pairs of children working on collaborative writing tasks, there was sometimes a tendency for one or other child to dominate the interaction. In the majority of these cases, this was the boy, but not in every case. The high ability writing pairs tended to have more problems in collaborating than the middle ability writing pairs and this may be because in the high ability pairs each child has developed a sense of themselves as a writer and "know" that they can write well alone. Thus the incentive to collaborate with another is less; in fact it is a distraction from simply getting on with the task and completing it. The high ability writers tended to show more impatience in negotiating with each other and were much more likely to work in relative silence, taking turns to write a section of the text. They were also less likely to comment on each other's work. This may be because they viewed each other as already competent writers and so felt less sure about providing feedback. However, this may also be due to social reasons, in that criticising another's writing can be viewed as breaking rank, especially when the high ability children already view themselves as different from the rest of the class.

Another way in which to facilitate the development of the social nature of writing and an understanding of writing as a communicative task is to engage writers in more authentic writing tasks. Galbraith & Rijlaarsdam (1999) suggested that using authentic tasks might ameliorate the problem of direct teaching about the nature of the writing community, its goals, purpose and genres. Through engagement in authentic tasks children will experience the process of constructing a text, transforming their knowledge into a form appropriate for a particular audience and to meet specific goals, which are themselves embedded in and emerging from the writing community. I believe this will also benefit the development of children's metacognitive knowledge of writing, of useful strategies, and of themselves as part of a writing community. Facilitating this knowledge through engagement with writing tasks rather than by direct teaching may overcome the problems associated with direct teaching of meta-cognition, which carries the danger of disassociation of knowledge and process. However, this is not only the case with writing; it affects the development of metacognition across the curriculum. The next chapter will highlight studies in other areas of the primary school curriculum which have focused on facilitating the development of young children's metacognition.

Chapter 6

Metacognition in other subjects

This chapter will focus on other areas of the primary curriculum and consider studies which have been undertaken by researchers and teachers into children's metacognition in a range of subject domains, including physical education (PE) and sport, religious education (RE), information and communications technology (ICT), history, geography and art, music and drama.

Metacognition, PE and sport

At first sight the idea of metacognition playing any kind of part in PE and sport appears problematic. Surely this part of the curriculum is about action, learning skill, competition and above all physicality, rather than cognition. However, developing metacognition allows us to make conscious decisions about life, which will influence our long term health and well-being. The goal of PE instruction in schools should be about fostering a long term commitment to a healthy life style. As we are aware, many countries are facing what has been described as an obesity epidemic. As nations become wealthier, the pace of life increases and people buy into convenience foods, which tend to have high levels of sugar, salt and fat. The need to juggle competing demands on our time means that for many people finding the time and motivation to exercise or take part in sport can be difficult. Through PE instruction in schools it is possible to promote healthier life styles. In the past PE instruction has tended to focus on skills training, rules of the game and technique. In this sense it has been largely content driven. However, just as there is a growing understanding of the need to develop self regulated learners who are self motivated and have metacognitive knowledge about themselves as learners in other areas of the curriculum, so there is a move towards this type of learning in PE.

Aspects of this more cognitive approach have been around in sport for a long time. For instance, there is a tradition of focusing on the mental processing of elite athletes in sport. World class athletes are seen to be "mentally strong" as well as physically fit; they are highly motivated and focused on a particular goal. Studies of athletes at this level highlight the distinction between novice participants in a sport and experts. A study of competition runners by Nietfield (2003) demonstrates this difference, with reference to the ways in which people think when running competitively compared to when they run for pleasure or training purposes. Nietfield suggests that runners have two different kinds of strategy thinking, differentiated by whether the thoughts are internally or externally focused. The internally focused thoughts tend to be metacognitive in nature. These thoughts are focused on monitoring and controlling fatigue, energy levels and pain, as well as ongoing evaluation of progress and selection of particular race strategies designed to give the runner a competitive advantage. Nietfield's study shows that these metacognitive processes increase as the competitive nature of the race increases. The more competitive the race, the more strategic the runner needs to be and the more thoughtful and metacognitive. When runners run for pleasure or training purposes, Nietfield found that they tend to focus on external thoughts, such as the scenery or their personal life. These externally focused thoughts seem to result in the runners feeling refreshed and enlivened by the run. This touches on an important point to consider in terms of metacognition and one that has been addressed many times in different domains: can metacognition be detrimental as well as positive? The simple answer, as the research on physical activity shows, is that yes it can. If we are running to invigorate ourselves or to clear our head, then it appears better to direct our thoughts to the immediate environment or externals, rather than focusing on monitoring our own physicality. However, knowing that different types of thinking are useful and appropriate in different types of settings is metacognitive knowledge. Thus in order to be able to make the choice of what to think about when running we need to be aware of how our thinking may affect the outcome; it helps to be aware of how we can manipulate our thinking to our own advantage. This is certainly the case for competitive athletes.

Nietfield's study delineates the different types of thinking of expert and novice runners. Expert runners show more deliberate and elaborate metacognitive knowledge about their sport. This is built through training and practice, but knowledge about the sport also impacts on the training and practice, so thinking and performance are linked in a virtuous circle. Nietfield's study also highlights another aspect of metacognition, which is its domain specificity. The competition runners focus their thinking not only on monitoring their energy levels, as other athletes would, but also on specific ways of viewing the race, such as breaking it up into sections. Different sports will therefore involve different kinds of metacognitive knowledge and different athletes may make use of this knowledge in different ways. For instance McPherson's study of tennis players found that expert tennis players mentioned three times more planning strategies than novice players. The expert players were unsurprisingly highly focused and strategic, but their focus was often on the metacognitive aspects of planning, monitoring and evaluating rather than on only performing the shot. The novice players were found to be less focused and often reported extraneous thoughts (McPherson, 2000).

One factor which is important in a consideration of developing expertise in sport, or in making the wise decision to continue with some form of physical exercise throughout life, is motivation. Motivation has been linked to metacognition across a number of domains. In a study of over 700 elementary, junior and senior high school students, Theodosiou and Papaioannou (2006) found that metacognition was a mediating factor between motivation and involvement in sport and exercise.

The study describes two different kinds of motivation – ego oriented and task oriented. A person who is task oriented is focused on learning and perfecting a skill and they equate their progress towards this goal with the amount of effort they put in. A person who is ego oriented will focus on how they are seen by others, whether they are viewed as having higher or lower skills than their peers or by being able to achieve high performance with little effort. A child's motivational orientation in PE may be a result of a number of social and environmental factors, including the classroom climate provided by the teacher. If teachers develop a climate of competition with others and evaluation by external rewards in PE then children are more likely to demonstrate ego oriented motivation. This can be useful for winning in competitive sports, but can have a detrimental effect on children who are not going to be competing athletes. However, teachers can provide a mastery oriented climate for PE which focuses attention on learning and perfecting skills without the need for comparison to external norms. Theodosiou and Papaioannou suggest that a master oriented climate results in the use of deep cognitive and metacognitive strategies and increased self regulation. On the other hand the ego centred students are more likely to use surface level strategies and try to complete the task as quickly as possible. Mastery oriented classroom climates build metacognitive knowledge and are more likely to lead to self regulated learners. Papaioannou and colleagues also found that task and mastery oriented students were more likely to take part in out of school sport and physical activity (Papaioannou et al., 2004). These two studies make a strong case for the role of metacognition in involvement with sport and as a mediator between motivation and performance.

However, children come to a PE class with a set of preconceptions, with different levels of knowledge and expertise and with different self concepts in relation to different sports and physical activities. Luke and Hardy (1999) developed a conceptual framework of metacognition for PE which takes account of wider social contextual factors, such as school and department culture. While the framework focuses on personal and cognitive activity of children, it also acknowledges the complexity of other social factors at teacher, class and activity level. They report that a large number of secondary school children are unaware of strategies they can use, or how and when they might use them. In PE lessons children tend to rely on the teacher to direct the activity. The researchers found that although children followed a teacher's counting strategy for throwing a discus, when asked about it later they were unaware that they had used a strategy.

There seems therefore to be a need to engage children in thinking about strategy use, to build knowledge of the sport or activity and also to build metacognitive knowledge about how and when to use this knowledge to best advantage. Skilled athletes have a great deal of knowledge about their sport as well as an ability to turn that knowledge to their own benefit during performance. Novices in sport tend to focus only on the goal, rather than bringing all of their thinking to bear on the task. There seems therefore to be a need to develop PE lessons which include metacognition. Yet the nature of many PE lessons means this may be more difficult to accomplish, as children and some teachers may find thinking in PE to be difficult or irrelevant.

One approach which has gained a good deal of success in this area is the PlaySMART programme, developed as "Thinking through Physical Education" at Manchester Metropolitan University. Tom Bell, one of the development team, describes PlaySMART as a challenge to the traditional teaching of PE as skill development. PlaySMART was designed to develop a combination of motor control and cognitive elements simultaneously. The emphasis is on thinking and problem solving; using tactical knowledge about the game, self and competition in a strategic and flexible manner. The programme steers away from teacher directed strategies, which tend to remain context specific, if remembered at all, to developing understanding at a conceptual level. In this way children will be able to adapt their thinking to different situations and to describe not only what to do, but also why this is appropriate (Bell, 2003). The PlaySMART programme owes much to the Cognitive Acceleration (CA) programmes of Adey and Shayer (see Chapter 4). In terms of PlaySMART, the SMART acronym refers to the different aspects of the method: Situation, Methods, Adaption, Reduction and Transfer, and these parallel the five pillars of CA: concrete preparation, cognitive conflict, construction, metacognition and transfer. Bell points out that while PlaySMART is based on CA principles it does not follow the five pillars exactly, and includes a Reduction section where children synthesise information into a principle solution which can then serve as an example and a shared mental model of a tactical plan. The procedure for using PlaySMART is detailed and involves students in planning, analysis, identifying strategies, visualising, imagining key moments and variables, testing their ideas, working with constraints, comparing and contrasting tactics, dealing with "what if" questions, constructing "if, then" rules and being able to transfer their knowledge to new situations. The aims of PlaySMART are not only to improve children's physical performance, but also to encourage them to take responsibility for their learning. This could be extended to include taking responsibility for making wise and thoughtful decisions about the place of sport in a healthy life style beyond school.

Metacognition and RE

Inherent in RE is the possibility for engagement with the moral perspective on making life decisions. In an education system which shuns philosophy as a curriculum subject, RE can become a space for philosophical speculation and development of self awareness and knowledge of beliefs, both individual and as systems of belief. Since the 1970s Michael Grimmitt has sought to connect religious instruction with children's own life experiences, in order to foster a critical consciousness of religious culture and of personal belief (see Grimmitt, 1989). RE can be about both learning about belief systems, their cultural and sociological contexts, and learning about oneself in relation to religious belief. The important difference between a content based RE and a more metacognitively focused RE is that the latter focuses on the learner and how the learner responds to and develops knowledge of self, others and religions, whereas the former relies on the learner absorbing knowledge about how different religions respond to the major issues of life.

In schools the nature of RE has changed over time, as has its name, and as a school subject it still invites controversy. What a RE curriculum should cover and in what manner is rightly discussed and contested both within and outside the education community. I do not intend to engage in those debates here, but instead to focus on how metacognition may impact on RE and how RE may facilitate the development of an ability to make wise and thoughtful decisions about life.

In his seminal article on metacognition Flavell (1979) described the circumstances which are likely to provoke a metacognitive experience. In his model, Flavell describes metacognitive experiences as arising from either a conscious search of metacognitive knowledge or a more automated process triggered by the task or context. Flavell describes the circumstances which may give rise to metacognitive experiences as situations which require highly conscious thinking; novel situations which require planning and evaluation, where decisions are "weighty and risky" and where there are few distractions. Some, if not all of these criteria may be met through philosophical speculation in RE lessons. I believe that the nature of the moral and ethical problems encountered here would call for deliberate and high level thinking and would involve drawing on one's own knowledge about the world, self and others. In addition, the problems posed in RE are likely to be open ended, complex issues which may be novel and require risk taking in terms of expressing opinion and values in a sensitive and appropriate manner. Engaging in discussion of weighty issues is also likely to promote cognitive monitoring processes as participants must monitor their thinking about the subject and take account of various external factors, such as right time to speak, the appropriate tone, whether to posit the thought as a question or a statement, consideration of the possible effect of the utterance on others and to participate in order to contribute to the content of the discussion. While metacognitive experiences can be triggered in times of individual study, when the task demands are complex, they can also be provoked through group discussion and both situations are relevant to RE lessons.

Mystery is a factor in all religious belief. In the Christian tradition, we are asked to hold different, often conflicting ideas, simultaneously. The mystery of the Trinity is not one which requires logical explanation, but rather one which necessitates believers being able to open their minds to the possibility of other ways of thinking. I would argue that religious thinking is different from both rational scientific thinking and philosophical exploration. Religious thinking involves rationality, but goes beyond logic to engage with thought which emanates from a complex interaction of feeling, experience and reflection. RE could engage children in different ways of thinking. Religious "problems" are not solvable in the same way as mathematical or scientific problems. They are not addressed either through creative, critical, analytical or philosophical thinking alone. Instead religious issues require a reflection on thought itself. Children and adults alike can become stuck in arguments about the existence of God, with both sides using specific but different ways of thinking about the subject. A metacognitive approach to RE would attempt to reveal these different ways of thinking and in doing so create a space for new ways of thinking to emerge. These new ways may be complex, involve exploration rather than explanation, but they should also provide a means for children to develop confidence in being able to hold competing thoughts at the same time. These new ways of thinking would involve a high level of abstraction and at present this is at odds with much of formal school learning.

In England and Wales the guidelines for RE (QCA, 2004) refer to both learning *about* religion and learning *from* religion. However, they omit a third goal, which should be to learn to think religiously. We can see how metacognitive skill, strategy knowledge, knowledge of self, monitoring of thinking and meta-comprehension can help with achieving the first target of learning *about* religion and religious beliefs. This is similar to metacognition in any curriculum area and allows for transfer of knowledge across subjects. In terms of the second target, learning *from* religion, I have outlined above how RE can enable us to reflect on what religion means for us and how we can connect it with our own lives. In this sense RE can help us to make wise and thoughtful decisions. We can learn from the lives of saints and religious figures, from parables and the teachings of prophets and gurus. We can encourage children to respond to and question religious beliefs. However, the third target, I am suggesting, is perhaps the ultimate aim of developing metacognition. In a recent article exploring children's difficulties with understanding Christian beliefs, the authors found that some students confused "understanding" with "belief". The authors link these difficulties to personal ontology, suggesting that it becomes difficult to understand a religious idea if one holds a radically different non religious view of the world. They argue that in order to understand belief, rather than understanding that some people hold these beliefs, one must share in the belief (Freathy & Aylward, in press). However, the mystery of religion means that it is possible through imagination and suspension of personal ontology to hold the possibility of a belief without necessarily believing it.

In a study of primary school children's beliefs about RE, Van der Zee and colleagues described seven categories of metacognitive beliefs of 10–12-year-old children. Metacognitive beliefs are described as a mixture of cognitive and affective aspects; they are beliefs about a particular subject in relation to self and others and they may be conscious or not (Van der Zee *et al.*, 2006). Such beliefs develop from experience, so situational and contextual factors play an important part. Some metacognitive beliefs may generalise across subject domains, while others may remain specific to a particular subject. However, there is no simple connection between student beliefs about a subject and their engagement with it – other task and contextual variables are likely to mediate. In their study Van der Zee and colleagues explored children's beliefs about the realistic nature of RE, which was conceived as the extent to which RE connects to real life issues; beliefs about the role of others in RE, including both peers and characters in religious stories; motivational beliefs towards the subject; and the role of the teacher. They found that the children were not fully convinced of the realistic aspect of RE, although they were more likely to agree that religion had the power to transform lives and help people to cope with life issues. The children were also ambivalent about the need to work with and learn from others. Responses to the motivational aspect of the questionnaire showed that the children were motivated to do well academically, but not specifically motivated towards the subject. The authors argue that this lack of subject motivation affects participation in group discussion and thereby development of more sophisticated subject knowledge. RE may have a particular issue with motivation, as arguably the connection between RE as a subject and personal identity is closer than in other subject areas. This can create an identity conflict and a split between children who practise or hold a religious faith and those who do not. There is a necessity to create learning opportunities in RE which will motivate children to engage with the subject regardless of background, rather than focus on academic success. This is a difficult task for educators, but one which can be informed by exploration of metacognitive beliefs of students.

Metacognition and ICT/e-learning

In the UK in-school use of ICT and e-learning seems to lag behind out-of-school and home use. Nichol and Watson (2003) suggested that while there are examples of excellent practice in some primary school subjects, in general there is little day to day involvement of ICT across the curriculum for younger children. Children themselves often view ICT as a means of finding material and presenting their work. This is often done at home as homework, with the product of the activity taken back into school in a printed form. Yet we know that by the time they reach school the majority of children in the West have some experience of using technology. In a report of ICT use in schools in Scotland, pre-school children were found to have already developed basic competency in the use of technology and were using it to support learning and for social reasons and play. However, the report suggests, these skills are not always fully recognised by schools (Learning and Teaching Scotland, 2002).

Technology and e-learning should enable children to take more responsibility for their own learning, provide the capacity to link formal school based learning with informal, out-of-school activities and also facilitate new and expanded communities of learners. E-learning has the potential to provoke metacognitive experiences but there is nothing inherently metacognitive about using technology. As with other classroom activities, opportunities for metacognition need to be built into the e-learning tasks. One way in which this can be done is if children are engaged in developing their own on-line learning activities. Kafai (1996) developed a project which enabled children to build a video game for learning maths. This taught mathematical concepts, engaged children in planning, monitoring and controlling their own thinking and led to increased motivation.

Many of the programmes designed to engage children in domain specific learning do so through a layer of interactive gaming or story telling. Learning progresses through engagement with the fun activities without the children being aware that they are learning particular subject knowledge and skills. The important aspect of these kinds of programmes is that at some point the children make a connection between the game and the subject, or the knowledge and skills they develop may not be useful for future learning in that domain. Huffaker and Calvert (2003) describe different projects which use these formats, including KineticCity.com designed by Malcolm. This programme uses an action game format to teach the science curriculum. It utilises some of the features of gaming such as offering rewards for achievements within the game, being accessible from home, and incorporating collaboration through real learning clubs which can interact with other clubs.

Many e-learning programmes are designed around problem solving. Monitoring thinking during problem solving; being able to hold different variables in the mind at the same time; selecting appropriate strategies; and reviewing and evaluating progress towards a goal are aspects of metacognition facilitated by these kinds of tasks. These programmes are often developed for older children, but much can be learned from how they incorporate metacognition into a particular curriculum domain. One study used what is described as the "infusion approach" to enhance secondary school children's learning of computer studies (Kirkwood, 2000). A particular goal of this project was to develop higher order thinking, metacognition and problem solving. Kirkwood bases her project on Resnick's model of higher order thinking (Resnick, 1987). She focuses on problem solving because it meets the criteria for necessitating higher order thinking: it requires judgement, is complex, requires the application of many and different criteria and has many solutions.

Metacognition is seen as a necessary part of problem solving when defined as self regulation and monitoring of thinking. Higher order thinking is also seen to develop understanding through analysis of the problem, creating order and constructing new meaning. As higher order thinking demands effort it is also linked to motivation. The computing studies programme involved specific problem based tasks which students could work through at their own pace, but which were introduced in a gradual way. The pedagogic principles of this project take account of the need to develop a language of both problem solving and higher order thinking. So emphasis is placed on teacher modelling, direct teaching of useful strategies, facilitating metacognitive talk and formative assessment. An interesting element of this study is the feedback from the students involved. They were pragmatic about collaborative working, suggesting that it can be useful to work with others on problem solving, but not always, and that effective problem solving requires planning, a step by step approach, time, organisation, keeping track of progress through notes, understanding that problems can be difficult and require effort, accepting and asking for help, and perseverance.

Advances in technology have given us the ability to track children's engagement within an on-line learning environment and this has given rise to a large number of studies which include keeping log files of how children are developing metacognition through shared on-line discourse. E-learning also has a good deal to offer in terms of socially constructed learning through collaborative projects and on-line discussion groups. Again much of this work has been undertaken with older children, but as technology becomes more user friendly and more ubiquitous, younger children are likely to have the skills to engage with similar projects, so it is worth highlighting some aspects of them. A project by Hurme and colleagues (2006) was aimed specifically at exploring the social nature of metacognition during collaborative problem solving in geometry through a computer aided interactive network. The project was designed for 13-year-old students who worked in pairs to both create and solve problems through writing computer notes. The researchers were able to analyse these notes and also track the discussion between different students and different pairs of students towards joint problem solving solutions. The study provides evidence of the students using metacognition in their interactions on the network as they compare their own thinking to the thinking of others and use monitoring and evaluating strategies directed at themselves and at peers. While not all the interactions could be described as metacognitive, the creation of a social network meant that by posting comments students were setting up an expectation that others would respond and that the more complex the interactions, the more need there is for monitoring and control. Different groups of students were found to engage in different amounts of metacognitive activity on the network. The researchers report that students who were interacting between student pairs or student pairs and the teacher were monitoring and evaluating their thinking more than their peers (Hurme *et al.*, 2006). This may be a result of taking on this mediating role, enabling them to use the contributions of others to develop their own thinking.

Primary classrooms these days include a range of new technology including interactive white boards and these can be tools to facilitate and promote metacognition. Researchers from Newcastle University have carried out an evaluation of the use of interactive whiteboards in upper primary classes. One aspect of this evaluation was to consider the role of interactive whiteboards in fostering metacognition (Wall *et al.*, 2005). In particular, the researchers used a think/speech bubble method for eliciting the views of children about both internal and external factors. The children were asked a series of questions about their own learning using the interactive whiteboard. The questions encouraged them to reflect on themselves as learners and to articulate in what ways the interactive whiteboard had impacted on their own learning. Other questions focused on external factors such as how others might benefit or not from interactive white boards. In order to stimulate talk about thinking and to mediate between the interviewer and the child, the researchers used simple outline drawings of children being taught using interactive whiteboards. The drawings incorporated speech and think bubbles which the children could complete in order to answer the prompt questions. The results showed that the majority of statements about the whiteboards were positive, suggesting that their use helped learning. The answers the children gave indicated that they are aware of how interactive whiteboards can impact on thinking. They referred to the way whiteboards use multiple methods of explanation, use different visual illustrations, and to how they aided concentration and memory. Motivation for learning seemed to be a particular feature of using interactive white boards, especially if the children were allowed to use them, rather than only watching the teacher use them. As well as highlighting children's views about the use of a piece of technology in the classroom, the study is a good example of how children can reflect on themselves as learners and articulate ways of enhancing their own learning experiences.

The area of ICT and e-learning is bound to grow as technology develops. Studies of virtual realities and on-line gaming are already in existence (see for instance the studies of learning in Second Life by the Open University, UK). Engagement in virtual communities may well facilitate the development of metacognition and lead to fostering wise and thoughtful decision making. Allowing children to practise problem solving and decision making and review the consequences of their actions in virtual societies may promote better decision making in the real world. I am optimistic that new technologies will impact on facilitating metacognitive development in formal and informal settings. However, the obvious dangers of substituting virtual worlds for real social interaction and the difficulties of transferring skills from virtual to real world settings suggest a cautious approach to using these technologies in education.

Metacognition and history

Although sometimes grouped together under the label of "Humanities", history and geography require different kinds of thinking. The teaching of both has changed considerably over the last 20 years and is perhaps set to change again with recent developments in the primary curriculum. In England, history is not a compulsory subject for school students after the age of 14, and while many children enjoy history at primary school, there is concern about the numbers who go on to study the subject at higher levels. A report by the Office for Standards in Education, Children's Services and Skills (Ofsted, 2007), into the teaching of history suggested that children should develop knowledge of historically significant people, ideas and events as well as understanding how events are connected. It suggests that one of the difficulties with a topic based approach to history is that children may have detailed knowledge of some areas, such as Ancient Egypt or the Victorians, but are less able to connect up historical events into a coherent time frame.

However, history is more than knowledge of what happened and when; it also involves understanding the relevance of historical events for our own time. Some of the skills required in thinking like a historian include: being able to ask relevant and purposeful questions, finding and evaluating evidence, constructing hypotheses, viewing an event from multiple perspectives, being able to compare across time periods and to evaluate historical sources. Early research on children's thinking in history, based on Piagetian stage development theory, often found that young children lacked the necessary cognitive ability to cope with historical concepts and that only in adolescence, with the onset of formal operational thinking, could history really be understood (Hallam, 1970). This has parallels with early research on metacognition which, also tied to a Piagetian framework, often reported that young children were not capable of reflecting on their own thinking. Both sets of findings have since been refuted, just as young children are seen as capable of metacognition, so they are also seen as capable of the cognitive skills necessary for studying history.

A research study by US researchers on children from kindergarten age to Grade 6 used pictures of American history and open ended interviews to explore young children's understanding of time (Barton & Levstick, 1996). The researchers criticise studies which focus on investigating children's understanding of time in terms of clock and calendar time or on asking children to estimate the length of a minute. They argue that there is no evidence to suggest that children need to be able to understand time in these senses before they can understand historical time. In fact, in their study, all the children were able to make some distinction between the time periods of the pictures. For the youngest children this was often encapsulated by simple references to "long ago" and "now", although children across all grades sometimes made finer distinctions than these. The children's understanding of time in this historical sense was not matched by their understanding of dates and this often revealed a lack of knowledge of what dates represent. While children's understanding of time is not a metacognitive process, it is an important one for this subject area. Historical thinking is not limited to understanding the past, it is also crucial for developing informed citizens who can make thoughtful and informed judgements about the world in which they live. In this sense history is crucial to a democratic society. The questioning and evaluating of sources of evidence and the ability to stand back and see the bigger picture, while attending to detail and maintaining a healthy scepticism, are habits of mind necessary for both the historian and the informed citizen.

Historical analysis involves interpretation of source materials, selection, evaluation and judgement. In terms of metacognition it involves understanding

understanding itself. Historians need to be aware of how they are interpreting the source materials, why they are selecting some and not others, what this means for the historical story they are constructing and understand that the story is a construction and not the "truth". They also need to reflect on what they already know and what may be left to know. This is the meta-knowing described by Deanna Kuhn (2000); an understanding of epistemology, in its widest sense. Historical thinking also includes taking different perspectives towards the subject. The ability to see that different perspectives exist and to make the imaginative leap to view the same issue from different positions involves a constructive theory of mind (Chandler & Helm, 1984). The task of sifting through and evaluating disparate pieces of information and constructing a coherent narrative involves the ability to select and use appropriate strategies, thus drawing on meta-strategic knowledge. Planning, another metacognitive strategy, is important for getting a sense of the whole while working on the details. Monitoring progress towards the goal of producing a story, solving a problem or seeking a missing piece of the puzzle is a metacognitive process which involves self questioning. The historian works at two levels, evaluating evidence, but also evaluating his/her own thinking about the evidence, at times controlling that thinking by making decisions about how best to progress the task. Thinking like a historian involves developing an understanding of people, their values, beliefs and attitudes and an understanding of others will inform the development of self and impact on self concept and self esteem.

Direct instruction for metacognition was recently included in a CA project for teaching history to gifted and talented 9–13-year-old children (Nichol, 2007). The project, based on the CASE programmes of Shayer and Adey and called CACHE, used an interview method to elicit the children's ability to think about their own thinking as they worked through a detective style task. The project demonstrates children's ability to reflect on their own thinking and suggests that the clearest responses to the metacognitive interview were provided by children who were working most effectively in groups, thus demonstrating the co-constructive nature of developing metacognition.

The construction of historical narratives by expert historians has been compared by Lang (2003) to how a film maker makes a film narrative. The historian as a story teller must be prepared to fill in the gaps of what is known with imaginative speculation. Thus children as developing historians need some understanding of the meta-theories of fact, fiction and the blurred boundaries of what is now often called faction. History also involves an understanding of causation and prediction and while this may be taught to children from a scientific perspective, a development of historical thinking requires the ability to view these concepts from a different perspective. Ultimately, the nature of historical thinking encourages a reflection on the nature of truth. It is this meta-cognitive speculation facilitated through the study of history and thinking like a historian which has the capacity to inform the decisions we make in other areas of life.

Metacognition and geography

A government report into the teaching of sustainable life styles in schools suggested that "Considering issues relating to sustainable development should be at the heart of geography teaching" (Ofsted, 2008). This is a long way from the kind of geography which I learned in school, with its emphasis on naming countries, capital cities and major rivers. Modern geography has much more to do with the lives children live and will live. In its widest conception it involves learning the effects of the decisions we make about the ways in which we lead our lives. Understanding the link between climate change and personal responsibility is one aspect of the subject which links geography with other subjects across the curriculum. This enables children to develop metacognitive knowledge about the knowledge they have gained from other subject areas, which they can then bring to bear on their thinking about sustainability. It also encourages children to draw on their own life experience and to reflect on themselves and others in terms of responsibility and values. However, the Ofsted report questions the extent to which this type of linking across subjects or to wider experience actually happens in geography classrooms. The picture seems to be patchy at best in primary schools.

As the UK National Curriculum links education for sustainable development with global citizenship within the geography curriculum, so researchers have turned their attentions to what these terms mean; the extent to which they are related and how schools can teach this more complex and inter-related notion of geography. An article by Morgan (2006) refers to "geographical wisdom". This is interpreted as a necessity to develop "post-formal thinking" about the world and our relationship with it, based on our understanding of the many different facets of sustainability and global citizenship. Post-formal thinking is viewed as counter to the Piagetian notion of formal operations being the end point of human cognitive development. Post-formal thinking has been conceptualised by Kincheloe and Steinberg (1999) and related to wisdom. It is viewed as a life-long developmental process involving understanding culturally situated knowledge, awareness of the deep patterns and structures shaping perception, and seeking new ways of interpreting the world around us. Geography is a curriculum area which has at its heart our relationship to the environment we live in. Geography can encourage children to explore relationships between themselves and their environment, seek understanding of the systemic patterns of nature, and develop a loving respect for the earth. Facilitating this kind of geographical thinking will entail developing metacognitive processing, a need to go beyond the cognitive level of the task demands to pursue these wider and deeper explorations of thought.

One approach to developing metacognition in and through geography is the use of specific tools such as concept maps and heuristics. Ahlberg and Ahoranta (2002) suggest using Vee diagrams to facilitate the shift to metacognitive processing. The Vee diagram is a kind of map in the shape of a large V. Completing a

Vee map is achieved through self questioning about the nature of the learning to be undertaken and about evaluating the outcome. Ahlberg and Ahoranta detail how the first Vee maps were described by Gowan (1981) and modified by Ahlberg in the 1990s. In Ahlberg's version the left side of the V corresponds to planning; the right side to evaluation and in the middle is placed the problem to be worked upon. The planning side requires children to think about why they are engaging in this particular learning task; what past knowledge they can bring to bear on it; what are the most important ideas for this problem; and how they might try to solve it. The right side of the V is constructed through responses to questions following the task. These include evaluating the new knowledge; expressing what the new knowledge is and how credible it is, given the evidence; what methods were used to achieve these findings; and what kinds of data were collected. Their study followed some fifth grade children engaged in a geographical project about their area. The researchers combined the use of Vee maps with concept mapping, so that the Vee maps relate to metacognitive processing while the concept maps concentrate on the cognitive aspects of the task. The researchers reported that the Vee maps provided detailed information about how the children in the project were thinking about geography and enabled children to monitor their own thinking towards a goal. Along with the concept maps, the tools seem to encourage children to make more sophisticated links between concepts, both within geography and beyond, in other relevant knowledge systems. In addition, they provide information to teachers about the depth of children's understanding in geography.

An approach which sits well with using these educational tools is inquiry based learning. Kriewaldt (2006) has suggested that an inquiry based approach to learning in geography is more likely to help geography teachers to rise to the challenge of educating children about the present and the future. The approach advocated in this study includes using and understanding maps. This is central to geographical knowledge but, as the author says, maps cannot be isolated from other knowledge. The interpretation of maps involves using other knowledge of the place or knowledge of similar places. The author suggests using "metacognitive questions" such as "How did I use elements of the map to make sense?" and "How have I improved in reading maps?", as well as more general questions based around evaluating strategy knowledge and evaluating methods of exploring and examining the map.

Kriewaldt also suggests strategies for developing metacognition through field work. She advocates using an inquiry based method where children decide on the questions they want to explore through a field work study. This involves them reflecting on the nature of inquiry itself, on how inquiries in geography can be conducted, reflecting on strategies for collecting and evaluating data and reflecting on how the study might be written up. All of these questions can be discussed collaboratively and involve children in planning, monitoring and evaluating their own learning.

Developing metacognition through geography seems to me to provide a unique connection to the world we live in. By reflecting on our thinking about the earth, by searching for deep patterns and connections, and by reflecting on different ways of interpreting the knowledge we already have, we have the power to alter our behaviour for the future. Metacognition in and through the geography curriculum can provide us with the skills necessary to make wise decisions about sustainability and what it means to be a global citizen.

Metacognition and art, drama and music

These three areas are grouped together here for convenience, although they have a thematic link in often being described as creative subjects. As such they also introduce the question of the link between creativity and metacognition. It is an interesting question since there is no necessity for the two to be linked. We can engage in metacognitive thinking without being creative and we can be creative without engaging metacognitively. Metacognition may even hinder creativity, especially at the generation of ideas stage. However, some thinking skills frameworks do combine creative thinking and metacognition. In this section I will concentrate on the subject domains rather than on these wider issues of the conceptual links between creativity and metacognition.

These subjects have the capacity to provide opportunities for multiple ways of seeing and understanding. They can provide openings for focusing on thinking while gaining understanding of the particular subject. In art education, a shift from individual self expression to understanding the intentions of artists, the social nature of art and developing critical thinking about art occurred in the UK in the 1980s and was prefigured by international work on the connection between art and cognitive processing undertaken particularly by researchers at Harvard, under the banner of Project Zero and led by Howard Gardner and David Perkins. This movement was paralleled by the development of more cognitive approaches to learning, including the development of theories of metacognition.

Gardner's work has led to many different research projects, not only in terms of his multiple intelligence theory but in other aspects of thinking. One such project in art education, created by Hoffman Davis (2000), uses Gardner's theory of entry points (Gardner 1991) to develop an inquiry based art curriculum and to enhance metacognition in Grade 5 children. In the project each child uses one of five frames as an entry into developing understanding and knowledge about the subject. So in examining a skull, for example, one child will make a drawing, one will make notes about the physical qualities of the skull, one will write a story about it, one will make a list of questions to stimulate further study of it and one will devise a performance piece based on it. Each frame is then passed on, so that each child is able to experience all entry points. The different frames represent different ways of thinking and include: aesthetic, which focuses on sensory data about the object; narrative, which might include the history of the piece of art or how it was acquired; logical quantitative, which focuses on problem solving including the choices an artist makes or the dimensions of the object; foundational, which takes a more philosophical approach including questions about what art is; and experiential which focuses on active learning and includes creating a performance piece based upon the object. Thus children experience how thinking differently about the same piece of art can provide different interpretations and deepen understanding.

In Davis's study, after each group of children had tried the different entry points they reflected on how they had gained understanding through discussing questions such as which frame worked best, which frame each person preferred and which was easiest and hardest, and over time the children were able to compare thinking in different subjects and to reflect on thinking itself. Davis reported that students would begin to differentiate between different ways of thinking and evaluate them in terms of the subject, particular task and context, thereby deepening their metacognitive understanding. As the author herself acknowledges, there is a danger that children will begin to connect one point of entry with themselves and begin to think of themselves as a particular kind of learner, and of course entry point theory does have connections to multiple intelligences. However, guarding against this closing down of metacognition will be an important aspect of how programmes such as these are developed with teachers and must include teachers re-evaluating and reflecting on the approach as it develops within their own classroom. The entry point approach seems to provide a particularly good way into developing metacognition in the classroom.

Drama provides an opportunity to develop the experiential entry point to any aspect of learning and as a subject in its own right it is very well placed to provide opportunities for understanding multiple perspectives. Through being in role children take on the perspectives of others, develop insight and social meta-cognition. A study by Johnson (2002) focused on developing drama activities for 9- and 10-year-old children which would also provide specific opportunities for fostering metacognition. An activity based on nineteenth century settlers in the Midwest of America involved the children in discussing the reasons for and against starting out on the journey. The metacognitive element was introduced by having the children in role reflect on how their thinking about setting off into the unknown landscape was being influenced by the thinking of others in their "family" group. When not in role, the children were also encouraged to relate their fictional experience to their real life experiences and to draw on their own past knowledge to inform their thinking in role. The author argues that drama can provide a space for children to explore their emotional response to real events, which they may never have discussed before. In addition to the role play aspect of the study, the children also kept reflective diaries to stimulate reflection on thinking between and beyond the dramatic session. The children were encouraged to create a still image from the drama, in the form of a tableau, which represented the aspect of the drama they felt was most important. In this way they had to collaborate and provide justification for what to focus on and how to create the image. The teacher asked each person in the tableau to speak the thoughts of the character they were portraying, thus encouraging another shift in perspective and in thinking. It is clear that in this study fostering meta-cognition is not left to the end of the session in terms of reflecting on what has been learned, but is infused into every aspect from inception to final reflection on the multiple perspectives employed.

A different approach to metacognition was taken by a study of the differences between novice and expert musicians in terms of the strategies they use for self directed practice (Hallam, 2001). Through conducting interviews with both sets of musicians following performance, Hallam records that there were clear differences in the way the expert and novice musicians approached practising. The professional musicians demonstrated far more metacognition than the novice musicians, including awareness of their own strengths and weaknesses, metacognitive task knowledge, metacognitive knowledge about strategies, and an understanding of the roles of planning, monitoring and evaluation of per-formance, concentration and memory. There was also a great deal of individual difference within the groups, suggesting that individual musicians develop metacognition about self in relation to their developing skill. Hallam suggests that teachers of music need to foster metacognition as well as specific skills. She suggests that they may do this by focusing on setting goals, encouraging students to monitor their own progress and evaluate their own performance. In addition, teachers should encourage reflection on individual strengths and weakness; suggest strategies to aid memory and improve concentration; and develop students' awareness of their own motivation and the strategies they might use for sustaining or increasing it. Above all, Hallam suggests a focus on planning in three areas: planning related to the task, planning as a characteristic of the individual, and conscious strategic planning, which may compensate for other planning deficiencies. This suggests that while some individual musicians may automatically plan and organise their practice, others, particularly novices, do not. An approach to teaching which makes this aspect overt may mitigate this deficiency.

Part III

Facilitating metacognition

Introduction

In Part II I concentrated on subject specific metacognition. In all of the subject areas discussed, the role of the teacher as provider of opportunities for metacognition or as instructor of metacognitive processes was apparent. In Chapter 7 I consider the role of the professional teacher in developing metacognition in children. However, professional teachers are not the only guides and facilitators of metacognition in young children. For pre-school children the role of parents is particularly important and Chapter 8 will discuss research on how parents, siblings and peers can contribute to developing metacognition in the youngest children. In addition Chapter 8 will consider how metacognitive environments can be created in different settings for children of all ages. In Chapter 9 I focus on policy both in the UK and around the world and consider the extent to which education policy supports metacognitive instruction in schools. This is particularly timely in England with the release of the Rose Review interim report into the structure of the primary school curriculum. I will return to this in Chapter 9.

Chapter 7

Teachers and metacognition

The success of any classroom intervention is to a large part dependent on the teacher. The teacher has the power to create an environment which will facilitate metacognition or one which will not. However, any teacher's behaviour is influenced by her own knowledge, beliefs and opinions. It can be difficult to differentiate between these three concepts; opinion and beliefs influence knowledge and knowledge contains belief. Nespor (1987) differentiates between belief and knowledge in a number of ways. Firstly, beliefs are dependent on feelings and on evaluating knowledge, so that a teacher's beliefs about the usefulness of a particular strategy or knowledge system will affect the way he teaches this area. Secondly, beliefs are thought to be stored in episodic memory and are drawn from previous emotionally charged experiences, whereas knowledge is thought to be stored semantically, in a more organised and objective manner. Thirdly, belief systems are not necessarily consistent, nor are they necessarily open to group consensus, whereas we would expect knowledge to have some kind of objective consensus and be accountable against evidence. Beliefs may be fickle, easily changed or long lasting. Opinion lies somewhere in between these two. Our opinions tend to be based on our value system, but they also usually make some claim to be rational or logical and draw on knowledge for support. Of course opinions are often biased in the way in which one selects aspects of a knowledge system and that selection can be driven by a strong belief. Possessing knowledge about something is no guarantee of how that knowledge will be demonstrated. Teachers possessing similar knowledge about a construct such as metacognition may act on this knowledge in very different ways, depending to some extent on how useful they believe this knowledge to be. Beliefs and opinions arise out of experience and all teachers were once students in classrooms. The experiences they had as students are likely to influence their beliefs and opinions about teaching; to affect their behaviour in their own classroom; and to influence the experiences they provide for their own students, some of whom will go on to become teachers. It is clear that any intervention into classroom practice must take account of the teacher's beliefs, opinions and knowledge about the proposed teaching strategy. Many researchers have bemoaned the fact that their carefully theorised and planned classroom intervention study looked completely different when implemented by different teachers across the sample. Changing well established classroom practice is a difficult and frightening prospect for many teachers, and researchers need to take account of the emotional effects of intervention studies on the teachers involved.

In the CASE@KS1 intervention outlined in Chapter 4, a great deal of thought was given to teacher professional development. This included whole day group sessions with the research team away from the classroom. In these sessions the researchers provided theoretical knowledge about the ideas underpinning the Cognitive Acceleration (CA) approach; some practical information about time-tabling and organising the sessions and, perhaps most importantly, plenty of time to meet and discuss with other teachers involved in the intervention. In addition to these sessions, the research team provided in-class coaching sessions, where we would model a sample CASE lesson with the teacher's own class and then support her through other sessions. Following the research part of the intervention, some of the teachers who had been involved became teacher tutors for the next group of teachers who were going to implement the programme. Teachers were also encouraged to team up with others from neighbouring schools to discuss the programme without the researchers being present and then to bring any questions back to the whole team during the next professional development day. While teachers were busy getting to grips with the programme and discussing it with each other, the researchers were interested in how the programme fitted with teachers' existing beliefs, opinions and knowledge of learning theory. In particular, I was interested in teachers' understanding of metacognition; if this changed during the year-long programme and how it affected their behaviour in the classroom. What follows is a condensed version of a research study into the teachers' beliefs, knowledge and opinions about metacognition before, during and after the CASE@KS1 intervention.

The study

The CASE@KS1 intervention was designed as a quasi-experiment which involved a number of schools running the programme and a matched number of control schools continuing with their normal curriculum. Teachers from both experimental and control schools were interviewed at the beginning and end of the intervention year. All the teachers were female and had a range of teaching experience from newly qualified to a great deal of experience in different settings. For this particular study, eight teachers were interviewed; four from the experimental schools and four from the control schools. The first four questions of the interview were designed to elicit some general opinions and beliefs about teaching Year 1 children. From their answers to these questions I loosely categorised the teachers as "Protective", "Child Centred" or "Disciplined". For instance, the teachers in the Protective group tended to emphasise the social aspects of teaching and the children's emotional development. Jane (an established teacher in St Hilda's school) said:

You have to remind yourself that they have been in school only a year, maybe less; they still need lots of reassuring, lots of encouragement. They are just kind of sensitive and they just fall back if you're not careful. They need lots of praise to build their confidence and you need to be really patient and repeat things often. I think helping them to develop social skills is the most important thing at this stage; helping them to listen to others and making sure that they feel safe in the classroom.

The Child Centred group focused on the child's individual development, on engaging their curiosity and using their own past experiences. Sarah (a teacher at Latimore school who qualified two years earlier) said:

It's important to really encourage the children to talk about their experiences, to enable them to really engage and interact with the life around them. My teaching is very much based on what I think they'd be interested in and what they already know. They bring a lot to the classroom from their own experiences and they have their personal fascinations. I think children always learn much more if they can relate it to themselves and I try to impress on them that the learning is for their own sake. You need to encourage the children to build on what they already know.

The Disciplined group tended to stress the need for organisation and routine. Bryony (in her third year of teaching at Merryfield school) said:

You need to set them up with skills that will help them to focus at school. Discipline and set routines and things that should be followed. That way you are helping them to achieve the best they can. The curriculum tends to dictate how I teach and I believe that being very organised from the start is important for small children, so that they know what is expected of them. The most important thing for me is planning, careful planning and organisation.

While I intended this tripartite categorisation to be a loose and flexible one, it was striking how, as the interviews progressed, the teachers' belief systems differentiated along these lines. All the teachers were very consistent during the initial interviews and often repeated the beliefs detailed here in answer to different questions. Of course it is possible that had I interviewed them on another day in a different place I may have got different answers, but the coherence of their beliefs within this interview frame was remarkable.

Metacognition

Question 5 of the interview asked the teachers if they knew anything about the concept of metacognition. These interviews were carried out before any of the CA professional development days, so unless they had come across the idea before, it was unlikely that the teachers would know much, if anything, about metacognition. Only one teacher, Jenny (categorised in the Protective group), was able to provide any explanation. She believed it involved "thinking about your own thinking". She said she knew little about it, but as her brother was a psychologist he had mentioned it and it had stuck in her memory. Bryony thought it had something to do with independent learning and Sarah linked it to Piaget but wasn't able to elaborate any further. What was striking about this part of the interview was that none of the teachers had come across the idea of metacognition during their teacher training. So it appears that metacognition is not something which is routinely included in teacher training courses.

I provided a brief synopsis of metacognition and asked the teachers to reflect on whether these ideas would resonate with their own views of teaching young children. All of the teachers suggested that metacognition would be an important aspect of learning, particularly for problem solving, for asking good questions and for making connections. One of the control school teachers, Yvonne, thought that while it would enable children to build on what they had experienced, her own class would not be up to this kind of reflective thought. Yvonne was very much of the mind that only older and more able children would be able to reflect at all. She remarked "some of my children just don't think at all".

In a following question I asked the teachers about their own metacognitive experiences and suggested that they reflect on themselves as learners rather than teachers. Their answers to this question fitted very well into the previous categorisation of Protective, Child Centred and Disciplined teachers.

Jane said that she was aware of not being very logical, "so it takes me a while to get to the answer and it would be better if I could speed up". Jane seemed to experience metacognition as exposing a flaw in her cognitive processing. It points to something that should be remedied. At times thinking seemed to her a bit hit and miss: "You're never quite sure you know; you didn't really see why you're doing it or how it fits in. Sometimes it comes to you and sometimes not." Interestingly, she changed the pronoun from "I" to "you" as she expressed more of her beliefs about her own difficulties with thinking.

Sarah, on the other hand, emphasised the positive aspects of metacognition. She believed that she had a "photographic memory", which she had become aware of during her own GCSE exams, as an adolescent. She said that she had always known she had a good memory and found tests and exams easy, but it was while sitting her GCSEs that she began to realise that she was visualising the text book and the page containing the information she needed for the test.

Jenny related metacognition to her own development as a teacher and said that she found it useful to reflect on her practice to "realise the gaps in my knowledge" and thereby to direct her attention to areas that she felt were weaker. Jenny seemed to be taking some control over allocating her own cognitive resources.

The Disciplined group of teachers tended to find the least use for metacognition. Bryony said that she was not conscious of being metacognitive and that she didn't believe that people did think about what they were doing while studying. The most important thing was to just get on and do it.

During the intervention year the experimental school teachers were able to discuss theories of metacognition with the research team and practise providing metacognitive experiences for their children through the CASE activities. Not surprisingly, the knowledge, beliefs and opinions about metacognition in this group changed over the year, while the control school teachers' ideas remained much the same as at the start of the year. However, there were differences among the teachers in the three categories.

The Protective group continued to emphasise the development of children's emotional life and sometimes felt that asking children of this age to reflect on thinking was too much. Jane said "I can see that it benefits the way they can think, but it is an awful lot to ask children to think about, it might be too much to expect them to understand this." When asked for any examples of children being metacognitive she provided the following:

> There was one golden moment when we were talking about bears, about polar bears living in the wild or in the zoo and one boy said "But how would they get polar bears to the zoo?" and I just thought what a lovely question, because normally you wouldn't go beyond the thought of polar bears being in the zoo.

The focus here is obviously on the questioning and the child's imaginative response to the theme, but it doesn't really provide any evidence of meta-cognitive processing. Jane went on to say that as her children had grown in confidence and maturity over the year they were more able to express their lack of understanding to her or to their peers. But she maintained that developing a reflective element to thinking was intuitive – "it's something you do without really thinking about it".

Sally, another teacher in the Protective group, changed most over the year. In her first interview she emphasised the child's individual emotional development, but by the end of the year she was emphasising group learning and the social construction of knowledge. She felt that she had a better grasp of how to facil-itate metacognition, but a closer analysis of her examples and answers suggests that she had focused particularly on the theory of mind aspect of metacognition. For instance, her explanation of metacognition was that it was "like being able to admit that another child has got another idea or see that they are looking at things from a different point of view". She added "I think it helps them to share because they have to work together and put themselves in another child's position." Sally also said that she had become more aware of her own thinking during the year: "I'm more aware that I don't always think about things. I'm more aware that I don't always think things through and I don't always approach things in a logical way."

The Disciplined group of teachers tended to maintain their focus on routines and behaviour. However, Bryony began to develop both her own awareness of metacognition and her enthusiasm for encouraging the children to be meta-cognitive by the end of the year, although she had yet to develop the strategies necessary to foster metacognition in the children. She made specific reference to the CASE professional development programme and said that it had made her teaching more interesting and more challenging: "My expectations of the children are probably higher. I'm expecting them to be able to explain things together, expecting them to get to a higher standard." She had come to distinguish rote answers from the children, such as "I worked it out in my head", from more genuine attempts to explain their thinking. Bryony said that she had become much more aware of how the children were working together and noticed that they changed particular strategies in order to be fair rather than logically choosing the best strategy. She related an example of a group devising a game together:

> They were trying to invent a game that they could all play, but when they came to discuss the rules they had a problem – not everyone agreed with one person's rules, so instead they decided to take it in turns to invent a rule for the game, but of course what happened was that the game was unworkable, but they were thinking about how they could collaborate all together. It was interesting that they all wanted to do it, but they were trying to be fair rather than use the best way to get a game. We talked about it afterwards and I think they realised that it wasn't the best strategy for that problem.

By the end of the year Bryony had certainly changed in her attitude towards fostering metacognition in the classroom. At the end of the programme she was planning to give a talk to her colleagues on the CASE project and on facilitating metacognition in the classroom. She related that the nursery class teacher was particularly interested in these ideas and it seemed that Bryony's new enthusiasm would ensure that the project would live on in her school.

Yvonne, in a control school, maintained her beliefs about ability and meta-cognition through the year and at the end of the year she said:

> Some children would think because they do think, some wouldn't whether I do a plenary session or not, so I don't know if this reflection on what you've learned is important at all. The less able children don't know how to answer those questions, they are too cryptic for them.

The biggest change over the year came from Sarah, one of the experimental school teachers who was categorised as Child Centred from her initial interview responses. Over the year she seemed to really seize the idea of metacognition and developed her teaching style around it. She related this development to both the CASE professional development and classroom support from the research team. She acknowledged that at first she had doubts about how the children would respond:

> Before it was so many whys – Why did you do that? – and whats – What made you do that? – and I didn't find those questions helpful at all. I just didn't because I'd say "Why did you do that?" and they'd say "Because that's the way I did it". But as soon as I asked "How do you know that's right?", "How did you get there?", suddenly all this information comes out. When I started asking questions like that it was really really unnatural, it just wasn't a question I would ask. It didn't make sense for me to ask that question. I didn't understand how children would relate to "How did you do that?" because I thought they were like building questions, like I would get answers about what they had done like "I did this and this and this", but that was what they answered to "what" questions, so when I started asking "how" questions suddenly they all started talking about how they did it in relation to their own thinking.

Sarah went on to suggest that at first she was just getting rote answers but by continuing she came to believe that the children were developing cognitively and not just linguistically:

> It's not so much a personal experience at first, you know, they just learn to say the answer to the question, but then they seem to engage with it and then they begin thinking about their own thinking in a much more personal kind of way.

Sarah developed her own strategies for creating metacognitive opportunities:

> We often have conversations about thinking … I give lots of rewards for thinking and lots of praise for the class if they are thinking. I don't say "Hey you've learnt something new" but I do say "Hey great thought, we can use that thought" and I've done a lot of modelling about thinking.

Sarah also believed that her own metacognition has developed as a result of her practice and this has motivated her to continue to develop her knowledge of teaching and learning: "I didn't use to engage with my learning at all, I just received the information and did the tasks but since doing this I've learned more about how to engage with my own learning."

The interviews with teachers showed that while some teachers appeared to develop their own metacognition and facilitated the development of metacognition in their children, others held on to their initial beliefs about teaching and learning and allowed little room for change. However, we also know that while people may say one thing, they may actually do something else, so it is important to corroborate the teachers' views expressed through their interviews with

Table 7.1 Codes for teacher metacognitive behaviours

Code	Explanation	Example
TS	Refers to self learning strategies	"What could you do if you've got problems?"
TK	Questions acquisition of knowledge	"How do you know that?"
TI	Seeks information	"What are you going to do now?"
TE	Aids explanation	"Jane explained how she has sorted these into colours"
TQ	Questions, comments on, or asks for explanations of strategies	"Why did you do it like that?"
TP	Asks for predictions of success	"Will this work?"
TL	Shows expectations of planning	"How are we going to do this, what do we need to think about?"
TO	Expects checking	"Check what you are counting in?"
TC	Refers to own cognitive processes	"I don't understand it either"
TT	Refers to cognitive processes in general	"We all need to think really hard about this"
TU	Refers to universals of cognition	"We are going to solve a problem"
TV	Prompts evaluation	"Was it difficult to do or was it easy?"

observations of their classroom behaviour. In order to do this I devised a coding scheme to label aspects of teacher's behaviour which appeared to be directed at facilitating metacognition.

A note of caution is necessary when using coding tables. Compartmentalising verbal interactions in this way is artificial. Boundaries are drawn around categories by the researcher, but in reality some categories will overlap. Categories are interpretations of behaviour. They have been interpreted as facilitating metacognition because they ask questions that require one to think not about the solution to a problem but about how to get to that solution. They also include prompts to reflect on feelings of knowing or to become conscious of thinking. Sometimes it is only clear from the context of the individual speech act that the teacher is engaging at a metacognitive, rather than a cognitive, level. For instance, a simple question taken in isolation such as "How did you do that?" could be referring to the cognitive strategy used to solve a problem and the answer might be "We put the biggest here and the smallest here." But "How did you do that?" could also be metacognitive if it refers to a metacognitive strategy. In this sense the question is a short form of asking "How did you know how to do that?"

This may get an answer referring to past knowledge or to an analogy – "Because it's the same problem as the sticks" – or a more general answer – "I had to think about it and decide how to organise it." Sometimes meaning is expressed by stress and tone rather than by the actual words and of course sometimes the teacher may have one meaning in mind but the question is interpreted differently by the children. One common problem with trying to facilitate metacognition in young children is the tendency to get rote answers such as "I think about it in my head." Children quickly learn the right kind of response to make using words such as "think" and so it is important that teachers also model metacognitive thinking, as well as ask questions. For instance, in the excerpt below Bryony models an aspect of metacognition, comprehension monitoring, to the group trying to sort buttons:

ANDREW: Oh these have got squashed up together, but we've got no more to go with it, so we could squash them up together.
BRYONY: I don't think I'm following what you're saying.
ANDREW: I think we should squash them all together because these are all squashed together.
AMY: Why do they have to be stuck together?
BRYONY: I don't understand why they have to be stuck together.

By participating in the group on a level with the children and verbalising her own incomprehension of Andrew's strategy, Bryony enables Amy to ask the question that had been bothering her and, as it turned out, was also perplexing the rest of the group.

In order to see the effects of the teachers' beliefs about metacognition on their behaviour and the behaviour of the children, it is necessary to also code the children's behaviour for examples of metacognition.

Using the two coding tables it is possible to see how children's metacognitive behaviour matches up with teachers' behaviour designed to facilitate metacognition. We might make predictions based on the teachers' interview responses and then test these out through analysis of the classroom observations. From the year's worth of observations of the CASE tasks in the experimental schools I have selected the last three tasks of the summer term to analyse. These tasks included the Transport task, which involves children in using rules to determine which kinds of transport are allowed into parts of town; the Farmyard task, which involves sorting animals by different variables – species, colour, size and deciding what to do about individuals which fit in two conflicting categories; and the Bottles task, which involves deciding on what causes some bottles to roll and not others (also referred to in Chapter 4). In the following table the teacher behaviours are totalled across the three tasks. The schools are referred to by name of teacher to make it easier to link this information to the earlier interview responses.

Table 7.3 shows counts of teacher behaviours interpreted as facilitating

Table 7.2 Codes for child metacognitive behaviours

Code	Explanation	Example
SELF	Shows knowledge of self in relation to cognition	"I know what to do" "I know I am good at writing"
OTH	Refers to what others think/ desire	"She doesn't know how to do it"
UNIV	Refers to universals of cognition	"We've got to solve a problem"
UND	Questions task information	"Something is missing, it doesn't make sense"
PRED	Predicts success/failure	"We'll be done in just a minute, if we do this"
RAT	Refers to ease/difficulty	"This is so hard to do"
COMP	Compares with other tasks	"This is just like the problem with the stairs we did last week"
EVA	Evaluates: indicates knowledge about what might be useful	"We should build up the boxes that will be quicker"
PLAN	Refers to planning the task	"We need to know which way to go round the table, we need to talk about it"
PAR	Paraphrases to confirm understanding	"Did you mean ...?"
SQU	Asks a question of self	"I think that's right, but is it?"
CHE	Checks work	"This one's good, this one's not"

metacognition over three half hour CASE@KS1 tasks. It is clear that while Bryony changed during the course of the year, she still employed fewer strategies for facilitating metacognition than the other two teachers. Bryony felt that she had a difficult, very mixed ability class to cope with that particular year. She had many children with English as an additional language and a small group with particular special learning needs. She felt she needed to establish a routine for these children before trying to encourage metacognition or self regulated learning.

Sometimes teachers felt that encouraging metacognition led them too far away from more traditional teaching and that this could be upsetting for children who didn't like change. In contrast, both Sarah and Jane employed more metacognitive behaviours over these three tasks. As I observed these classes on a regular basis over the whole year, I could not see any great difference between the make up of Sarah's class compared to Bryony's. Both schools were in a deprived part of inner city London and both included some children of asylum seekers and refugees from war torn areas. Sarah's class had a small number of traveller children who joined half way through the year and then left again a few months

Table 7.3 Teacher metacognitive behaviours across three CASE tasks

Totals of teacher metacognitive behaviours across three CASE tasks: Transport,
Farmyard, Bottles

Code	Sarah	Jane	Bryony
TS	1	0	0
TK	13	10	2
TI	0	0	0
TE	2	0	0
TQ	5	1	5
TP	3	0	0
TL	1	0	0
TO	0	0	0
TC	3	0	0
TT	21	17	8
TU	0	0	0
TV	2	5	1
Total	51	33	16

later and both teachers were helped by teaching assistants, language specialists
and sometimes voluntary helpers. The difference between the two appeared to
be in the belief of the teacher concerned of the need to develop metacognition.
One striking aspect of this analysis is that many of the codes, which represent
types of behaviour teachers might employ to facilitate metacognition, were not
seen across these three tasks. Certainly, different tasks tended to provoke different kinds of teacher strategies for encouraging metacognition. The one code
which remained constant through all tasks was TT – teacher refers to cognitive
processes in general. This included teachers encouraging children to think about
how they were thinking about the task. This seemed to be the easiest strategy
for the teachers to employ, closely followed by TK – questioning acquisition
of knowledge. Asking children to reflect on how they know something comes
fairly easily to teachers but the problem can be that the answers remain at the
cognitive level of describing how something was worked out rather than a
reflection on knowledge itself.

There are a growing number of studies of teachers' metacognitive behaviour
and how this impinges on how they facilitate metacognition in the classroom.
The literature has a good deal in common with literature on reflective practice, which often details strategies for uncovering our own assumptions about
our professional practice and challenges us to think about the sources of those
assumptions. For instance, a paper by Watson and Wilcox (2000) suggests that
practitioners need to pay attention to the ordinary and habitual everyday

experiences, to reflect on them and to see them anew. They suggest two methods for doing this. One involves sharing our stories of practice in a more organised way than the normal staff room chat. They detail a method of sharing a story of practice within a group. Each member of the group reads the story quickly at first to get a sense of the content and note points of recognition. A second reading involves what they term "zooming in", where the readers pay attention to the details of the story and add their reflections to the text. A third reading, or "zooming out", invites others to comment on the story and add their own insights. A second method for reflection uses hypomnemata. Hypomnemata are notebooks in which are kept the details of actual experience of day to day activities. These include no reflection or commentary but a simple assemblage of artefacts, lists and texts showing what a job actually entails. In particular, this involves collecting lesson plans, details of how lessons are normally begun or ended, timetable details, notes about how marking is undertaken etc. Many of these practices become so familiar and habitual for teachers that they no longer become part of reflective practice. After collecting these items, the second stage is again a "zooming in" where the teacher herself begins to reflect on these, asking self directed questions such as "What are the origins of this convention?", "How does the convention relate to my personal philosophy?", "What values shape the convention?" etc. Following this annotation of the items, the authors suggest that we play with reassembling the items in different ways to see what aspects of practice connect up with others and which parts are disparate. This process of assembling, annotating and re-assembling can occur many times until the individual feels that some insight is gained into the connection between personal beliefs, opinions, knowledge and conventions of practice.

Of course developing metacognition about ourselves as professionals as well as about ourselves as learners takes time and motivation. If we expect our students to develop metacognition about themselves as learners, then we must also engage in the process ourselves. In a demanding profession such as teaching this can be particularly difficult. Adey and colleagues highlighted the role of the school culture in changing teacher practices. A teacher who wishes to engage in developing her own metacognition and that of her students may find this hindered or supported by the culture of the school (Adey *et al.*, 2004). It can be very difficult to engage in practices which are different from those of other teachers in the same school. In primary and early years settings there may be a small number of full time staff, often working closely together, sometimes re-creating a "family" atmosphere for the children in their care. While this may have positive emotional benefits for the children, it can also hamper any one individual teacher's intention to alter the conventions of practice. Teachers need to feel supported by colleagues if they are to embark on more metacognitive approaches to teaching. For Joyce (1991), collegiality is one of the primary "doors to school improvement". The literature on reflective practice discussed above suggests that real change comes from more structured reflection on practice than just staff room collegiality.

A recent study of nursery school teachers' metacognition and meta-learning also focuses on the connection between teachers' own metacognition and their practice in supporting play based learning of very young children. In the study by Cheng Pui-wah (2008), a "meta-learner" is defined as someone who engages in the metacognitive behaviours of self questioning, monitoring, reflecting and evaluating and someone who is aware of themselves as a learner and therefore someone who has developed a base of metacognitive knowledge. As the study was located in Hong Kong the author was able to track the developmental change of teachers' practice in the light of recommendations in the 1980s to incorporate play based learning into the early years curriculum. The findings from this small scale qualitative study of four teachers' practice highlight different beliefs and conceptualisations of play based learning held by the different teachers.

One view is described as a technical approach to teaching and learning, where play is seen as a pre-cursor to more didactic teaching. These teachers relied heavily on teaching aids, such as using puppets to engage the children's attention, but there was no real change to the usual teaching practices. While these teachers could see when things didn't work quite so well in the classroom, their own strategy for change involved waiting for the next round of professional development courses when they hoped to be told how to make their practice better. Thus their own views of how learning is a process of soaking up knowledge from expert others influenced their own way of teaching the children. Pui-wah details the response of one teacher who broke this mould. This teacher, rather like Sarah in my own study, was initially unable to articulate a coherent theory of play based learning, but she was motivated to reflect upon her own assumptions and came to a personalised and situated theory of play based learning, which she could enact within her own classroom. She allowed the children to take part ownership of the curriculum and to take charge of a particular project. She also consciously drew on all of her own experience, including mothering her own child, to inform her practice. She sought out different views on play based learning and increased her knowledge of theory through independent study. Pui-wah highlights the way in which this teacher's own metacognitive development impacts on her practice and suggests that studies of professional development of teachers which are based on length of experience fail to acknowledge the extent to which novice teachers can develop expertise through developing metacognition.

Lin, Schwartz and Hatano (2005) suggest a critical event strategy for increasing the metacognitive awareness of teachers. They argue that teaching requires particular types of what they call "adaptive metacognition", which takes account of the variety of different activities and situations which teachers face. These real situations are not necessarily akin to the problem solving type tasks which are often the basis for metacognitive interventions for students. This is a valuable contrast to make. I have often found that classroom metacognition interventions are heavily reliant on problem solving and as such tend to focus on strategy selection, monitoring progress towards the goal of solving the problem and then evaluating the solution. These can, as the authors point out, become a check list of skills to be employed given any task. This is not only repetitive and probably de-motivating, but also gives a false impression of metacognition as useful for real-life situations in which problems do not necessarily have a solution.

In their study Lin and colleagues, in a similar way to Watson and Wilcox (2000), highlight the need to challenge assumptions about everyday conventions of practice; to see anew routines of behaviour; and to reflect on hidden value systems which underpin these. However, the authors also make the valuable point that teachers must also be able to connect with and communicate with children and students who have very different values from their own. They argue that the features of many successful metacognition interventions, such as a clearly defined problem, a stable environment and a shared value system with others, are not features of teaching practice. They describe one teacher's attempts to adapt a new curriculum to her own practice through periods of "off-line metacognition", i.e. reflecting and evaluating after the class. This type of reflection requires teachers to reflect on established practice and to be open minded to the possibility of new ways of approaching familiar situations. The difficulty here is that if nothing is obviously wrong with a practice, the tendency is not to reflect any deeper or seek ways of altering that practice. This can lead to very routine ways of teaching which become more embedded and no longer serve the developmental needs of the teachers concerned. In Lin et al.'s study the researchers used examples of recurrent but everyday classroom problems as a focus for reflection. However, rather than categorising these according to their own value systems, the researchers encouraged people with different values, goals and experience to comment on the same event. In this way they sought to develop a multiplicity of voices about this issue. They also asked people to search for additional information which might impact on the issue, thus involving the teachers in a more elaborate conceptualisation of the problem and allowing them to challenge their own assumptions about the issue. This method helps people to understand what kind of extra information may be needed to see an issue more clearly. The problem is thus made more complex, rather than simpler, and the aim of the reflection is not to seek a simple solution but to examine the problem from different perspectives. This type of programme, I believe, has more in common with the goal of metacognition as facilitating wise and thoughtful decision making for real social situations, rather than the often cognitive based models of metacognition for problem solving.

Leat (1993) made the point that competence based teacher education should be viewed within a framework which includes metacognition. Moreover, teacher training should consider the interaction of cognitive and metacognitive processes with emotions and behaviour. Teachers may experience a downturn in performance as established patterns of behaviour are disrupted by reflective and metacognitive practices. This is likely to cause an emotional response and requires recognition and support for feelings from mentors during this phase. Teacher development based on metacognitive theories must also take account of self esteem and self concept. A study by Salonen, Vaurus and Efklides (2005) makes similar points in terms of co-regulation of learning and scaffolding metacognition. While this study was based on teachers or others scaffolding the learning of students, the points are relevant for all learners, including trainee teachers or established teachers undertaking professional development. The authors argue that socio-cognitive learning processes must take account of affective and motivational processes as well as metacognitive ones. They suggest that there may be a mismatch between the teacher and student's metacognitive experiences. Scaffolding learning can therefore be open to difficulties such as over control, where the teacher is too quick to step in and help. This may be the case with some experienced teacher mentors who find it difficult to step back from the classroom situation they are observing and allow the student teacher to work out the situation for herself. According to Salonen *et al.*, scaffolding learning can also be intrusive and block the learner's growing independence or be asynchronous, in that the support is poorly timed or misplaced. They suggest that if these difficulties persist there can be a knock on effect on the students' emotional and motivational states and decrease their sense of autonomy and control.

This study is particularly interesting as it highlights a little researched area of metacognition which is relevant to teacher education, i.e. constructing and maintaining a shared discourse about education. Socially constructive learning involves a continuous effort to share meanings and match discourses with others. This can be difficult when one partner is more expert than the other and when one is in a position of power. Meanings need to be negotiated and altered during the process of teaching and learning. The aim must be to achieve a regulatory balance between the partners. Salonen *et al.* point out that in these situations, partners often experience temporary imbalances caused by misunderstandings and this can lead to feelings of insecurity and lack of confidence. The need to restore this balance felt by both partners may result in them engaging in more personal metacognitive activity to reflect on and seek understanding of the problem and more metacognitive activity aimed at understanding the other's perspective and metacognitive experiences. These metacognitive behaviours which are aimed at regulating and commenting on the ongoing communication between people are often called "meta-communicative". These are not divorced from the ongoing communicative act but seek to regulate it in order to bring about a more positive experience for both partners. Thus when we relate this theory of metacognition to teacher development, it becomes apparent that teacher trainers must also be aware of, and seeking to develop, their own metacognition and regulatory behaviours in order to support similar development in novice teachers.

It has often been noted in studies of metacognition that teachers find it difficult to implement research driven theories of metacognition in their own classrooms. In a study of some different thinking skills programmes which include aspects of metacognition, Baumfield and Oberski (1998) reported some of the most common obstacles teachers found to implementing these programmes. One complaint was that they were often repetitive and children would get bored with the set tasks; other reasons revolved around finding the time for the extended group discussion work required and the difficulty of working with open ended problems, when children are used to seeking the correct answer. These factors were common to my own research with teachers and suggest that established patterns of teaching, supported by the curriculum and culture of the school, can make it difficult for individual teachers to change their practice enough to use metacognitive intervention programmes creatively. Rather than creating more intervention programmes designed to facilitate the development of metacognition in children and teachers, it seems more appropriate for researchers to help teachers to identify opportunities in their everyday practices, which may become sites for greater metacognitive engagement. In addition teachers, teacher trainers and researchers also need to find opportunities and ways of developing their own metacognition before attempting to implement strategies aimed at children.

Here is an excerpt from my interview with Sarah, a Year 1 teacher, back in May 2000:

ME: Do you think metacognition can be taught?

SARAH: Absolutely. I didn't use to engage with my learning at all, I just received the information and did the tasks, no personal engagement. I feel I was so let down by my own education, so I'm thankful for having been involved in this project because I think I might not have stayed if I hadn't. I wasn't sure how to be involved and engaged. I spent years just writing out the same information in different ways, but I did well because I had a very good memory. I engaged with the people, but not with the learning. But now I impress on my class that we are all doing it together, we are all learning together, we are all sitting together, and they know that I'm thinking and they are thinking. And then you know sometimes it's "Great thought, I would never have thought of that, that's brilliant, wow, how did you think of that", you know, and so on. They've started asking more challenging questions now and also seem to have gained some confidence about speaking up. They don't wait for me to give them the right answer as much now and sometimes I have to really think hard about how to answer their questions, so that I don't shut them down.

Certainly some of what Sarah says about her time in higher education, writing out the same information in different ways, resonates with my own experiences of studying for higher qualifications. If teachers at all levels of the system pursue the development of their own metacognition we may just break this cycle of disengagement with learning and re-connect learning with feelings, behaviour and cognition.

Of course trained teachers are not the only teachers of children. Long before they enter the school system children have learned many things from parents, other adults and peers. In the next chapter I'll consider how we might create metacognitive environments for children both before and during school.

Chapter 8

Context and metacognition

No one method of facilitating metacognition in young children will suffice for all contexts. We know that learning is influenced by many factors, some of which may appear to be individual, but all are related to the learning environment in one way or another. In the last chapter we saw how teachers' beliefs might impinge on the way they construct learning environments conducive to developing metacognition. However, before children ever get to school they have been immersed in learning environments provided at home, play groups and informal play situations with peers and siblings. Learning is always situated in a context and the features of that context can have marked effects on the way learning happens and on what is learned.

Context

Okagaki and Sternberg (1990) detailed ways in which context impinges on thinking skills (of which metacognition is a part). They argue that task materials can affect the way a task is undertaken; material which is unfamiliar may make a task more difficult than completing a similar task with familiar material. It is likely that materials which have real world relevance to the task set will aid the type of thinking necessary to complete it. For instance, ordinary and everyday problem solving is contextualised and specific; cues are provided by the environment and people seek out information from the context which will simplify or solve the problem as quickly and easily as possible. Sometimes school type learning breaks with this convention, often for broader educational reasons, but if these reasons are not adequately explained, children can become de-motivated. Okagaki and Sternberg suggest that the particular contexts in which thinking skills are learned also include beliefs about appropriate behaviour and social roles. When the context changes and those other contextual factors no longer match the original setting, children may be unable to activate the appropriate type of thinking and become confused about what is required. Similarly, different cultures have different theories of what constitutes good thinking in any particular area and developing metacognition may not be part of the general view of educating children. Thus children may come into school with very different backgrounds in terms of the importance given to higher levels of thinking. Some children will devise ways of negotiating these differences by adopting different styles of thinking in home and school contexts, but for other children the mismatch between home and school can be an obstacle which is never overcome. If the goal of facilitating the development of metacognition is to make good life decisions then there must be some coherence between the learning environments provided by the school and those found outside of formal schooling.

A number of ethnographic studies carried out by Sternberg and Suben (cited in Okagaki and Sternberg 1990) explored the differences between home and school contextual factors on the thinking skills of children. They detail how ideas of time, and therefore how time is allocated, differed in home and school contexts for a particular community. When a child from that community enters school the idea of having to think through a problem in a given time may be completely alien. The researchers suggest that the child may have developed metacognitive processes related to allocating resources to a task but the rules that the child is using to make those metacognitive decisions will not include time as a factor in the decision making. Similarly children may have metacognitive knowledge about strategies for completing certain tasks in the home context which do not transfer to similar tasks in a school context. Thus children may develop metacognitive knowledge in one context but this does not necessarily mean that they will be able to transfer that knowledge to other contexts. Further studies by Sternberg and colleagues, of parental beliefs about learning in different ethnic groups, found varying views about the importance of teaching children to become independent learners. For some groups this was rated as highly important while for others teaching children to listen and conform were rated more highly. The researchers point out that this does not mean that these parents are not interested in their children becoming independent learners, but that wider social and political factors may make conformity for one group of children particularly desirable as parents seek to ensure that their children fit in with the dominant culture and thereby enhance their future life and employment opportunities.

Parents

A study of the skills mothers taught to their pre-school children by Sonnenschein, Baker and Cerro (1992) found that no metacognitive or self regulation skills were included in the list. However, when the researchers deliberately asked about "learning to learn" skills all the mothers claimed that these were important, and either believed that they taught their children these skills or that their children already had these skills. Yet when asked for examples, mothers returned to talking about basic cognitive skills rather than about how they facilitated the development of metacognition. These findings parallel some of my own findings when talking to teachers about metacognition. Both parents and teachers tend to be positive about facilitating metacognitive development when asked about it but they often relate cognitive rather than metacognitive activity. These findings highlight one of the problems of researching beliefs about metacognition. Given that most people outside of academia are unfamiliar with the term, researchers often have to substitute other terms such as "learning to learn" or "self regulation" but these terms imply more than "metacognition". Interviewees may focus on the aspects of these broader concepts which they feel most able to articulate and this can skew findings from self report studies. However, studies which break metacognition down into component parts and ask parents to comment on the importance of those have yielded some interesting results.

In an earlier study Sonnenschein and colleagues asked mothers to comment on how their 4 to 6-year-old children learned a variety of metacognitive skills such as planning and comprehension monitoring. Regardless of the age of the children, the mothers believed that these skills were developed through everyday experiences and that teachers were not responsible for this development (Sonnenschein *et al.*, 1991, cited in Baker, 1994).

Other studies have concentrated on observing parents and children in interaction, when solving a problem. The interaction patterns are analysed in terms of how the parent is scaffolding the child's metacognitive behaviour. It seems fairly obvious that social interaction with a more experienced other would support a child's learning and that the same would be true for developing metacognition. However, as Baker suggested, findings from a number of different research studies shows a more complex picture. While children seem to benefit from working with the support of a parent on some aspects of a task, on others they do not. In particular it seems that some of the metacognitive processes such as planning are not necessarily fostered by social interaction (Baker 1994). A body of research based on Wertsch's social interactionist model of learning found evidence for the importance of mothers' skill in matching their support to a child's age and developmental level and lent support to the idea that children develop self regulation through appropriate interaction with parents on problem solving tasks. However, as Baker pointed out, it has never been clear how and at what point the child moves from the position of having the metacognitive functions scaffolded and supported by a parent to one of independent metacognition.

The theory of social interaction and support for developing metacognition was also called into question by Susan Kontos (1983), who conducted studies into the metacognitive environment of young children and its effects on how the children performed on a problem solving task. Kontos used familiar problem solving tasks in the form of peg board puzzles which were designed to be difficult for the young children to solve on their own, but not impossibly so. She tested thirty-nine 3- to 5-year-old children and their mothers. The children were first encouraged to attempt the puzzle alone and asked a series of questions to elicit information about any metacognitive strategies they may have used to aid them in the tasks. Then the mothers were encouraged to help their child to solve a new, similar puzzle. The mothers were free to help their child solve the puzzle as they would at home and finally the child was asked to complete a third similar puzzle alone. The mothers' instructions and help were analysed for metacognitive content. Categories such as goal direction, passing on relevant information about the task, focusing on task specific knowledge and reminders of the steps in problem solving were related to Flavell's task related aspect of metacognitive knowledge. Other instructions focusing on strategy selection and use, monitoring progress towards the goal and evaluating the success of particular strategies were related to Flavell's strategy aspect of metacognitive knowledge. The results of the analysis showed that while there was a good deal of meta-cognitive content in the mothers' guidance, this was split fairly evenly between task and strategy information. Mothers tended to alter their talk depending on the child's age. Although mothers talked more to younger children, the amount of metacognitive content in their talk was about the same as for older children. The study found that mothers do use metacognitive talk with young children to regulate their performance on problem solving tasks.

However, in a follow up study with fathers and young children, Kontos found that children performed equally well on the peg board tasks if they were given time to practise alone as they did when supported by their fathers, even though fathers used instructions with similar metacognitive content to those used by mothers. Kontos makes the point that individual practice is at least as important as social interaction in terms of developing metacognitive skills related to prob-lem solving. Thus it seems that we can support young children too much and that it is sometimes better to give them the opportunity to work on tasks alone, to fail and to try again in order to develop their own regulation of cognition and to build a base of metacognitive knowledge.

The parents in Kontos's studies were mainly white, middle class and educated. Until relatively recently studies of metacognition have not overly concerned themselves with wider social contextual factors such as socio-economic status (SES) of the participants. However, a study by Pappas and colleagues (2003) made SES a central feature of the research. Over one hundred 4- to 5-year-old children participated in this study of children's metacognition during mathematical prob-lem solving. Here metacognition was defined in three categories: recognising errors, adaptability in selection and use of strategies, and awareness of thinking processes. Basing their hypothesis on studies of language which have shown that children from lower SES backgrounds fall behind their peers from higher SES backgrounds on language competence and vocabulary, the researchers suggest that lower SES children would also fall behind their peers on the development of metacognition. Language may be the mediating factor of course and may impact on understanding the task and self directed monitoring of the task.

It is difficult to categorise people in terms of SES and the categories employed will impinge on the interpretations of the findings of such studies. In the UK one measure often used by researchers is allocation of free school meals. Only chil-dren from low income backgrounds, often those on means tested state benefits, are offered free school meals. However, this may not mean that the parents are uneducated or of low SES background themselves. Yet, in the absence of other measures of SES, qualification for state benefits is used as a proxy measure. So it is with the Pappas study in New York. The background of the low SES children was determined by their qualification for subsidised day care, whereas the middle SES children were determined by whether their parents were working and the high SES children were those who went to an exclusive fee paying pre-school. The children were presented with mathematical problems to solve and their behaviour and responses to questions about solving the problems were categorised by the kinds of metacognition they displayed. The study describes levels of metacognition within each category. So in terms of recognising mistakes, spontaneous correction of an error is viewed as a higher level of metacognition than a display of uncertainty about the answer; similarly a spontaneous change of strategy is seen as a higher level of metacognition than a simple awareness of a strategy not working. The findings from this study showed that all three groups of children, regardless of SES background, were largely unaware of the mistakes they had made. However, in terms of adaptability, while most children displayed some adaptability in their use of strategies, a significantly higher proportion of children in the high SES group displayed independent adaptability at least once, i.e. spontaneous change of a strategy which was not working, although this was a relatively rare occurrence for any of the groups. In the third category, awareness of thinking processes, the researchers found a significant difference between high SES children and the other two groups. In general, neither middle nor low SES children were able to articulate their thinking processes to the extent that the high SES children could. However, once again it seemed that none of the three groups showed high levels of metacognition.

This research confirms my own findings, that while young children may display some metacognitive processing such as detecting errors, articulating thinking processes during problem solving is not a frequent activity, unless prompted by an adult. In the years before formal schooling it is parents who can give children the opportunities to develop metacognition. The Pappas study has shown that while there is not a great difference between children of different SES background in terms of metacognition, the high SES children have some advantage by the time they reach school age. The ability of these children to articulate their own thinking processes will advantage them in the classroom and may impact on teachers' beliefs about their ability in specific subject domains. If children are to become independent learners the development of metacognition must be supported before the onset of formal schooling.

A factor which appears to be instrumental in providing a metacognitive advantage for some children is the ability to articulate thinking processes. Children from poorer backgrounds may have less developed language skills, so while they may not lack metacognitive development, their inability to articulate their own thinking may lead us to believe that they are also deficient in metacognition. Developing good language skills is important for all children, but in terms of developing metacognition this requires the development of understanding of what are usually called mental state words. In Chapter 2 I described some of the theoretical research on language development, however it is worth mentioning here research which has highlighted children's understanding of their own mental processing.

Work by Estes, Wellman and Woolley (1989) in particular showed the extent to which young children can differentiate between ideas and things. In their classic studies of children's ontological and epistemological beliefs they hypothesised that while Piaget's view of young children as realists may relate to children's beliefs about knowledge it is unlikely that children believe that mental states are real in the same way as objects in the world are viewed as real. These theorists distinguish objects from mental states using the following criteria: that objects provide sensory data, i.e. can be touched or seen; that the sensory data is available to others as well as to oneself; that objects have a temporal existence. In tests of 3-, 4- and 5-year-old children the researchers presented either descriptions of real objects, e.g. a boy with a dog, or thoughts, e.g. a boy thinking about a dog, or they contrasted people who were dreaming, remembering or pretending. The children had to decide in each case whether the dog was real, based on the three criteria above. They found that even the youngest children gave correct judgements about the reality of the objects in over 70 per cent of cases. The errors did not show a consistent pattern, suggesting that on the whole even young children distinguish between real objects and mental entities. In subsequent experiments where the researchers checked their findings and ruled out other interpretations of the children's responses, they still found that even the youngest children made correct judgements about objects and thoughts most of the time. When asked to explain their answers, children were able to provide rational explanations, such as a thought of an apple cannot be eaten because it is imagination and not a real object. In follow up studies Estes and colleagues tested children's understanding of what they termed "close imposters" (ibid.). These included intangible objects such as air, representations such as drawings and sensations such as pain. Their findings showed that children provided different explanations for the different types of phenomena. Even the youngest children in their sample (3-year-olds) provided different explanations for mental entities and "close imposters", suggesting that young children are able to distinguish the mental realm from the physical world. However, they also found a developmental progression in terms of consistency of explanation. The 4- and 5-year-olds were more consistently correct in their explanations for the different objects. The researchers suggest that rather than these inconsistencies providing evidence for child realism, the errors that 3-year-olds make in their explanations for mental phenomena may be a result of focusing on only one part of the question, e.g. focusing on the object "dog" rather than the first part of the question "thought of a …".

In later work, Estes (1998) investigated the extent to which children are aware of their own mental processing following a mental rotation task. Using the form of a computer game, children were asked if two monkeys which flashed onto the screen were holding the same arm in the air or different arms. While one monkey was always upright the other monkey was rotated clockwise through 30° intervals until it was upside down. The research showed that 6-year-olds were similar to adults in terms of having access to their own thought processing and explaining how they had rotated the image in their mind. In addition, a majority of the 5-year-olds and a large number of 4-year-olds also used mental imagery to explain their performance on the task.

I repeated Estes's study (with his permission) with some minor changes. While keeping the task the same, I used cards rather than a computer programme and focused on the children's explanations of their performance on the task. I used Estes's scoring categories of 0 for a non mental answer; 1 for a general mental answer and 2 for explanation of mental rotation. Of the 39 5-year-olds in my study only 9 children were able to provide mental rotation answers. The major-ity of the children (unlike in Estes's study) provided only physical answers even when I attempted to lead them towards more conscious mental interpretations. For instance, here is Sarah explaining how she worked out the answer to the card where the monkey is upside down:

ME: Can you tell me how you worked out this one?
SARAH: Because there was one the right way up and the other upside down, I got up and looked at it like that [she moves around the table and twists her body to look at the card upside down] and I knew them two were not the same, cos that one is a little bit longer.
ME: Why did you get up and move around like that?
SARAH: Because that one was upside down
ME: If you move around that side of the table won't the other one be upside down?
SARAH: Yep.

Our conversation continued along these lines, with Sarah providing no further explanation. She seemed to have guessed the right answer for this card as she got all the other cards incorrect.

In contrast, Pritti got all the cards correct and also gave mental rotation answers:

ME: How did you work out the answer to this one?
PRITTI: I imagined this monkey was like that [she uses her fingers to indicate turning the upside down monkey upright] and then I know the answer.
ME: Which bit of you did all that working out?
PRITTI: My brain.

For the children who scored 2 on my version of Estes's test the explanation appears to be easy, obvious and a natural thing to do. They often used "just" as in "You just need to turn the monkeys over in your brain and put them together again" or "You just need to use your brain to move the monkeys around then you will get the correct answer." They also referred to practice, although to my knowledge none of the children had been set a problem like this before. Some of the children speculated on what aspects of cognition may be involved, for instance: "It may be your memory that helps you to do this", "I think you have to use your imagination", "Your eyes help your imagination to see things the other way round". However, the children in this category agreed that once they could solve these problems using mental rotation they wouldn't need to use any other method.

In contrast the children who scored 0, getting most of the cards incorrect and giving non mental answers, often focused on their knowledge of their own physicality. For instance, responses included "Standing on your head or twisting your body so that you could see things upside down would help you to solve the problem" or "I know left and right so I can tell which one it is." The emphasis with this group was on the solver paying close attention to the task to search for clues to its solution. For instance, saying "They may have different feet or different colours" would mean that they could say that the monkeys were different from each other without having to turn one around. Some children thought up other types of strategies for solving the problem such as cutting one monkey out and then turning it around or re-drawing the monkeys the right way up. One boy thought that thinking about monkeys in the zoo might help him to solve the problem, but he wasn't sure how, only that monkeys shouldn't stay upside down for too long. Another child said "Clever people would just know how to do this and wouldn't need to work it out."

The children in the middle group, who scored 1, gave what Estes called general mental answers to the problem. They also had mixed results in terms of the numbers of cards they got correct. There was some understanding that problems had to be worked out using your brain and that this takes effort and some children thought that concentrating hard on the problem was necessary. George, who got the answers to the cards wrong, thought speed of thinking was important: "You have to think about it and I thinked about it quickly, if you do that you can work it out." Some children thought that you might be able to use your hands to help you, but in the end it was thinking which would really solve the problem. Explanations such as "I thought about it", "My brain helped me", "I worked it out" were common in this group, although many of their answers to the problems were incorrect. When I asked about mental rotation more specifically, the children in this category denied that it was possible to solve the problem purely by rotating the image mentally. They were usually unable to provide any clarity of answer to the question beyond "thinking about it" and although they got some cards correct, it remained largely a mystery to them how they had achieved this.

The difference in my results compared to Estes's may be accounted for by the smaller number of cards used in my study and the lack of the computer image. Estes suggested that his computer task may have promoted more active engagement and mental effort than problem solving tasks used in earlier studies.

Younger children who do not yet understand that people are always thinking, even when resting, may need to be prompted by tasks which make thinking effortful in order to be able to reflect on their thinking. Antonietti *et al.* (2000) highlighted the importance of visualisation in problem solving. Their research suggests that visual representation of problems encourages people to view the problem holistically and to take different perspectives on it. Helping students to visualise also helped them to re-structure the problem, to see it anew and to seek other solutions. The mental rotation task required this kind of visual representation and many children referred to using their eyes to solve the problem. Becoming consciously aware of using strategies such as visualisation is a development of metacognition.

Pramling (1988) argued that simply teaching metacognitive strategies to young children is unlikely to facilitate development of independent metacognitive processing. Instead, such methods may produce children who are aware of the kinds of answers required and respond in an appropriate way without ever having internalised the thinking process. We often see this when children are first prompted to talk about their own thinking and they begin to preface every answer with "I thought about it" or "I used my brain to think about it." Secondly, teaching general metacognitive strategies suggests that these are transferable to different subject specific domains, however different subjects draw on qualitatively different kinds of thinking and lead to building different features of the metacognitive knowledge base. Pramling's study sought to develop the metacognitive ability of pre-school children through a shop activity. In this study, one teacher focused on engaging the children in metacognitive talk about learning during the children's work on the shop activity. The children were encouraged to reflect on what they were doing and why. In particular, the teacher focused the dialogues on learning in terms of the specific activity of the shop, rather than on learning in general. Another teacher used more traditional question and answer techniques to aid learning about the shop activity but with no focus on metacognition and the third teacher was allowed to choose her own way of working on the shop activity. This teacher used traditional pre-school type activities such as using clay, cutting and sticking and play based learning, but did not encourage reflection on the activities. The study showed that where the teacher focused on asking the children to reflect on their learning in terms of the activity, these young children were able to describe their own learning in terms of either personal experience, by actively doing something, or by reflection. The study suggests that helping children to develop metacognitively requires a re-structuring of learning activities so that content is not divorced from reflection.

These studies of children's development of understanding about mental states and processes suggest that in order to develop metacognition, children need to be provided with opportunities for individual practice on tasks which require effortful thinking. In addition they should be given the opportunity to discuss their solutions with others. This is where parents can scaffold their child's metacognition by asking questions which prompt reflection on how they have thought about the particular task, rather than on the step by step solution to the problem.

Peers

Developing the social skills of young children is high on the list of parental beliefs about what education for young children should be. Many children enter into some form of pre-school activity, where they get the opportunity to play with a wide range of peers. In recent years attention has been paid to how children in social situations regulate their own behaviour and that of others. A major factor in such studies is the extent to which these young children demonstrate metacognitive processing. In particular Whitebread and colleagues (2005) conducted a two year project in over 30 nursery and reception school settings to explore the development of self regulated learning in 3–5-year-olds. Through detailed analysis of video data they devised an assessment check list (CHILD) which includes statements related to self regulated learning under four headings: Emotional, Cognitive, Prosocial and Motivational. While not all of these statements correspond to metacognition, some, such as "is aware of own strengths and weaknesses" clearly are related. The video data from this project shows young children engaged in learning through play and spontaneously regulating their own behaviour and that of other children in their group. The researchers highlight the co-learning of these children, showing them learning from and with each other. They also suggest that on occasions when an adult intervened the children retreated to a position of incapability and looked to the adult to direct the activity. It can be particularly difficult for adults to stand back and allow children to struggle with tasks. It is not only that adults seek to protect children from harm and distress by intervening, but they may also intervene for more practical reasons, such as time and efficiency. In addition, in play situations adults often intervene simply because they too want to play. Making the imaginative leap back in time to our own childhoods can help us to empathise with children's position of powerlessness, but it can also create in us a desire to become re-involved in the child's world out of some more hidden drive to realise tasks we failed at the first time around. Sometimes a conscious effort is needed on the part of adults to restrain their own need to take a part in children's activities and allow children to work through situations in their own way.

Many studies of young children developing metacognition have highlighted the need for collaboration and group work, so that children engage in meta-cognitive dialogues with each other. A distinction needs to be made between co-operative group work and collaboration. Galton and Williamson (1992) defined co-operative groups as those where each child takes on an individual task necessary for the completion of a project. The project comes together at the end of the session when all the individuals pool their knowledge. Collaboration, however, involves all the children in a group working towards a single outcome through continued discussion and sharing of ideas. Many of the tasks in schools which are set up as group work involve co-operation rather than collaboration. Kutnick & Rogers (1994) highlight the need for teachers to organise tasks which require collaboration, tasks for which multiple perspectives are an advantage, and ones where there may be more than one solution.

Collaborative group work is not easy to set up in formal school settings (see the latest book by Baines, Blatchford and Kutnick (2009) for effective ways of establishing collaborative learning). In play situations children are very often found collaborating to agree on rules for games, or planning play activities. Some of the variables we might consciously take account of in school settings, such as group size, ability level, friendships, age, gender and personality, are often self selecting in more informal settings. There is no definitive answer of what constitutes the most effective groups in terms of metacognition. My own recent research on children collaborating in writing tasks indicates that the nature of the relationships is of major importance in effective reflection. This work focused on girl/boy pairs of children and it became clear that while some partnerships were effective at creating metacognitive dialogues, others either inhibited reflection or never really got started. Ability level and verbal fluency were not as important as the way in which pairs reacted to each other's ideas (Larkin, 2008). This is a line of research which requires further exploration.

There have been studies of the effects of friendship on group effectiveness, but while some research has shown it to have a limiting effect (Webb, 1991), other research such as that by Hockaday (1984) found friendship groupings to be advantageous. In her study, Hockaday explored the verbal behaviour of two groups of infant school children while they solved problems designed to necessitate discussion and thinking about how to solve the task. Friendship groups may work more efficiently together or find that their friendship gets in the way of critical reflection on ideas put forward. The study revealed that the non friendship group took longer to come to a solution primarily because they spent longer on deciding how to organise themselves as a group and when they were working together they often ignored each other's suggestions and pushed individual ideas. They also became focused on peripheral matters rather than staying focused on the problem. The friendship group worked more effectively together, although at times they were less critical of each other than they could have been. In a correlation analysis of the roles children took in the discussion with personality factors established through a personality questionnaire, Hockaday found that members of the friendship group shared many of the same personality characteristics, whereas the non friendship group demonstrated more variance in individual personalities, thus providing further evidence of the old adage that "birds of a feather flock together". The friendship group was more effective in terms of reflecting on their problem solving behaviour. This may be a result of collaborating in informal play. However, formal school settings often do not take account of friendship when organising collaborative group work.

There is also a need for young children to learn how to listen and discuss. Hardman and Beverton (1993) suggest that to work effectively as a group children need to be made aware of what they term "metadiscoursal skills". These include showing children how to question or challenge, how to listen and take a positive interest in the group, skills of turn taking, including yielding a turn and maintaining or holding the floor, using discourse markers to aid the flow of the discussion and using non verbal communication. Becoming aware of these features of discussion requires children to engage metacognitively, to monitor and regulate their own contribution to the discussion, as well as become consciously aware of other people's needs within the group. This seems like a great deal to ask of small children, but many of these skills are taught in early years settings as part of developing good social skills. What tends to be missing is a focus on encouraging children to reflect on developing these skills rather than just repeating instructions to "listen to each other". As with all attempts to facilitate metacognition, this is probably best done through a content based approach, so that tasks are set up to deliberately provide opportunities for children to practise and reflect on their discussion skills. The focus would then move away from the solution to the problem and to how the solution came about.

It is clear that task is an important variable in providing opportunities for peer to peer construction of metacognition. Not only is task type important, but so is the way the task is structured. Meloth and Deering (1994) showed that children who were made aware of task structures and given models of how to ask questions developed better metacognitive awareness than children who were simply allowed to work co-operatively. Yussen (1985) described different types of puzzles and problems and their possible effects on developing metacognition. He argued that solving puzzles, such as those often used in earlier cognitive research like the Tower of Hanoi puzzle or jigsaw type puzzles, provide little sense of risk or reward. Rewards are seen as twofold – either external praise from another for having completed the task or internal feelings of satisfaction. Puzzle type problem solving tasks are low on reward because they are removed from every day life; they provide no authentic sense of reward or risk associated with failure. In addition, once completed, puzzles such as these require little reflection. Children may learn some cognitive strategies about the best way to approach a jigsaw puzzle but the puzzle will not provide much opportunity for developing metacognition beyond this. In contrast, open ended tasks such as writing a story or planning a journey entail more risk, as more resources need to be allocated and more thought is required before beginning the task. If you begin too quickly, without adequate planning, you run the risk of your story grinding to a halt midway or of losing your direction. Once more resources are allocated, more investment is made in the activity and the rewards for successful completion are greater. Rewards can also be increased in relation to the authenticity of the task, so planning a real journey and then completing it is likely to lead to greater feelings of satisfaction than planning a journey which is never undertaken. As degree of risk and reward increase so does the need to engage metacognitively:

to plan; to monitor progress; to bring metacognitive knowledge to bear; and to evaluate performance.

Different tasks are likely to involve different combinations and amounts of these metacognitive processes. In order to facilitate the development of meta-cognition in young children we need to provide many and varied tasks which require metacognition. In some classrooms, teachers try to engage children in reflection on tasks which really don't require reflection. The result is often a very superficial question and answer session, where children repeat what they know to be the right answer, often using cognitive strategies which were provided by the teacher at the start of the task.

In Chapter 6 I suggested a cautious approach to using virtual reality software to facilitate metacognition in children, but I also acknowledge that computers have provided us with many more ways of providing opportunities for children to develop metacognition. In particular, they can provide tasks which are open ended, have multiple entry and exit points and which require planning and monitoring of thinking. Work by White and Frederiksen (2005) shows how software can be used to facilitate metacognition and collaborative working in inquiry based tasks. Their "Inquiry Island" software includes a community of learning advisors who provide support for children to conduct their own inquiry based project. Different kinds of support are provided at different levels and for different purposes. For instance, there is a top down approach which helps children to structure their project around a cycle of inquiry, so they are guided towards planning their project through developing an appropriate ques-tion, formulating hypotheses, collecting and analysing data and evaluating the findings. However, as well as this, at each stage of the process there are other advisors, whom children can turn to for information about how to carry out that particular part of the investigation. In this way children gain knowledge about strategies for completing a step of the process, as well as an understanding of the criteria to be used to evaluate that aspect. The authors argue that these advisors are providing cognitive models for the children to follow in carrying out their own project, thus adding to the child's metacognitive knowledge base. Their package also includes a third level of advisors, whom they term "general advisors". These provide information on more general aspects of learning such as creating new ideas, synthesising or fitting ideas together, strategies for planning and monitoring and "social advisors" for collaborative working and negotiating working relationships. Children can take on the roles of the advisors and begin to investigate these roles in an inquiry based fashion. By playing roles the children are developing metacognition through socially constructed means. They begin to see the difficulties of monitoring thinking in collaborative groups or of working towards a common goal and, using the general advisors as role models, they begin to take on the language of the different aspects of metacognition.

In collaborative and social metacognition both talk and non verbal com-munication are important. There is little research about the non verbal aspects of developing metacognition and yet young children often communicate non verbally. Some research, such as that by Karl Wall who was a member of the original CASE@KS1 team, has found that whereas teachers use gestures to *support* their speech, young children use gestures *instead* of speech. In addition, Wall's research has shown that children's interaction is often determined by where they are seated, by whom they believe they are working with and by friendship groups. Children's gestures towards each other can aid or disrupt the collaborative work of the group (Wall, 2002). Gestures may indicate loss of attention and off task behaviour or be used to indicate a desire to take part in the group. Lack of ability to verbalise thinking does not mean that an individual is lacking in metacognition and adults need to be aware of the different ways in which young children may communicate their thinking to themselves and to each other.

Whitebread and colleagues also researched young children's non verbal communication in relation to metacognition and found a rich source of indications of metacognitive features such as planning, monitoring, control and evaluation. Children were seen to use comparison non verbally to aid decision making or to detect errors. Pauses were often used to reflect and alter the course of an action and children checked their work against external models. Much of this individual metacognition was done silently (Whitebread *et al.*, 2007). In my own research on paired writing in young children there were many instances of children using non verbal communication to correct each other's work or to draw attention to new strategies, such as re-ordering items in a list (Larkin 2007). It seems clear that research on young children's metacognitive development should include an account of non verbal as well as verbal communication.

However, a great deal more work has been carried out in terms of children's verbal communication and the development of metacognition through collaborative working. An important but less researched aspect of this is children's listening skills in group work. Anderson and Sangster (2006) have investigated listening practices in schools and detailed how teachers communicate the norms of listening in their classrooms. Listening is undertaken for a number of different reasons including aiding independent thinking, aiding comprehension, evaluating others' ideas, and preparing to take part in the discussion. Listening is also made more complex as we become aware of the need to use memory, to pay attention, to regulate our listening and re-focus it. Listening is also connected with understanding the bigger picture, for instance understanding how listening alters depending on the type and structure of the information being conveyed. Sometimes we need to listen to details, sometimes to the main point; we may need to listen in order to question or in order to reflect on our own thoughts. Listening is an important feature of developing metacognition and our classrooms need to become places where the act of listening is also investigated, so that models and frameworks for listening can be provided to guide children towards effective listening. Developing good listening skills is part of developing good dialogue skills.

Developing metacognition through social collaboration includes more than just talking and listening. Effective communication involves an ability to monitor and regulate one's own activity in relation to the group. Talk must be co-ordinated to fit in with the group interactions. Garrod and Clark (1993) investigated the way children develop these skills of group dialogue through a collaborative computer based problem solving task. The intricacies of the task require that participants, who cannot see each other, engage in computer based dialogues to establish their own and their partner's position in the game. In the younger children (7–8-year-olds) the researchers found that they often used a partner's way of describing their position as a basis for their own response regardless of whether the partner's contribution was really effective. So these younger children failed to monitor or evaluate the partner's contribution or to override it and begin a more effective dialogue. This failure often led to long and confusing dialogues which did little to further the goal of the task. In contrast, the older children (11–12-year-olds) were able to overcome the pressure to comply with a partner and to re-focus the dialogue using more effective language, thus aiding the joint goal of completing the task. These older children have developed some metacognitive knowledge about how language works in context to achieve a particular communicative goal.

A further study by Mercer, Wegerif and Dawes (1999) described 9–10-year-olds' use of "exploratory talk". This is described by the researchers as talk which constructs knowledge through reasoning, so that children are expected to give their views and suggestions supported by evidence or reasoning and that these are open to scrutiny by others in the group, who add to and evaluate the talk. They found that little of this type of talk took place during normal classroom activities; instead children often used talk to compete with each other, or to construct knowledge in an uncritical fashion. Moreover, there was little focus on how to talk or models provided by the teacher. However, once children were provided with this guidance they were able to develop effective ways of using talk to aid collaborative reasoning and this development had an effect on children's individual reasoning ability as measured by Raven's matrices.

Many studies of language and metacognition are carried out with older children because of the difficulties of researching two concepts with different developmental trajectories. However, a study by Glaubman and colleagues directed attention to young children's questioning and the effects of metacognitive instruction. The researchers note that while young children are known for their spontaneous questioning, this tends to diminish with age and the onset of formal schooling when questioning becomes less a search for knowledge and more often directed at social interaction (Glaubman *et al.*, 1997). The role of questioning for knowledge seems to be taken over by teachers.

In a study with Ros Fisher, we found that children's understanding of the role of talk and who controls the talk increased with age. The younger children held to a belief that their teachers liked them to talk, while older children voiced some of the contradictions in teachers' attitudes towards talk in the classroom (Fisher & Larkin 2008). The study by Glaubman *et al.* compared using an active processing theory, which is based on the quantity of questions asked about an object, and a metacognitive theory, which includes knowledge of the task, self and strategies. Their findings showed that metacognitive instruction in questioning enabled children to ask better questions and this had a long term effect, suggesting that even young children can internalise such training for later use. Their study also suggested that simply getting children to generate more questions did not raise the quality of the questions asked or have a lasting effect. In addition, the metacognitive instruction had a positive effect on the children's acquisition of skills, which enhanced their motivation, curiosity and self directed learning.

It seems clear that even very young children can begin to develop metacognition if given the right kind of environment and where attention is paid to instruction for general skills, such as asking good questions, listening, monitoring thinking, planning, and evaluating. There is a long history of research into effective classroom environments which takes account of both the features of a classroom which can be observed and the interpretations of those features by individual members of the class.

It is often self regulation of class members which is evaluated but some of this research includes metacognition. The work of Thomas in Hong Kong has made explicit the link between learning environments and developing metacognition. Thomas and Mee (2005) developed a scale to evaluate the metacognitive elements of a Year 3 general studies classroom. The "General Studies Metacognitive Orientation Scale" (ibid.) is a development of Thomas's earlier Metacognitive Orientation Scale (MOLES–S, Thomas, 2003). Thomas bases his scales on an understanding that the ways in which communities of practice operate will impact on children's development of metacognition. The scales ask children to comment on the metacognitive features of their classroom environment. In this study the scale was developed and used to mark any changes the children perceived in their classroom environment after a short intervention where teachers were asked to alter their teaching to a more metacognitive approach. The teachers were encouraged to model and discuss strategies related to learning; discuss their own learning and how they made use of such strategies, providing a common language for discussing metacognition; and provide opportunities for students to practise metacognition (Thomas & Mee, 2005).

An interesting feature of this study is that rather than being given the strategies to use by the researchers, the teachers were helped to develop their own strategies based on the metacognitive framework provided and to relate these to their own experiences of learning. The findings show that, even in this short term study, the students did perceive a difference in their learning environments in terms of metacognition and this was supported by interviews with the students. It is interesting that in this study not all the metacognitive changes were seen as valuable by the students. Resistance to some aspects of metacognitively oriented teaching is a fairly common finding in qualitative research studies and suggests that change needs to be gradual, long term and embedded in normal classroom practice.

The complexity of many of the studies of metacognition and children highlights the difficulties of researching in this area and the many different factors which may affect metacognitive processing on any given day. It is difficult to isolate the way children demonstrate their use of metacognitive processes on a task from the factors in the school, class or group context in which they are working. Some teachers, and classroom environments may support metacognitive processing, whereas others may unintentionally hinder it. In addition, larger external factors including culture, family background, and adult–child relationships impinge on the development of metacognition. If we plan learning environments which support metacognition from the earliest ages then these will become the norm and the goal of education then becomes to develop independent learners capable of making wise and thoughtful learning decisions. While individual teachers may pursue this goal, often a change in education policy is also necessary. The next chapter considers the role of policy in fostering metacognition.

Chapter 9

Policy and metacognition

Many intervention studies show an improvement in children's metacognition by the end of the intervention period and some show an improvement in various performance and outcome measures. However, these gains are rarely maintained over longer periods of time. In higher education teachers often address metacognition again, as they seek to encourage independent thought and reflective questioning. In my experience many students on undergraduate and post graduate courses still find reflecting on thinking difficult and even frightening. The external examination procedures they have come through to enter higher education rely on an ability to remember information, to discuss that information in the light of a pre-set question and to demonstrate skills of critical analysis and synthesis. These are good skills to have developed through years spent in formal education. However, what is often missing from higher education students' repertoire of skills is metacognition. In my experience of teaching these students, a metacognitive deficit is demonstrated in their inability to make connections between different aspects of the topic, and more often between the academic topic and life outside academia. Teaching on courses concerned with education or childhood, I am often struck by students' lack of thinking about the implications of different theoretical positions for real children in real schools or childhood settings. In addition, news items, whether about child poverty or changes to education policy, often fail to register with the students. This is not an intelligence gap, nor is it about simply a lack of thought – instead I believe it has more to do with a lack of confidence about their own ability to think around the subject matter. There seems to be a block between thinking about the subject and thinking about where their own thinking is leading them. The lack of confidence comes from lack of practice and support for thinking.

Many higher education students have developed ways of thinking which have served them well in the past, allowing them to pass the examinations necessary to get into higher education institutions. Yet they have rarely had to link their knowledge to knowledge about themselves in any overt way. While most teenagers do reflect on their own values and morals, and develop opinions about the world around them, they rarely reflect on their thinking. They tend to stop at the point of what Deanna Kuhn has referred to as "multiplist thinking"

(Kuhn, 2000). Multiplists have come to understand that there are different views on subjects and that even experts can disagree. Higher education students in my field often give their opinion on a particular theory and sometimes debate these with other students, in the end agreeing to disagree, since all opinions are valid. However, what they, and multiplists generally, tend not to do is to reflect on why they hold their particular opinion; on what wider contextual factors may have influenced their opinion; and on whether or not the sources of their beliefs are trustworthy.

Reflecting on knowledge and the sources of knowledge requires a shift in thinking, from the cognitive level of the topic to the metacognitive level of evaluating knowledge and thinking about thinking itself. It is this step change to what Kuhn referred to as an "evaluative epistemology" (ibid.) which I often find lacking in higher education students. She describes an evaluative epistemology as one which seeks to make judgements about different claims through debate and argument. Some students do begin to develop this through the three years of an undergraduate degree, but many still do not, and I believe that this is due to a lack of practice in questioning knowledge and thinking. The earlier education system has left many students unprepared for this shift in thinking in higher education. Yet this is the type of thinking which leads wise people to acknowledge when they are mistaken and when their opinions are based on shaky foundations; the type of thinking which enables them to open their minds to new ideas and to perceive merit in different views. Wise people are most often perceptive people. They see beyond the surface and make judgements about the worth of something based on knowledge of sources of knowledge. If we want to educate for wise and thoughtful adults we must begin with developing a love of thinking in young children. In the next sections I will consider the different ways in which this goal is aided or hindered by education policy and other initiatives.

Foundation Stage curriculum

From September 2008 the Early Years Foundation Stage (EYFS) became the statutory framework in England for all early years providers, bringing together earlier guidance on the care and education of pre-school children, such as Curriculum Guidance for the Foundation Stage (2000), Birth to Three Matters (2002) and the National Standards for Under 8s Day Care and Childminding (2003). The aim of the EYFS (QCA, 2008) was to provide a coherent approach to both care and education across pre-school provision.

The EYFS is based around four themes: the uniqueness of every child; positive relationships; enabling environments; learning and development. Under the learning and development theme there is a concern with learning through play, extending and developing the spontaneous play of children to create learning situations. The EYFS details six areas for learning and development. These are: personal, social and emotional development; communication, language and literacy; problem solving, numeracy and reasoning; knowledge and understanding of the world; physical development; and creative development. In each of these areas early learning goals are identified and staff in early years education must complete an observation profile for each child in the year before they enter formal schooling. In order to do this an assessment scale is provided which breaks down the themes further and details nine levels of achievement under each heading, against which the children can be scored. The assessment sheet details 117 points of achievement and of these none are overtly metacognitive. Under the umbrella theme of Personal, Social and Emotional Development there is a reference to taking account of the ideas of others – a nod in the direction of theory of mind perhaps. Yet in the thematic areas of Language for Communication and *Thinking* (my emphasis) there are no references to understanding mental state vocabulary such as "think", "know", "dream", "guess", "imagine", "remember" etc. although we know that young children begin to develop understanding of these words before the age of five. There is one reference under this theme to "talks activities through, reflection on and modifying actions", which indicates some form of regulation although this is about regulating behaviour rather than thought. Under the general theme of problem solving, reasoning and numeracy, where we might expect to see some reference to strategy selection or monitoring progress towards a goal, there are no references to anything which could be described as metacognitive. However, under the general theme of Knowledge and Understanding of the World, a Level 9 assessment point refers to simple planning, evaluation and explanation of thinking. This is probably the most metacognitive of all the statements in the profile. Throughout the assessment framework there is a heavy reliance on measuring cognitive skills based on understanding number or assessing traditional literacy skills.

An international review of early years provision commissioned by the Qualifications and Curriculum Authority (QCA, 2001) provided knowledge of early years provision in 20 countries around the world in order to inform the early years and primary curriculum in England. While not directly referring to metacognition, the review mentions two aspects of international curricula which are necessary for facilitating metacognition. These are collaborative peer group learning and opportunities for children to self manage and self direct their own learning. However, neither of these has been particularly highlighted by the EYFS, nor are there overt references to developing regulation of thinking or to building metacognitive knowledge about self, tasks or strategies.

The EYFS framework has been heavily criticised by a number of high profile academics and writers for its focus on cognitive skills and its usurpation of spontaneous play by cognitive development. The critics of EYFS have launched a campaign (Open EYE) which highlights seven points of criticism of the framework. These include the focus on early literacy, which they believe is too much too early and could have a detrimental effect on children's development; the loss of play for play's sake; the move towards an audit culture of early years provision, which is also assessment and target led; an obsession with developmental norms; and the compromising of parental rights to not have their young children educated in such a way (Open EYE Steering Group, 2008). The campaign has gained ground: a partial review of some aspects of the EYFS is due to take place and there is scope for providers of early years education and care to opt out of the framework if they can garner parental support to do so. From the point of view of developing metacognition, it would seem that neither the EYFS nor its detractors show any concern for it at this early stage of learning. For the critics of the framework, metacognition would probably indicate an even more cognitively based curriculum and detract from experiential learning and for the government advisors on early years education, metacognition would probably seem a distraction from focusing on literacy and numeracy skills.

However, fostering metacognition need not be at odds with either of these positions. I agree with the critics of the EYFS that the strong focus on literacy and numeracy may well be detrimental; research from other European countries suggests that children learn to read more easily at a much later age and there seems to be no good evidence that early instruction in these areas is necessary or beneficial. Instead, very young children should be given opportunities for play and peer collaboration and it is through these interactions that children can be helped to reflect on their thinking. This should not be in terms of formal instruction or teaching of particular strategies, but through conversation about their experiences both inside and outside of school. Collaborative group work on open ended tasks, such as play acting, making and creating new things, joint painting or telling each other stories, are the kinds of activities which will begin to facilitate metacognitive skills of planning, monitoring and evaluating, as well as lay the foundations for development of metacognitive knowledge. Through conversations about experience adults can help children to make connections between disparate areas of their lives. This involves reflecting on experience and using knowledge from one activity to aid progress in another. These metacognitive processes are not reliant on, or developed from, cognitive skills of literacy, numeracy and problem solving; instead they have a reciprocal relationship with cognitive skills. Engaging children in conversation about experience is likely to have a positive effect on their language skills as well as the development of metacognition. Young children often communicate non verbally and metacognition is not wholly reliant on language fluency. Above all, metacognition relates to understanding of self and others and is part of social and emotional development, as well as cognitive development. Theory of mind tests show that children as young as 3 or 4 consistently show understanding of others as thinkers, and this developing faculty can be fostered through early years education and through peer collaboration.

A major criticism of the EYFS is that while it claims to be a play based curriculum, play has become so structured and used as an instruction tool to foster cognitive development that it has lost its meaning as spontaneous child led play. The problem is an old one, which permeates our culture – the differentiation made between work and play. We all learn through play, adults and children alike, but at some stage of our education play becomes defined as a reward for having worked at something else. In schools, play time is often at the discretion of the teacher; non completion of work can lead to loss of time to play. Yet at the same time adults admire and respect those people who are lucky enough to make a living from something they enjoy and would probably do regardless of the monetary incentive. To find a career which marries play and work is the ultimate prize. As we progress through the education system work and play become more and more differentiated rather than less so, thus making it more difficult to achieve a working life which also functions as play. Metacognition cuts across both work and play; we develop metacognition in order to understand ourselves better and to aid us in making good life decisions. A change in the direction of education from the work/play distinction to a more integrated project which seeks to develop metacognition alongside foundation skills and to dissolve the boundaries between work and play may help more of us to achieve a balanced life. The new primary phase curriculum which is due to come into effect in 2011 begins to dissolve some of the boundaries created by a reliance on subject based teaching.

The primary curriculum in England

At the time of writing Sir Jim Rose has just released his interim report of his review into the primary curriculum (Rose, 2008). The full and final report is due for release in Spring 2009. However, the interim report gives a good outline of how primary education is set to change under the new curriculum framework. The review makes a point of saying that a new thematic based approach to primary education should not be at the expense of good quality specialist subject teaching but the new curriculum, like the EYFS, will be based on six thematic areas. These are: Understanding English, Communication and Languages; Mathematical Understanding; Scientific and Technological Understanding; Human, Social and Environmental Understanding; Understanding Physical Health and Well-being; and Understanding the Arts and Design. There is no "Understanding" of what it means to understand, however. The review claims its aim is to foster a love of learning and a good attitude towards learning. The six areas of the curriculum will be underpinned by subject teaching, but there is also a focus on making links across the subjects and on aiding transfer of learning from one area to another. However, to date there is no clear guidance on how that transfer will be achieved other than by gaining practice in similar skills – by repeating them in different subject domains or through some cross curricular project work. The primary review so far omits any overt reference to developing metacognition, yet the goals of producing "confident individuals" and "responsible citizens" (p. 39); fostering "communities of learning" (p. 46); and encouraging "greater flexibility in personalised learning" (p. 55) are all linked to developing metacognition. Confident learners are those who know what they know and can use their knowledge appropriately, as well as knowing where there may be gaps in their knowledge or understanding and are able to choose appropriate strategies to remedy that. Responsible citizens are those who can see things from different perspectives; who are able to take account of the thoughts and feelings of others; who understand how opinions are formed; who can make rational decisions. Communities of learning are formed through collaborative activity, which involves monitoring and regulating one's own thinking to serve a group goal. Becoming a flexible learner involves developing metacognitive knowledge about one's self in relation to different tasks and experiences. As yet, it is unclear whether the final primary curriculum will include any reference to developing metacognition or higher order thinking skills. It appears that the curriculum will give greater independence to schools and teachers to create opportunities for learning within the overall framework. However, there is little mention of children devising their own learning opportunities. If the final curriculum omits any guidance on fostering the development of metacognition in children, it will be an opportunity lost.

In contrast to the English curriculum, the New Zealand curriculum, which has also undergone a review and revision in the past few years, details a framework for all schools based on a set of values, key competencies and learning areas (Ministry of Education, 2007). Schools are then free to develop each of these aspects to suit their own contexts. The guidance states that the values, competencies and learning areas are those that students will need for "real-life situations" (ibid.) and that education for life will involve learning across subject boundaries. What distinguishes the New Zealand curriculum from the framework for the English primary curriculum is the detail of key competencies. Five key competencies are described. These are: thinking; using language, symbols and texts; managing self; relating to others; and participating and contributing. The key competencies connect with the values and learning areas, rather than stand alone. They are described as more complex than skills and key to learning in every area. They develop through social interaction, through modelling and through internalisation of once external processes, and develop over time and with practice in a wide range of complex situations. These are conditions necessary for metacognitive experiences and it is no surprise that the key competencies guidelines make specific mention of thinking and metacognition. Below is a direct quotation from the New Zealand curriculum, key competencies:

Thinking is about using creative, critical, and metacognitive processes to make sense of information, experiences, and ideas. These processes can be applied to purposes such as developing understanding, making decisions, shaping actions, or constructing knowledge. Intellectual curiosity is at the heart of this competency.

Students who are competent thinkers and problem-solvers actively seek, use, and create knowledge. They reflect on their own learning, draw on personal knowledge and intuitions, ask questions, and challenge the basis of assumptions and perceptions (Ministry of Education, 2007).

In addition, "managing self and relating to others" – one of the key competencies – appears to be based on theories of self regulation and theory of mind. "Managing self" means that students should be able to "establish personal goals", "plan and manage projects", "have strategies for meeting challenges" and be self motivated. While "relating to others" means students should be able to "recognise different points of view", "take different roles in different situations" and collaborate to devise new ways of thinking. Thus there is a good deal more of a focus on metacognitive aspects of learning in the New Zealand curriculum than in the English curriculum as outlined in Rose's interim review.

Rose's review of the curriculum is not the only review of the primary curriculum being conducted. A large scale review of childhood and primary education is also being carried out by a team of researchers led by Robin Alexander at Cambridge University. Different aspects of the project are detailed in a number of briefing documents and interim reports. One such report, by Goswami and Byrant (2007), gives an overview of theories of children's cognitive development and learning, including the development of metacognition and executive functioning. Executive function is described as the monitoring and control of mental processes. The report states that metacognition and executive function develop during the primary years of education and that learning in formal settings can be fostered by developing self reflection and control. The authors state that good metacognitive skills help children to improve their learning by becoming aware of what they do and do not understand, and of appropriate strategies to employ. A common thread across some reports for this review and one detailed in a summary conference paper is the importance of learning outside of formal school settings (Alexander, 2008). I have already discussed how parents and home background can impinge on the development of metacognition in young children and Goswami and Byrant reflect this view, stating that children need "diverse experiences … to help them develop these self-reflective and self-regulatory skills" (Goswami and Byrant, 2007, p. 20). In addition, the summary report highlights Howe and Mercer's thoughts on the need for young children to collaborate on joint goals and to develop the language of discussion and negotiation.

Alexander also highlights the work of Robinson and Fielding (2007) on children's voice and their desire to have more control over their own learning. It is my view that developing metacognition gives children more autonomy over learning, enabling them to set their own goals, use strategies for finding information, monitor their own learning and achieve a sense of satisfaction at having developed new knowledge or skills. The Rose interim report of the review of primary education states that it will take account of the Alexander review, along with other reviews taking place at a similar time. The extent to which the evidence from over 30 reports for the Alexander review will make their way into the final review of the primary curriculum is not yet clear.

Thinking skills

One difficulty with acting on evidence of the positive effect of fostering metacognitive development on learning in the English education system is the tendency to merge theories of metacognition into the bigger and less differentiated field of thinking skills. While there are many educationalists in the UK who work on different thinking skills projects, there are few who research metacognition specifically. This is underscored by the fact that the only academic conference to host a special interest group on metacognition is the European Association for Learning and Instruction (EARLI). In contrast, the British Education Research Association (BERA) has no specific group for metacognition or self regulated learning. The only academic journal dedicated to metacognition is *Metacognition and Learning* (Springer), a journal set up by members of EARLI. The nearest British academic journal is *Thinking Skills and Creativity* (Elsevier). For some working in the English education system, the idea of metacognition appears too tied to cognitive psychology to have relevance to education. While thinking skills programmes have flourished in the UK, specific research on metacognition, especially in primary and early years education is scarce. Yet many of the thinking skills programmes include, or are based upon, theories of metacognition.

At the end of the 1990s a review and evaluation of research into thinking skills was carried out for the UK Department for Education and Employment by Carol McGuinness (McGuinness, 1999). One aspect of the review was to clarify what is meant by thinking skills. Thinking skills were seen to be based on theories of constructivist learning which foreground the learner as an active participant in creating knowledge and understanding. Their effect on learning was to give children the skills of inquiry enabling them to go beyond the given; to cope with new and complex tasks; to take a critical stance towards material; and to communicate ideas. While there are many different frameworks for thinking skills, McGuinness highlights the common features which contribute to many of them. These include cognitive skills of classifying, comparing, identifying cause and effect relationships, synthesising information, developing new ideas, testing hypotheses, drawing conclusions and making decisions. The report discusses different ways in which thinking skills programmes can be incorporated into the curriculum. General thinking skills, usually in the form of some intervention programme such as Instrumental Enrichment (Feuerstein *et al.*, 1980), are given a separate space on the timetable, so that time is set aside to think and learn about thinking itself, with the intention that what is learned in these sessions will become a habit, a way of thinking which will transfer to the rest of the curriculum. In contrast, other thinking skills programmes or approaches such Cognitive Acceleration (CA) (Adey & Shayer, 1994) are designed to work within a subject curriculum. The original CASE programme was set in the context of secondary science lessons but the approach has developed beyond science and beyond the secondary age group so that now there are a number of CA programmes focused on different curriculum areas and designed for early years, primary and second-ary education. McGuinness also describes a third approach to thinking skills, which she calls an infused approach, where thinking skills are adopted across the curriculum through the creation of classroom environments where talking about thinking and practising thinking skills are actively encouraged.

A second review of thinking skills programmes carried out for the Evidence for Policy and Practice Information and Co-ordinating Centre (EPPI-Centre) by a team from Newcastle University stated that:

> There is certainly mounting evidence that adopting approaches which make aspects of thinking explicit or which focus on particular kinds of thinking are successful at raising attainment – particularly metacognitive approaches ... The meta-analysis described in this review adds weight to this growing body of evidence (Higgins *et al.*, 2005, p. 36).

Their meta-analysis of the main effects of a range of thinking skills programmes found that those studies which focused on metacognition had a greater impact than those based on other frameworks of thinking. The authors suggest that there is a fairly consistent message from educational research about the positive benefits of thinking skills programmes on educational attainment. However, the review also points out the difficulties in undertaking a statistical meta-analysis of highly differentiated programmes, especially as the results of the meta-analysis are dependent on the information provided in each individual study.

Thinking skills though are not synonymous with metacognition. It is possible to design a thinking skills programme which pays little attention to meta-cognition. See, for instance, the number and different types of thinking skills approaches detailed in the book *Frameworks for Thinking: A Handbook for Teaching and Learning* (Moseley *et al.*, 2005). Yet a metacognitive approach does seem to have a positive impact on learning.

McGuinness suggests that acquiring and using metacognitive skills is a powerful approach for developing a thinking skills curriculum and she goes on to employ this approach in her own thinking skills programme, Activating Children's Thinking Skills (ACTS). This programme includes a range of think-ing skills: searching for meaning; critical thinking; creative thinking; decision making; and problem solving (McGuinness, 2006). At the heart of the ACTS programme is the facilitation of metacognition. Metacognition is described as including planning, monitoring, redirecting and evaluating. The teachers in the programme encouraged metacognition through providing supportive classroom environments through which children engaged in tasks requiring a good deal of thought and discussion. The teachers also modelled thinking and helped children to develop a language to describe their thinking. The reported findings from the project show that children in ACTS classrooms demonstrated a positive approach to hard work, to putting in more effort and rated themselves higher on the use of cognitive and metacognitive strategies, when compared to control classes.

However, the effects seem to take a considerable amount of time to show. The children who took part in the programme for three years showed the most benefit while those who participated for only one or two years showed little difference from children not on the programme. In addition, the programme had differential effects for children of different abilities. Those with moderate to high ability as measured by verbal and non verbal reasoning tests benefited the most whereas the children with poor attainment on these measures did not show the same advantage from being part of the ACTS programme. While children's self ratings showed a positive trajectory, the effect on attainment in reading and mathematics, while still positive, was small. These findings highlight the difficulties of devising metacognitively based programmes which have a statistically positive effect on attainment in cognitive domains.

I have no doubt that developing metacognition has benefits for some aspects of education, but it remains difficult to find conclusive evidence of the effects of metacognition on attainment in particular subject domains. It seems that we are missing a piece of the jigsaw here. It may be that while metacognition is beneficial for life skills and for developing wisdom and thoughtful decision making, it has little to offer in terms of acquiring subject specific knowledge. Or it could be that the measures of subject specific attainment used in education take no account of metacognitive processes and so any increase in metacognition is subsumed into cognitive measures. For instance, two students may gain 8 out of 10 on a test, but student A may be using a simple memory strategy to regurgitate information, while student B is thinking about and reflecting on the question, drawing on knowledge of similar questions in order to achieve the same answer. We may wonder then if it matters – if both students do well on the test, why would it matter how they had arrived at their answers? This only matters if you believe that education is more than about passing tests and remembering information for the short term. If this is the case then assessment across subjects would need to reflect the student's thinking processes rather than only the outcome of the performance. Here we meet the difficult problem of assessing metacognition.

Assessment

A good deal of research has now been carried out around assessment of metacognition and much of this is based on assessment for use in research studies. There are five main ways of tapping into students' metacognitive processing. These are observation, questionnaires, interviews, tests and think-aloud protocols. Each method has its strengths and weaknesses, and suitability for different contexts. Observation is the most obvious way of assessing young children's metacognition. It is easier to observe children working in collaborative group settings on complex tasks, working towards a joint goal, because these situations are more likely to require metacognition and the group nature of the task requires that thinking is revealed, shared and co-constructed. In order to assess metacognition through observation, some kind of observation check list or schedule is required. I have devised schedules from my own research, as have other researchers. Observation has the benefit of tapping into the metacognition that children are actually displaying in natural classroom settings. It avoids the difficulty of asking children to verbalise their thinking out of context and consistent observation over a period of time can provide a developmental profile of metacognition in individual children across different settings. However, real time observation is time consuming and difficult to maintain. It is easy to lose concentration when observing for long periods of time. It is difficult to record all instances of metacognition apparent in group discussions. Children move in and out of metacognitive reflection, begin to talk about thinking and then change to some off task behaviour, or are interrupted by other children. Knowing what to record and how is a major challenge for observational research. For instance, if using some kind of check list deciding when one metacognitive episode begins and ends is difficult, some instances of metacognition are so fleeting it is hard to compare those with other longer episodes, although they may be just as meaningful. In my own research I have often used video recordings of children working collaboratively to give me the relative luxury of analysing the interactions later and through repeated viewings. However, even this proves challenging; the natural flow of a conversation is not necessarily amenable to being sectioned up into different meaning units and the act of videotaping the interaction will have an effect on the outcome. Observer effects are a common problem with this type of research and as Gussow (1964) pointed out "when the observers are physically present and physically approachable, the concept of the observer as non-participant, though sociologically correct is psychologically misleading". In the case of observing young children it is impossible to remain at a distance and adequately record their interactions. Thus observations by class teachers, who are normally present, are likely to be just as effective as those by the unknown researcher. Of course the caveat is that children view teachers as judging behaviour and may alter their behaviour in the presence of the teacher, looking to her to contribute or guide the discussion. While observation may be the most relevant way of collecting information about young children's metacognitive behaviour, other methods should be used to produce a more complete picture.

Questionnaires have frequently been used in metacognition research. These differ depending on whether they are prospective or retrospective, i.e. they ask questions about what children normally do or they ask children to reflect on a task they have completed and report on their thinking at the time. Both kinds of questionnaires create problems for young children. They require comprehension of the question and the language skills to respond to it. Sometimes questionnaires use pictures of smiley faces so that children can indicate their feelings towards a statement. However, my own experience of using these with 5–6-year-old children is that even though they recognise the different facial expressions, it is not always clear that they are choosing the face which represents their own feelings, rather than a face they like or a face they haven't chosen for some time.

In addition, retrospective questionnaires pose the challenge of asking children to remember, as well as report on their thinking.

Interviews also have the difficulty of asking children direct questions about mental processes, which may be hidden from them. In my research with Year 1 children I carried out interview type conversations with children about a task they had just completed and which remained on the table in front of us. The presence of this concrete stimulus helped to keep the conversation on track, but even so I needed to be aware of the different ways in which children talked about their own thinking. For instance, during an interview conversation with a child about how she had remembered a number of items in a memory task she began to talk about a bus journey. This seemed to have little to do with the subject matter, and I was eager to ask my next question to turn the conversation back to talking about her knowledge of her own memory. Luckily, I waited a little while longer and as she talked I realised that she was in fact answering my question about memory, relating to me a story of how she remembered the bus journey, what factors had stuck in her mind and why. She went on to talk about different members of her family and their tendency to forget different things and her mother's need to make lists to remember shopping. Through the conversation she demonstrated a knowledge of remembering, showed she was aware of different strategies for remembering and described a basic theory of how memory might work (see Larkin, 2007a for other examples of children's understanding of memory).

In conducting interviews about declarative metacognitive knowledge of young writers it became clear that not all children had the same conception of writing (Larkin, 2008). However, the interview method, which this time used a drawing to elicit information about "good writers", indicated that young children do demonstrate a metacognitive awareness of their own knowledge, skills and writing strategies and can delineate a theory of how people learn to write, including understanding the wider contextual factors which may affect learning.

Conducting interviews with children has the benefit of developing a relationship and, unlike administering a pre-set questionnaire, an interview can go where the child leads. The interviewer can pick up on specific elements of an answer and ask follow up questions. It is best with small children to have a stimulus, either a completed task, picture or story to base the questions around, but interviews conducted at regular intervals can provide valuable information about how children's metacognition is developing. In my experience, even young children sometimes remember being asked the questions before, even if the second interviews are a year later. Interviews are time consuming, however, and may be difficult for teachers to carry out, given that they are also in a position of authority and may get acquiescent answers.

Tests have been used in a variety of ways to measure metacognitive development. These tend to focus on one element of metacognition, such as metamemory, theory of mind or mental rotation. A study by Thorpe and Satterly (1990) used a battery of tests under the headings of generating strategies, word list generation, organisation of prose, and judging task difficulty to investigate metacognition in 7–11-year-old children. Their findings suggested that while there were some common features of metacognition across the tasks, the lack of a statistically positive relationship between these features indicates that metacognition is specific to the task. The researchers also argue that results from self report measures of metacognition may in fact be a result of language development rather than metacognitive development. They conclude that metacognition may be a general term to describe different higher order thinking skills which may not be related in primary age children.

It is difficult to find tasks which draw particularly on metacognitive rather than cognitive skills and which do not require a high level of verbal fluency. However, some computer based studies which track children's thinking as they make various moves through a problem based task may provide one kind of solution to direct assessment of metacognition. Schraw and colleagues (2000) suggest that computer based testing provides greater control over the administration of the test, so that individuals receive exactly the same amount of information over the same time period, thus eliminating some of the difficulties of producing a fair test to different participants. It also enables the collection of a great deal of data about how the participant behaves on the test and can produce accurate timings for different aspects of the test session. Both teachers and researchers may benefit from computer based assessment of metacognition, as data from one test can be selected for different purposes.

The final most common method of assessing metacognition is the use of think-aloud protocols. This method requires people to think aloud while completing a task. These "thoughts" are recorded and transcribed to form a think-aloud protocol. The protocols are then analysed in a qualitative manner through coding and categorising sections of the text. Individual protocols can be compared with others and analysis continues in an iterative manner until more general themes emerge. Pressley championed this method of assessment of metacognition in reading at the Buros-Nebraska Symposium on the measurement of metacognition (Pressley, 2000). Through analysing the verbal protocols of skilled readers, Pressley suggested that he would gather rich data about reading and the conscious processes skilled readers use to understand text. This method of analysis produced large amounts of detailed data which demonstrate the variation of processes and the complexity of the reading process. Through a meta-analysis of verbal protocol studies of reading, Pressley and colleagues produced a catalogue of conscious reading processes. This catalogue could be used as a guide for further think-aloud protocol studies and assessment of metacognition in reading.

The Buros-Nebraska symposium on assessment of metacognition highlighted the main difficulties which challenge researchers and practitioners. Summarised by Schraw *et al.* (2000), these include the need for a comprehensive theory of metacognition, so that assessments can be standardised. While work since 2000 has gone some way towards this, there are still very many different terms used for different aspects of metacognition and not all theorists hold the idea that there is a unified concept of metacognition which will serve assessment needs at different ages or in different contexts. Connected to this is what Schraw calls "grain size", i.e. that different researchers investigate at different levels of analysis from overarching theories of conscious processes employed in a particular domain, such as reading, to micro analysis of specific monitoring or control strategies in a particular condition. The practitioner equivalent is whether we are trying to assess strategy use in one aspect of mathematical calculation or whether we are trying to assess self regulatory behaviour during a discussion.

At present there is little in the way of classroom assessments for metacognition in young children across a range of subjects. The research studies which use metacognitive interventions to foster children's development of metacognitive knowledge, regulation and control processes tend to use pre- and post intervention tests of cognitive skills or intelligence. If they use metacognitive assessments these are either questionnaire based or variations on the test/interview procedures described above. Research studies of metacognition in young children often produce categories and lists of metacognitive behaviours grounded in those contexts and linked to theoretical frameworks of metacognition, such as those used by myself and by Whitebread and colleagues (2007). I believe it is problematic to then use these as assessment tools in classroom practice. The danger is that we end up with a deficit model of metacognition in young children, which focuses attention on what they can't do, or what the next step in developing metacognition should be. Instead there is a great opportunity in metacognition research to devise assessment procedures which are more holistic and contextualised and give credit for thinking and monitoring thinking in a formative manner rather than ticking off different itemised aspects of metacognition. The difficulty with using lists of metacognitive processes in classrooms is that teachers can become blinkered to new and unique demonstrations of metacognition which do not already appear on the list. Instead it may be better to include instruction on theories of metacognition in teacher training and development and encourage teachers to develop good metacognitive skills themselves, which they can model for their students. Assessment of metacognition would then become part of a teacher's judgement and normal classroom practice. If a more formal method of assessment is required then a computer based problem solving task, which includes collaboration with others and which can provide data about the way children are thinking about the task, is more likely to produce valuable information for fostering future development of metacognition. Such tests would probably need to link to specific skills used in different domains, but these need not be tied directly to specific subjects; instead it would be possible to create tasks which require skills used in a number of similar subjects. This would enable assessment of metacognition in each of the thematic pathways of the new English primary curriculum.

The Assessment Reform Group (ARG), a group of scholars in the UK who are concerned with the links between pedagogy and assessment, argue that test based measures of attainment omit many other educational benefits. The researchers go on to suggest that attainment is only one of seven different outcomes which could be seen as important indicators of learning. The others are described as Understanding; Cognitive and Creative; Using Higher-Order Learning (which includes metacognition); Dispositions and Membership, and Inclusion (Daugherty et al., 2007). In addition, research projects aimed at different stages of education depend more or less on test data as assessment tools, so that early years education stands out as using other methods of assessment, such as self report and creative outcomes. In their review of assessment practices the ARG highlight "learning to learn" as one area of education which causes great difficulty for assessment. Many of the problems described above with assessing metacognition are rehearsed in terms of learning to learn, which appears to be an even more difficult concept to pin down. One of their comments strikes me as particularly relevant for developing educational policy which includes metacognition. In trying to create an assessment process for a construct such as "learning to learn", the researchers suggest that the construct itself is likely to be shaped by the requirements of the assessment process which, if it is to be included at policy level, would need to be robust and transferable across different education systems. Thus the construct can end up serving the needs of assessment of education systems rather than fostering the development of individual learning. This is obviously a danger for assessment processes of metacognition, especially ones that seek validity and reliability at a macro level. In trying to incorporate metacognition into education policy we run the risk of devising closed assessment procedures which alter and shrink the construct of metacognition to a narrow check list of learner attributes. This may create a unified concept of metacognition on which educationalists and psychologists can agree but it may also close the door to new and different ways of conceptualising metacognition which are yet to emerge.

In addition to formal assessment methods, there has been a great increase in peer and self assessment strategies in UK education across all age ranges. An EPPI-Centre review of 26 studies of peer and self assessment in secondary schools in the UK reported a mixed picture for the positive benefits of peer and self assessment on learning to learn, although this area of research used these methods of assessment more often (Sebba et al., 2008). In peer assessment students assess each other's work in relation to a particular goal and the processes required to achieve it. Peer assessment may be done in groups or pairs, during or after performance on a task, and may also be encouraged in order to develop better group working skills, rather than being solely for assessment purposes. Self assessment involves students making judgements about their own performance and learning and encourages them to be involved in decisions about future learning targets. Both these practices are related to policy decisions to promote personalised and independent learning, with students taking more responsibility for their own education. The EPPI-Centre review suggests that these assessment methods do improve students' abilities in setting goals, clarifying learning targets and in taking responsibility for learning, with an attendant increase in self confidence. There were also reports of positive outcomes in terms of improvement in study skills and talking about learning, although some studies reported no increase in metacognition following self assessment practices. While these practices may have a positive effect on some students, a lack of focus on fostering metacognition may lead to such practices being viewed as just another task by students who have not developed the capacity to reflect on their own learning in a meaningful way. The conclusions of the EPPI-Centre review suggest something similar, in that the authors recommend that if self and peer assessment practices are to continue to form educational policy, more instruction for students on the skills required to work with others and to engage in assessment dialogues is necessary. This would, in my view, require modelling of metacognitive practices such as reflecting on what has been learned, on how it has been learned, on how deep one's understanding goes, and on what future learning is necessary to progress. This also involves developing the ability to make good and thoughtful decisions about one's own learning, including micro level skills such as time management, organising resources and planning etc. as well as macro level reflection on what to learn, how deeply, for what purpose and when to move onto something else.

The review also highlights the need for teachers and other classroom staff to gain training on self and peer assessment procedures. Moreover, and I believe more importantly for fostering metacognition, the review suggests that teachers need to develop a classroom language for talking about learning and create an environment where teachers relinquish control to the learners, so that an "interdependent relationship" is created between teacher and students (Sebba et al., 2008, p. 9).

At present, education policy in England for primary education does include aspects of metacognition, although the word itself is rarely used. For instance, the policy document *Excellence and Enjoyment: Learning and Teaching in the Primary Years. Creating a Learning Culture: Conditions for Learning* (DfES, 2004) highlights developing self awareness and self knowledge for learning. Strategies for fostering self awareness and self regulation, including the ability to reflect, self evaluate and "think about their own thinking" (DfES, 2004, p. 15), are described and reference is made to background information on metacognition. While these aspects of policy go some way towards encouraging a metacognitive approach to the education of young children, the lack of detail about different aspects of metacognition and the use of the overarching term "thinking about thinking" are likely to make fostering metacognition in the classroom difficult to put into practice. The conflation of metacognition with developing self awareness and other social and emotional attributes makes it unclear what the policy is aimed at, e.g. educational attainment; self regulated learners; wise and thoughtful adults or some combination of these and/or other outcomes. In the next chapter I will consider some different views of metacognition and developments in metacognition research.

Part IV

New thinking

Introduction

In this section I will consider some of the ways in which research on meta-cognition has diversified and developed and suggest new areas for work on metacognition in young children. In the second half of Chapter 10 I return to consider some arguments about the place of metacognition in a wider context, along with theories from other areas of psychology, philosophy and education, and share my thoughts on new ways of thinking about metacognition. I then return to Flavell's call for the potential of metacognition to foster wise and thoughtful life decisions and suggest ways in which we may come closer to realising this goal.

Chapter 10

Developments in metacognition research

We have seen a great increase in the amount and types of research into meta-cognition since Flavell first put out the call for researchers to investigate metamemory (Flavell, 1971). Metacognition has been explored in a wide range of areas and positive effects of developing metacognitive awareness have been reported across most academic subjects, in health related areas, in social relationships, in law and other social science fields, and in all age groups. Metacognition is linked to big questions around intelligence, consciousness and emotions. A great deal of theoretical work has delineated and described the different components of metacognition, how they work together, and their effect on cognitive processes. From its initial conceptualisation, metacognition was seen as incorporating both declarative knowledge, referred to as metacognitive knowledge, and procedural knowledge aimed at monitoring and controlling thinking. Procedural metacognition has also been referred to as metacognitive skills. Many other terms are used to refer to different kinds of metacognitive processes, so we might refer to meta-strategic knowledge to indicate knowledge about strategies and ability to select the most appropriate strategy. Terms such as meta-knowing have been used to refer to the development of knowledge about sources of knowledge and understanding of epistemology. Metacognitive awareness is often used to refer to knowledge about when and how to use metacognitive knowledge. Researchers from different branches of psychology and social sciences may use the terms slightly differently, but there is a growing consensus that metacognition is important for self regulated learning, learner autonomy and educational achievement.

Links have been made between metacognition and theory of mind research, demonstrating a developmental trend and, as this book has shown, there is now a solid body of research which demonstrates that young children also display metacognitive awareness in social and educational settings. This is contrary to earlier views that metacognition was not possible before the Piagetian stage of formal operations. This stage of development was usually attributed to late childhood/early adolescence. Other studies have indicated that adulthood does not necessarily bring with it a development of metacognition. Instead metacognition needs to be encouraged and fostered through carefully designed environments, where the focus is not on the outcome of learning, but on the process.

One area of metacognition research which I have not covered so far but which is growing is non human metacognition. There are two distinct areas here: animal metacognition and artificial intelligence (AI). It is perhaps not so surprising that investigation of animal metacognition has developed because theory of mind research has its roots in the early work of Premack and Woodruff (1978) on the possibility of chimpanzees having an ability to take account of mental states. Animal studies provide an evolutionary perspective on the development of theory of mind, which can be informative for studies of human theory of mind development.

Baron-Cohen (1995) proposed a modular development of theory of mind in children. He describes four developmental modules beginning with the "Intentionality Detector". This primitive skill is thought to be possessed by animals as well as humans. It proposes that something moving towards us has an intention to do us harm or good. The second module, termed the "Eye-Direction Detector" detects the presence of eye-like features, detects where the eyes are looking and infers that the individual can see the thing it is looking at. Both these modules develop in early infancy and are quite primitive. In his research with autistic children Baron-Cohen found that these children could pass tests based on these two modules. The later developing modules, termed "Shared-Attention Mechanism" and "Theory of Mind Mechanism", are more sophisticated and involve the ability to interpret information from different perspectives. Children with autism routinely fail on tasks involving these latter two modules.

More recently, work on animal metacognition has explored uncertainty monitoring and animal self awareness. In a fascinating study with rhesus monkeys, Kornell, Son and Terrace (2007) demonstrated that monkeys could both monitor and control their own thinking. The monkeys were trained on perceptual discrimination tasks, such as choosing the longest line from a number of different lines. After completing each task the monkeys had to respond to one of two confidence icons, which represented high or low confidence in the accuracy of their performance on the task. In training, if the monkeys chose the high confidence icon when they had given correct answers on the task or the low confidence icon when they had given incorrect answers on the task they were rewarded with tokens, which were banked to be exchanged later for food treats. Tokens were subtracted from the bank if the monkeys failed to make an appropriate confidence judgement. In the experimental phase the monkeys were found to be able to make appropriate confidence judgements and to be able to transfer this skill to a new and different task. The researchers suggest that monkeys can make metacognitive judgements which are similar to those made by humans. Furthermore, in a second experiment other rhesus monkeys were given a task of responding to pictures of natural objects in a particular order, regardless of where the pictures appeared on a screen. The monkeys would learn the correct order by trial and error, but in this experiment they were also offered the opportunity to ask for a hint for the next picture in the sequence by responding to a hint icon on the screen. If the monkeys performed the task correctly without using any hints they got a better reward than if they used the hints. The hints were also limited in number. The monkeys asked for hints when they did not know what came next, but did not ask for hints as they became more familiar with the task. The researchers suggest that the monkeys were able to differentiate between knowing and not knowing and take remedial action, thus demonstrating that monkeys can monitor and control their thinking and that they are capable of transferring these skills to new and unfamiliar tasks. As the researchers point out, this does not mean that monkeys are doing this consciously, but the study does suggest that language is not a pre-requisite for metacognition. This has implications for the study of metacognition in young pre-verbal children and may provide insight into the beginnings of metacognitive development in humans.

In a review of studies of animal metacognition, Smith, Shields and Washburn (2003) suggested that these studies also have implications for the social scaffolding view of metacognitive development, which draws on theories of learning from Vygotsky and Bruner. In this view metacognition is developed through a more experienced other serving as an external monitor and regulator of the child's thinking, until the child begins to internalise this role and begins to function independently. The study of metacognition in monkeys, who have different parenting patterns from humans, suggests that there may be other independent ways of developing metacognitive awareness. Flavell and Wellman (1977) also suggested this, when they wrote that what children come to understand about their own memory could just as easily be achieved through abstraction from their own individual experience, to form a more general view of their own cognition, as it could from social interaction. However, in both monkeys and humans, this development would take place within a social context and the context itself may provide opportunity and necessity for the development of metacognitive awareness, without direct instruction, scaffolding or modelling from others.

The research on animal metacognition has covered many species apart from monkeys and apes. There is research on dolphin, bird and rodent metacognition. These studies can help in understanding the evolutionary necessity for metacognition – in familiar tasks where there is no risk metacognition is unnecessary and unhelpful but in uncertain and new situations where there is risk and where a decision needs to be made, higher levels of cognition are necessary. These studies also bring into question the role of language in the development of human metacognition and thus pave the way for studies of child metacognition which do not rely on verbal fluency. Finally, the studies of animal metacognition raise again the problem of whether metacognition is necessarily conscious or not. The animal studies do not suggest that animals are consciously metacognitive, but they highlight the possibility of implicit metacognition whereby animals may monitor and control their cognitive behaviour without full consciousness. Similar issues are highlighted in studies of metacognition and AI.

One area of growth in cognitive research over the past few years has been in cognitive neuroscience or studies of the brain. The beginning of the twenty-first century seemed to bring with it a desire among brain researchers to connect their findings to applied fields, particularly education. Blakemore and Frith (2000) suggested that neuroscience studies might inform educators about aspects of learning which are counter-intuitive. They cite implicit learning and brain plasticity as two such areas. The hope was that studies of how the brain works would transfer to education and, rather than confirm what teachers and educators already know about learning, these studies would add valuable new information which could be translated into new and different ways of teaching and learning. In terms of metacognition, a great deal of work had already been done on understanding the executive control mechanisms of the brain, which regulate and control other cognitive functions. The pre-frontal cortex of the brain is particularly associated with the executive functions. However, Darling and colleagues (1998) suggest that the evidence from brain damaged individuals describes a less consistent pattern and belies the idea of a single executive monitor which oversees all cognitive functions and it may be more appropriate to consider different executive functions monitoring specific areas of cognition.

An interesting feature of much of the research investigating metacognition from a neuroscience perspective is that metacognition in terms of regulation of cognition is being increasingly linked to emotional factors and emotional regulation. Researchers have argued that the brain area and activity associated with metacognition is also associated with regulation and control of emotion (Fernandez-Duque *et al.*, 2000). As technology provides us with more and different ways of looking at how brains function, it is likely that this area of metacognition and neuroscience will grow.

However, the link between cognitive neuroscience and education has been critiqued by a number of scholars. In particular, Bruer (1997) highlighted the deficiencies of translating findings from brain science into practical application in the classroom. He demonstrates how results from neuroscience which show that early childhood marks a period of rapid increase in the numbers of synaptic connections made by the brain and the laying down of neural pathways are picked up by education policy makers to give scientific support for different education policies. This finding suggests that early childhood is a window of opportunity for educators to intervene and provide learning opportunities for very young children in a wide range of subjects from music to languages and mathematics. If we miss these opportunities for teaching children very early on, then we are doing them a disservice and programmes designed to intervene in children's cognitive development which start too late are unlikely to prove successful. In particular, Bruer rejects the idea that the biological growth spurt in synapses in early childhood can be translated as a critical time for learning. While this period may see the beginning of new skills and capabilities, these continue to develop after this period. In addition, other studies have shown that environmental conditions are crucial for the development of sensory systems, motor skills and language and also that the plasticity of the brain means that it can overcome some environmental or biological disadvantage. The conditions needed for children to develop these faculties are present in normal social environments and not dependent on particular teaching and learning materials or practices. Only if children are subject to sustained abuse is this development likely to be affected.

Bruer criticises the way in which sound scientific understanding of how the brain works is then taken out of context and parlayed into objectives for early years classrooms, and particularly the view that these early years are more important than later years for educational policy initiatives. Bruer suggests that what educators cite as enriched environments for young children, which neuroscience suggests is necessary for development, also happen to be those provided by middle class and Westernised homes. Bruer does not dismiss the potential of neuroscience for education, but rather insists on caution in applying early findings from this developing area of study to education policy.

This area of study is growing, however. New centres of cognitive neuroscience, such as the one led by Uta Frith at Cambridge University, are forging new links between brain science and education. The academic journal *Mind, Brain, and Education* (Blackwell) was launched in 2007. In the preface to the first edition entitled "Why *Mind, Brain, and Education*? Why now?", the editors (Fischer *et al.*, 2007) suggest that new technology has opened up new possibilities for the development of a new science and practice of learning. Educational interventions, they claim, can be observed in terms of their biological effects and these can be related to learning outcomes. They claim that this new science will provide insight into how we acquire knowledge, how we transfer knowledge to new areas and how learning environments can be designed to optimise learning. This may be the birth of a new science which takes account of all biological process, including genetics, and relates this to social and educational environments. Grigorenko (2007) suggests that we will soon understand the genetic base for memory development and the development of literacy, mathematics and language. It is proposed that this knowledge will provide parents with evidence for supporting a claim for personalised and individualised learning plans based on their children's genetic make up. There is no doubt that this area of research is growing in popularity and that cognitive neuroscience may provide us with a better understanding of metacognition and begin to answer some questions, such as the relationship between cognition and metacognition and the role of consciousness in metacognitive skill, but whether it is desirable for this to influence our education policies is another question.

In the second part of this chapter, I will go on to consider some of the criticisms of the scientific approach to metacognition research and begin to open up other pathways on which research on metacognition could develop.

Possible futures

In earlier chapters I may have implied that the study of metacognition began in the 1970s with the work of Flavell and Brown. Certainly the word was coined by these researchers at that time, but as Brown herself pointed out, metacognition has a long and rich history. In the seminal paper which provides the theoretical framework for much contemporary research on metacognition, Brown traces speculation on the capacity of humans to reflect on their own thinking back to Plato and Aristotle (Brown, 1987). In her outline of the historical roots of metacognition she contemplates the views of philosophers such as Locke, who believed that children's minds were incapable of reflective thought and psychologists such as Buhler who, at the turn of the twentieth century, used think-aloud protocols to understand the thinking of adults.

The development of the conceptualisation of metacognition is connected to developments in theories of intelligence. Recent developments in this area include Demetriou's model of intelligence, which posits the idea of a tripartite hierarchical system consisting of specialised cognitive systems and a domain general system operating under a central processor. In this model, the components of metacognition are part of the domain general system, and are termed "hyper-cognitive" (Adey et al., 2007). The link between theories of intelligence and metacognition proves problematic since the concept of intelligence itself is disputed and new and different models are put forward. This link also means that metacognition research is formally located within a cognitive psychology paradigm. The contribution of philosophers to thinking on metacognition is less apparent in the educational literature than that of psychologists. Thus educationalists who view learning from a socio-cultural, humanist, embodied or other non cognitive perspective find that the dominant psychological approach to research on metacognition is problematic. Yet there is a great deal of work from philosophers and theorists which is either directly concerned with metacognition or relates to metacognition. I believe that it is timely that we acknowledge, consider and include this work in our understanding of how developing metacognition can help us to become wiser.

In this section I will put forward some areas of possibility for how metacognition research may develop and enter into dialogue with other theories of learning. I suggest these links in terms of opening up a space for discussion between these different research traditions based on the premise that fostering metacognition is essential to developing wise and thoughtful citizens. Metacognition involves thinking about different perspectives; reflecting on the sources of knowledge; and abstracting from the surface level of thinking to draw connections between different bodies of knowledge. I have tried to use my own metacognition to do just that, in terms of thinking about the field of metacognition research at the present time. These are tentative suggestions for ways in which we might think again about metacognition and develop new understandings, new possibilities for facilitating metacognition in ourselves and others and new connections with other theoretical frameworks of learning.

A specific criticism of metacognition theory is the use of the metaphor of the mind as an information processor. Models of metacognition tend to be drawn using the standard information processing diagrams of boxes and arrows. While some frameworks include emotions and perception, these are often peripheral and outside of the main focus on cognitive processes. The aim has been to describe the different elements of metacognition and their relationship to other cognitive processes. Thus the theoretical frameworks of metacognition appear to perpetuate the split between mind and body which has dominated Western psychology and philosophy. While theories of metacognition have been applied to social constructionist views of learning since the beginning, with the work of Brown and colleagues on reciprocal teaching and learning, the main focus of theoretical models of metacognition has been on the cognitive and metacognitive processes which are developed and built through these interactions with the environment and with others. In contrast, a Dewyan pragmatist view of learning would focus not on the cognitive processes but on how the individual learns from action in and on the world, so that habits of learning are formed unconsciously. Dewey suggested that the focus on cognitive development at the expense of an understanding of the embodied nature of learning has dominated Western thought, including education systems, and is responsible for many of the problems education faces.

In their criticism of metacognition, Kivinen and Ristelä (2003) make both theoretical and practical arguments against the focus on conscious learning. In terms of theory, they argue that it makes no sense to think of cognition on two levels since our access to the metacognitive level can only come about through introspection and in order to view our metacognitive level we would need another higher level and so on. The problems of infinite regress and homunculi driven cognition imply that theories of metacognition rely on there being a unified monitor of cognition or that it is necessary to have processes which monitor the monitoring processes. However, if we shift our thinking from focusing on the content of a story, for instance, to being aware that we no longer understand what is going on in the story, then we have made a shift from one way of thinking to another. For the second type of thinking to interrupt our reading flow there must have been some monitoring process going on in the background as we read. It is only necessary for that monitoring to become conscious when it is needed to provoke us into taking action, either pausing and thinking or re-reading. In this way metacognition is another way of thinking, one which focuses on our own thinking processes rather than on the task. Nelson and Narens (1990) described a reciprocal relationship between cognition and metacognition which has no need for another level of cognition, since all monitoring processes are described under the term "metacognition". Kivinen and Ristelä's criticism of the way that metacognition theory has been incorporated into educational practice is based on Dewey's view that learning should be unconscious and result from immersion and engagement with the task. They express the pragmatists' fear that engaging children in metacognition is asking them to become psychologists and reflect on their own actions and thinking at the expense of immersion in an activity. The criticism can be seen as a fear of introspection, where thoughts are de-contextualised and the aim is to think only about thinking itself. While this is a valid point to highlight, it misses the way in which metacognition research has developed in some areas and fails to acknowledge that Dewey too was interested in how the mind operates, how thinking changes with context, and how humans reflect on their own thinking. The difference between the functionalist approach of Dewey and the largely cognitive approach of metacognition theorists lies in the way that cognitive psychologists reduce thinking to a set of discrete processes and ignore the embodied nature of consciousness. This is a problem for theoretical models of metacognition, but not one that is usually adhered to by educationalists who understand the contextualised and situated nature of learning. There is a need to re-establish the link between embodied learning and metacognition, rather than to see them as discrete and contradictory.

Bresler (2004), drawing on phenomenological philosophy, defines embodiment as an integration of the phenomenological self and the physical self. Embodied learning acknowledges that the mind is inherently embodied. The ways in which we perceive the world are dependent on physiological and biological constraints. Only a certain range of sound frequencies, for instance, are audible to the human ear; the way we perceive colour is dependent on the physiology of the human eye and the neural network. Moreover, what and how we perceive is related to our bodily position, our location in space and time. Embodied learning acknowledges that we make meaning and learn through, and as a result of, our lived experience. This refers to our physical, social and temporal immersion in the world.

Tobin (2004) has argued that the body is no longer central to early years education. Young children are encouraged to engage with technology at the expense of physical activity and teachers are discouraged from making any physical contact with children. He traces this movement back to a number of causes. The fear of child abuse in educational settings affects both parents and teachers. Teachers fear accusations of abuse and parents fear the numbers of child predators at large in our society – both fears are fuelled by tragic and high profile cases. We might also add that the decline, or at least perceived decline, in the extent to which people know and interact with their local community has increased the fear of predatory strangers. However, school is not home, nor is it an extension of home. School should provide space and opportunity for children to interact with each other, in situations where the power dynamic approaches equality and where children can learn the subtle nuances of social communication, without too much interference from adults. Bringing teachers' awareness about physical contact with children into the open has enabled teachers to reflect on how they might manage difficult behaviour or soothe an anxious child without an unconscious reliance on an instinctual response of engaging physically. I am not suggesting that teachers should never touch a child under any circumstances, but in the past when physical contact between teachers and children was more prevalent, there was little conscious appreciation of the inequality of the power dynamic in the act. The teacher who cuddled you when you cut your knee would also be the teacher who smacked you for fidgeting.

We know that we all communicate with and through our bodies and this is even clearer in young children who have yet to become consciously aware of this and learn how to mask or suppress these signals. Tobin's view that a focus on getting young children to talk rather than to communicate physically is symptomatic of a view that words are more important than the feelings they refer to, and that words can adequately reflect those feelings. There is a need to redress this balance in education and allow children to communicate in a variety of ways. We might, for instance, engage children in metacognitive reflection about the ways in which people communicate, so that rather than talk being at the centre of early years education, we give equal status to physicality and to silence. For many children understanding and reading non verbal cues is as problematic as speech, and it would be relatively easy to create fun activities for young children which focus on non verbal communication. This kind of work is often done with children who have learning difficulties, particularly those on the autistic spectrum, but it is less apparent in mainstream education and even less so as children grow older. Yet becoming wiser about making life decisions involves being able to fully "read" the situation as it presents itself. Developing a conscious awareness of the ways in which we interact and react to each other is likely to develop our skills of social perception.

Non verbal communication is bound up with the notion of silence. Communicating through gesture and physicality frees us from having to verbalise our thinking before we are ready to. Silence is a difficult area for education. We are used to theories of learning through dialogue and through collaboration; an active, lively classroom appears to be a good learning space for young children. It also accords with our cultural view of the importance of discourse, the need to talk things through. There is less emphasis, however, on contemplation – on using silence to reflect on our own thinking, to play with our own thoughts and to follow our own mental journeys. Children are encouraged to talk, discuss, criticise and analyse, but rarely to contemplate or to take more than a few minutes to think. Silence is often used in educational settings as a form of punishment, so that the norm of the classroom environment is to be engaged with learning through talk. Much of the talk that happens in classrooms, however, is not connected with thinking about the topic or problem set by the lesson. Instead there is a great deal of talk about resources and procedures. In addition, much talk is teacher directed or children talking to each other for social reasons. Silence may be found in periods of quiet reading or in test situations, but there is rarely silence purely for contemplation.

While studies of collaborative learning have demonstrated how metacognition can be socially constructed, there is less investigation of how this socially constructed metacognition becomes internalised and accessible for individual use in new situations. The difficulty for programmes of metacognition instruction or facilitation is in how individuals make use of their metacognitive skills in new and different situations. Periods of silent reflection and contemplation may well assist this internalisation process. Silence can provide us with periods of rest from the busy active process of learning new things. In silence we may reflect on our learning, make new connections, contemplate the possible or simply rest our thinking, allowing new thoughts to emerge. If we wish to foster metacognition then building periods of restful silence into the rhythm of the school day may prove productive.

In recent years there has been a move towards a more inclusive view of cognitive psychology which values the importance of understanding cognition as situated and views thinkers as acting in and on the world. A great amount of this theorising has been undertaken by scientists working in AI with the development of systems based on the notion of the active agent – of situated and embodied cognition. Anderson (2003) provides a comprehensive review of the work on embodied cognition. This work emphasises the complex nature of thinking in the real world, which cannot be reduced to a set of algorithms or formal symbols. This approach views cognition as intentional and reasserts the position of the thinker. Anderson argues that models of cognition must take account of the embodied thinker interacting with the other and with the world. Models of cognition which fail to acknowledge this are inadequate for explaining intelligence. From an embodied cognition perspective, intelligence is no longer seen as a function of an individual brain but as a function and product of brains interacting with each other and the wider world. Anderson suggests that the traditional divide between the social sciences and cognitive sciences is no longer tenable. The work from AI has much in common with the move towards a cognitive psychology which takes account of how the individual experiences the world.

The "I" is being reinstated in cognitive psychology through a focus on understanding the personal lived experience of individuals. Velmans (1991) has argued that cognitive psychology which fails to take account of the individual's experience can only give a partial account. However, a phenomenological approach which focuses wholly on the personal is also incomplete. What is required is a view of cognition which sees these two perspectives as complementary. Chamberlin (1974) argued that the phenomenological method encourages educationalists, who come to a subject with predetermined theories and with their own experience of the structures of education, to look at their subject afresh. The methodological procedures of phenomenology encourage investigators to seek new understanding from analysing "the essence of things". In attempting to re-connect cognitive science with phenomenological understanding of the lived world, a revision of both fields is necessary. Recent years has seen a growth in conferences and academic communities concerned to formulate theories of cognition which account for phenomenology. Yet it is still unclear where metacognition would fit within these emergent theories of cognition. There is the obvious connection with consciousness in the sense of metacognition re-defined as reflexivity. However, this poses problems since the phenomenological idea of reflexivity is not viewed as a separate act of introspection in the way that metacognition proposes a distinct level or shift of thought, to reflect on thought itself. The philosophy of phenomenology, particularly that of Merleau-Ponty (1962), can help us to return to a focus on experience itself, including the way we experience cognitive states such as remembering. Varela and Shear (1999) state that the phenomenologist and the psychologist are interested in the same mental content, but whereas the psychologist is "motivated by research … to establish empirical results", the phenomenologist is interested in the "broader meaning and place [of mental content] in ordinary human areas such as temporality, intersubjectivity and language" (p. 8). Perhaps it is timely to consider how metacognition research might create a dialogue with phenomenology. The development of similar connections with AI and embodied cognition might show the way.

If we relate the ideas of embodied cognition and phenomenology back to learning we find a link with the work of Bruner. Bruner has suggested that cognitive psychology has lost its focus on the bigger picture of the search for how humans make meaning from experience and instead has focused on the mental structures and components of information processing (Bruner, 1990). In an interview with Bradd Shore (Shore, 1997), Bruner speaks of the unique and irreducible quality of sensory experience, the knowledge that our ways of making meaning are essentially embodied. Yet, he says that we make meaning from our experience through some other medium – language, thought and reflection. He refers to going "meta" as the transduction of sensory experiences into thoughts and reflections. Moreover, Bruner argues that we never operate on a purely perceptual or sensory basis – we always either implicitly or explicitly take account of our own knowledge of the world. He rejects the notion of a split between the senses and the mind, suggesting that all sensory experience is also mindful experience and that the phenomenological immediate experience cannot be captured except through reflection. While acknowledging the unique quality of sensory experience which cannot be captured through language, he regards the translation of experience into thought as a positive trade off. It is this translation of experience into a form which creates a basis for reflection which drives human knowledge. "I'm mad for the notion of 'going meta' that gets you beyond the information given […] it is just that kind of search for meta-cognition that has pushed my own career, and I think that its cultivation should be a central task of education" (p. 16).

When Bruner refers to metacognition he refers particularly to seeing things anew, to making new metaphors for understanding and for making the familiar strange. He refers to science as being not only about verification of hypotheses but also about finding new ways of thinking about and communicating ideas about things. In this sense he is referring to what others have called "mindful activity" or "mindful learning". Langer has argued that much of what passes for education in schools is mindless learning (Langer, 1997). The opposite approach is an education based on mindfulness, where mindfulness is defined as seeing new things, drawing new distinctions and making new connections. Langer argues that the level of importance of the new observation is irrelevant; trivial observations are as relevant as major observations as long as it is new to the individual learner. Seeing the new in the familiar ensures that we stay in the present and heightens our awareness of context and perspective. It is easy to become familiar with a subject or area and to continue to always look at the topic from the same perspective, sometimes at the expense of understanding different and new contextual factors. This habitual way of living in the world can blind us from making use of new information, seeing different perspectives and making new connections. Langer argues that our education systems and policies create an environment where mindless learning is praised and rewarded. Children are taught to repeat and remember, whether this is in terms of facts or ways of thinking. I would argue that some attempts to include thinking skills in classrooms have just this effect, especially when they are based on teaching children ways of thinking for certain situations or use check lists so that children can ensure that they have completed all the thinking steps required.

Langer (ibid.) suggests that we are all prone to drawing on established ways of thinking when set a new learning task. She suggests that a mindset, such as having to learn the basics thoroughly when we begin a new learning task, is a mindset which we have been taught and which may be relevant for some tasks but not for others. We rarely question who taught us that this was the correct way to learn, why they did this, or whether this way of learning is helping or hindering our progress. We become stuck in ways of thinking, which are no longer conscious, unless we bring them back to consciousness by reflecting on them. Langer's work has shown how with relatively small changes mindless learning can be altered to mindful learning. For instance, a change in language from presenting information as definite and closed using words such as "is" to presenting information in a more conditional way by using words such as "could be" changes the nature of the learning environment. Rather than a closed space, the use of more tentative language opens the space for new and different ways of seeing.

It is not just in the process of learning that we can effect a shift from mindless to mindful thinking. Langer also considers what learners know about learning processes. This is akin to exploring the metacognitive knowledge base of learners in terms of what we might call universal skills. For instance, in one study Langer investigated teachers' and students' definitions of paying attention. She found that both groups thought of paying attention as being still and focused; probably something they had been taught early on in school. How many times have we all been told to "sit still and pay attention"? However, Langer cites a number of studies where if people are taught to actively look for new things in the information, their attention actually improves and people tend to find more enjoyment in the learning process. We know of course that learning is an active process, that children construct and re-construct their understanding and interpretations of material, and small children are encouraged to participate actively in doing things rather than absorbing information. However, we do not often focus children's attention on how they might learn something by attending to what is new in it, rather than in going through a series of steps. We may often ask children to remember something, but how often do we ask them to make it mean something to themselves? These are the kinds of ideas Langer has expressed in her work on mindful learning. She puts forward the view that most of what we learn in school is context-free information; we are not expected to question the source, nor relate the information to our own lives. This is not always the case, but in my own experience education is still dominated by this kind of pedagogy. A metacognitive approach to education would be more aligned with mindful learning as described above rather than a prescriptive differentiation of different types of thinking, such as creative thinking differentiated from critical thinking and so on. A metacognitive approach to learning which is in line with mindfulness would not exclude a reflective phase at the end of a task to evaluate the process of learning, but the main focus would be, as Langer says, on responding to the task anew.

While I have concentrated on ideas of metacognition and learning above, another perspective on metacognition which may be ripe for exploration is the political. Metacognition, like many psychological theories, appears to work outside of, or with little regard to, bigger political and social contexts. In this sense it is context-free. However, if theories of metacognition are to influence pedagogy in any major sense, then socio-political factors need to be considered. At a local level we see studies of metacognition which touch on some such factors, for instance studies of the impact of metacognition on disadvantaged children or the effects of disadvantaged home life on the development of metacognition, yet there is little theorising of the connection between developing metacognition and the politics of education. At one level of analysis, a theory of metacognition which defines metacognition as a process whereby a shift of thinking takes place from the cognitive to the metacognitive level has the potential for developing greater autonomy in the learner. Individual awareness of how we think brings with it the possibility of thinking differently. Developing meta-knowing (Kuhn & Dean, 2004) enables understanding of epistemology not just as an abstract field within philosophy but in terms of self. The process of "going meta" in its broadest sense requires introspection, but not in terms of de-contextualised thought. The object of thinking may be another thought but this thought is ultimately about and related to something external of the self.

At an individual level, metacognition allows us to evaluate our own thinking and to make choices about what and how to learn. Becoming knowledgeable about ourselves in relation to different learning situations is akin to having internalised our own guide or teacher. A consequence of this, and one which is political, is the change in relationship between the professional teacher and the learner. This is not simply an argument for progressive education, nor for de-schooling (Illich, 1973), because this view of learner autonomy rests on self knowledge and having the skills to make choices about our own learning. In order for this to happen, we need to become aware of the choices open to us and the constraints under which education systems operate. Increased awareness of the socio-political context of education complements increased awareness of our own learning needs. In reflecting at both the individual level and the political level, learners develop the ability to become more independent and to make better use of the educational system as it stands.

A fourth avenue for the future of metacognition research is the contribution of developing metacognitive awareness for personal and transpersonal growth. This whole area is one which moves metacognition away from the constraints of cognitive psychology and instead explores the value of metacognition for finding meaning in life and achieving greater awareness of the world around us. Transpersonal growth has been described as referring to a sense of being in touch with one's inner self – the unification of the self and the "I" – and has been characterised by metacognition and "metamotivation". Here metacognition is described as "objective consciousness" or acute awareness and metamotivation as understanding and acting based on the connection between self and spiritual values. Both terms refer to a unification of consciousness and self, so that the "I" feels more complete and more real. There is also a movement and growth beyond the self and personal metacognition to acknowledge spiritual values within everyday life.

In their analysis, Hamel and colleagues (2003) describe four components of metacognition and metamotivation in a matrix. Under metacognition they place "In-Depth Perception" – this emphasises details and refers to the ability to go beyond the surface to find and explore deeper aspects of self and of life. This element requires concentrated attention, knowledge of personal resources and the willingness to take different perspectives and to engage in contemplation of reality. In-Depth Perception is located at an individual level and is related to self knowledge and knowledge of self in the world. "Holistic Perception", their second category of metacognition, is based on detachment and relates to viewing self and life from a detached standpoint, one that is not encumbered by attach-ments, fears or beliefs. The two components categorised under metamotivation follow a similar pattern of focus on either the individual level or the global level. The first category "Presence of Being" is an inner search of "knowing how to be rather than only how to do and to get something" (p. 13). The second category of metamotivation, "Beyond Ego-Orientation", refers to a focus on others rather than self, a sense of belonging to something outside of self and an appreciation of the connectedness of everything. The authors state that to be transpersonal all four factors must co-exist in an active, interdependent relationship. The development of research in this area of spiritual growth and the understanding of metacognition as necessary for that growth indicates a broad and profound direction for future research on metacognition.

The areas of embodied learning, phenomenology, political awareness and spiritual growth provide us with new ways of conceptualising metacognition. They develop understandings of metacognition beyond its inception in cognitive and developmental psychology and broaden its influence beyond education.

Throughout this book I have shown how important metacognition is for learning in both formal and informal settings. In order to develop independent and self reliant learners we need to provide opportunities for children to develop metacognitive awareness. Flavell's hope that metacognition might be used to make wise and thoughtful life decisions is perhaps more likely to be met through these four less common areas of metacognition research. Wisdom, I believe, comes from and with spiritual growth. When we know ourselves, can engage with the world with a sense of detachment, have an understanding of how to be in the world and can engage with others while leaving aside our own preoccupations, we are more likely to be able to make wise and thoughtful decisions about ourselves and others. In this sense the development of metacognition, which begins in childhood, is a life-long pursuit, but one that is worthy of pursuing.

References

Adey, P., Csapó, B., Demetriou, A., Hautamäki, J., & Shayer, M. (2007). Can we be intelligent about intelligence? Why education needs the concept of plastic general ability. *Educational Research Review, 2*(2), 75–97.

Adey, P., Hewitt, G., Hewitt, J., & Landau, N. (2004). *The Professional Development of Teachers: Practice and Theory*. Dordrecht: Kluwer.

Adey, P., Robertson, A., & Venville, G. (2001). *Let's Think! A Programme for Developing Thinking in Five and Six Year Olds*. Slough: NFER Nelson.

Adey, P. S., & Shayer, M. (1994). *Really Raising Standards: Cognitive Intervention and Academic Achievement*. London: Routledge.

Ahlberg, M., & Ahoranta, V. (2002). Two improved educational theory based tools to monitor and promote quality of geographical education and learning. *International Research in Geographical and Environmental Education, 11*(2), 119–137.

Alexander, R. (2008, 17 March). *The Primary Review: Emerging Perspectives on Childhood*. Paper presented at the Childhood, Wellbeing and Primary Education Conference, Central Hall, Westminster.

Anderson, C., & Sangster, P. (2006). Listening practices in classrooms. *International Journal of Reading, Writing and Literacy, 1*(2), 27–45.

Anderson, M. (1989). New ideas in intelligence. *The Psychologist, 2*(3), 92–94.

Anderson, M. (1992). *Intelligence and Cognitive Development*. Oxford: Blackwell.

Anderson, M. L. (2003). Embodied Cognition: A field guide. *Artificial Intelligence, 149*, 91–130.

Antonietti, A., Ignazi, S., & Perego, P. (2000). Metacognitive knowledge about problem solving methods. *British Journal of Educational Psychology, 70*, 1–16.

Armbruster, B. B., & Brown, A. L. (1984). Learning from reading: The role of metacognition. In R. C. Anderson, J. Osborn, & R. J. Tierney (Eds.), *Learning to Read in American Schools. Basal Readers and Context Texts* (pp. 273–281). Hillsdale, N.J.: Erlbaum.

Baines, E., Blatchford, P., Kutnick, P., Chowne, A., Ota, C., & Berdondini, L. (2009). *Promoting Effective Group Work in the Primary Classroom: A Handbook for Teachers and Practitioners*. Abingdon, Oxon: Routledge.

Baker, L. (1985). How do we know when we don't understand? Standards for evaluating text comprehension. In D. L. Forrest-Pressley, G. E. MacKinnon, & T. G. Waller (Eds.), *Metacognition, Cognition and Human Performance* (pp. 155–206). New York: Academic Press.

Baker, L. (1994). Fostering Metacognitive Development. In H. W. Reese (Ed.), *Advances in Child Development and Behaviour* (Vol. 25, pp. 201–239). San Diego: Academic Press.

Baker, L. (2005). Developmental differences in metacognition: Implications for metacognitively oriented reading instruction. In S. E. Israel, C. C. Block, K. L. Bauserman, & K. Kinnucan-Welsch (Eds.), *Metacognition in Literacy Learning Theory, Assessment, Instruction and Professional Development* (pp. 61–79). Mahwah, N.J.: Lawrence Erlbaum Associates.

Baker, L., & Brown, A. L. (1984). Metacognitive skills and reading. In P. D. Pearson, R. Barr, M. L. Kamil, & P. Mosenthal (Eds.), *Handbook of Reading Research* (pp. 353–395). New York: Longman.

Baltes, P. B., & Smith, J. (2008). The fascination of wisdom. Its nature, ontogeny, and function. *Perspectives on Psychological Science, 3*(1), 56–64.

Baron-Cohen, S. (1995). *Mindblindness.* Cambridge: Bradford Books, MIT Press.

Barton, K. C., & Levstick, L. S. (1996). "Back when God was around and everything": Elementary children's understanding of historical time. *American Educational Research Journal, 33*(2), 419–454.

Baumfield, V., & Oberski, I. (1998). What do teachers think about thinking skills? *Quality Assurance in Education, 6*(1), 44–51.

Beeth, M. E. (1998). Facilitating conceptual change learning: The need for teachers to support metacognition. *Journal of Science Teacher Education, 9*(1), 49–61.

Bell, T. (2003, December). *The PlaySMART Programme. Thinking through Physical Education.* Paper presented at the Australian Association for Research in Education Conference, Auckland, New Zealand.

Bereiter, C., & Scardamalia, M. (1987). *The Psychology of Written Composition.* Hillsdale, N.J.: Lawrence Erlbaum Associates.

Blair, C., & Razza, R. P. (2007). Relating effortful control, executive function, and false belief understanding to emerging math and literacy ability in kindergarten. *Child Development, 78*(2), 647–663.

Blakemore, S.-J., & Frith, U. (2000). *The Implications of Recent Developments in Neuroscience for Research on Teaching and Learning.* London: Institute of Cognitive Neuroscience.

Bless, H., & Strack, F. (1998). Social influence on memory. In V. Y. Yzerbyt, G. Lories, & B. Dardenne (Eds.), *Metacognition: Cognitive and Social Dimensions* (pp. 90–106). London: Sage.

Boekaerts, M. (2002). Bringing about change in the classroom: Strengths and weaknesses of the self-regulated learning approach – EARLI Presidential Address, 2001. *Learning and Instruction, 12,* 589–604.

Boekaerts, M., & Corno, L. (2005). Self-regulation in the classroom: A perspective on assessment and intervention *Applied Psychology, 54*(2), 199–231.

Borkowski, J. G. (1996). Metacognition: Theory or chapter heading? *Learning and Individual Differences, 8*(4), 391–402.

Bresler, L. (2004). Prelude. In L. Bresler (Ed.), *Knowing Bodies, Moving Minds. Towards Embodied Teaching and Learning* (pp. 7–11). Dordrecht: Kluwer Academic Publishers.

Brown, A. (1987). Metacognition, executive control, self-regulation and other more mysterious mechanisms. In F. E. Weinert, & R. H. Kluwe (Eds.), *Metacognition, Motivation and Understanding* (pp. 65–116). Hillsdale, N.J.: Erlbaum.

Brown, A. L. (1978). Knowing when where and how to remember: A problem of metacognition. *Instructional Psychology, 1,* 77–165.

Bruner, J. (1990). *Acts of Meaning.* Cambridge MA: Harvard University Press.

Bruer, J. T. (1997). Education and the brain: A bridge too far. *Educational Researcher, 26*(8), 4–16.

Bryant, P., & Bradley, L. (1985). *Children's Reading Problems.* Oxford: Blackwell.

Burman, E. (1994). *Deconstructing Developmental Psychology.* London and New York: Routledge.

Carpendale, J. I., & Chandler, M. J. (1996). On the distinction between false belief understanding and subscribing to an interpretive theory of mind. *Child Development, 67*, 1686–1706.

Carr, M., Alexander, J., & Folds-Bennett, T. (1994). Metacognition and mathematics strategy use. *Applied Cognitive Psychology, 8*, 583–595.

Carr, M., & Biddlecomb, B. (1998). Metacognition in mathematics from a constructivist perspective. In D. J. Hacker, J. Dunlosky, & A. C. Graesser (Eds.), *Metacognition in Educational Theory and Practice* (pp. 69–91). Mahwah, N.J.: Lawrence Erlbaum Assocs.

Cavanaugh, J. C., & Perlmutter, M. (1982). Metamemory: A critical examination. *Child Development, 53*, 11–28.

Chamberlin, J. G. (1974). Phenomenological methodology and understanding education. In D. E. Denton (Ed.), *Existentialism and Phenomenology in Education, Collected Essays* (pp. 119–137). New York: Columbia University.

Chandler, M. J., & Helm, D. (1984). Developmental changes in the contribution of shared experience to social role-taking competence. *International Journal of Behavioural Development, 7*, 145–156.

Chi, M. T. H., Feltovich, P. J., & Glaser, R. (1980). Categorization and representation of physics problems by experts and novices. *Cognitive Science, 5*, 121–152.

Clay, M. M. (1991). *Becoming Literate. The Construction of Inner Control*. Birkenhead, Auckland: Heinemann Education.

Covington, M.V. (1984). The motive of self worth. In R. E. Ames, & C. Ames (Eds.), *Research on Motivation in Education* (Vol. 1: Student Motivation, pp. 78–113). London: Academic.

Darling, S., Sala, S. D., Gray, C., & Trivelli, C. (1998). Putative functions of the prefrontal cortex: historical perspectives and new horizons. In G. Mazzoni, & T. O. Nelson (Eds.), *Metacognition and Cognitive Neuropsychology* (pp. 53–95). Mahwah, N.J.: Lawrence Erlbaum.

Daugherty, R., Black, P., Ecclestone, K., James, M., & Newton, P. (2007, 6 September). *Investigating the Alignment of Assessment to Curriculum*. Paper presented at the BERA Annual Conference, London.

Davidson, J. E., & Sternberg, R. J. (1984). The role of insight in intellectual giftedness. *Gifted Child Quarterly, 28*, 58–64.

Deci, E. L., & Ryan, R. M. (2003). On assimilating identities to the self: A self-determination theory perspective on internalization and integrity within cultures. In: M. R. Leary, & J. P. Tangney (Eds.), *Handbook of Self and Identity* (pp. 253–272). New York: Guilford Press.

DeLoache, J., Cassidy, D., & Brown, A. (1985). Precursors of mnemonic strategies in very young children's memory. *Child Development, 56*, 125–137.

Desoete, A., Roeyers, H., & Buysse, A. (2001). Metacognition and mathematical problem solving in Grade 3. *Journal of Learning Disabilities, 34*, 435–449.

DfES – Department for Education and Skills (2004). *Excellence and Enjoyment: Learning and Teaching in the Primary Years. Creating a Learning Culture: Conditions for Learning*. Primary National Strategy, DfES 0523-2004 G, Crown copyright 2004.

Diener, C. I., & Dweck, C. S. (1978). An analysis of learned helplessness: Continuous changes in performance, strategy and achievement cognitions following failure. *Journal of Personality and Social Psychology, 36*, 451–462.

Dimaggio, G., Semerari, A., Carcione, A., Nicolo, G., & Procacci, M. (2007). *Psychotherapy of Personality Disorders. Metacognition, States of Mind and Interpersonal Cycles*. London and New York: Routledge.

DDA – Disability Discrimination Act 1995, Chapter 50. Retrieved October 2008 from http://www.opsi.gov.uk/acts/acts1995

Dweck, C. S. (1999). *Self-Theories: Their Role in Motivation, Personality, and Development* Philadelphia, PA: Psychology Press Ltd.

Education Act 1996, Chapter 56, part IV, chapter I. Retrieved October 2008 from http://www.opsi.gov.uk/ACTS/acts1996

Efklides, A., Kourkoulou, A., Mitsiou, F., & Ziliaskopoulou, D. (2006). Metacognitive knowledge of effort, personality factors, and mood state: their relationships with effort-related metacognitive experiences. *Metacognition Learning, 1*, 33–49.

Efklides, A., & Petkaki, C. (2005). Effects of mood on students' metacognitive experiences. *Learning and Instruction, 15*, 415–431.

Estes, D. (1998). Young children's awareness of their mental activity: The case of mental rotation. *Child Development, 69*(5), 1345–1360.

Estes, D., Wellman, H. M., & Woolley, J. D. (1989). Children's understanding of mental phenomena. In H. W. Reese (Ed.), *Advances in Child Development and Behaviour* (Vol. 21, pp. 41–87). San Diego: Academic Press.

Fabricius, W. V., & Imbens-Bailey, A. (2000). False belief about false beliefs. In P. Mitchell, & K. J. Riggs (Eds.), *Children's Reasoning and the Mind* (pp. 267–279). Hove: Psychology Press Ltd.

Farrant, A., Boucher, J., & Blades, M. (1999). Metamemory in children with autism. *Child Development, 70*(1), 107–131.

Fernandez-Duque, D., Baird, J. A., & Posner, M. I. (2000). Executive attention and metacognitive regulation. *Consciousness and Cognition, 9*, 288–307.

Feuerstein, R., Rand, Y., Hoffman, M., & Miller, R. (1980). *Instrumental Enrichment: An Intervention Programme for Cognitive Modifiability*. Baltimore: University Park Press.

Fischer, K. W., Daniel, D. B., Immordion-Yang, M. H., Stern, E., Battro, A., & Koizumi, H. (2007). Why *Mind, Brain, and Education*? Why now? *Mind, Brain, and Education, 1*(1), 1–2.

Fisher, R., & Larkin, S. (2008). Pedagogy or ideological struggle: An examination of pupils' and teachers' expectations for talk in the classroom. *Language in Education, 22*(1), 1–16.

Fisher, R., Myhill, D., Larkin, S., & Jones, S. (2007). *Talk to Text: Using Talk to Support Writing*. Exeter: Esme Fairbairn.

Flavell, J. (1971). First discussant's comments: What is memory development the development of? *Human Development, 14*, 272–278.

Flavell, J. (1979). Metacognition and cognitive monitoring. *American Psychologist, 34*(10), 906–911.

Flavell, J., & Wellman, H. M. (1977). Metamemory. In R. V. Kail, & J. W. Hagen (Eds.), *Perspectives on the Development of Memory and Cognition* (pp. 3–33). Hillsdale: Erlbaum.

Fox, R. (2001). Helping young writers at the point of writing. *Language and Education, 15*(1), 1–13.

Freathy, R., & Aylward, K. (in press). "Everything is in parables": An exploration of students' difficulties in understanding Christian beliefs concerning Jesus. *Religious Education (USA), 105*(1).

Galbraith, D., & Rijlaarsdam, G. (1999). Effective strategies for the teaching and learning of writing. *Learning and Instruction, 9*, 93–108.

Galton, M., & Williamson, J. (1992). *Groupwork in the Primary School*. London: Routledge.

Gardner, H. (1993). *Frames of Mind* (2nd ed.). New York: Basic Books.

Garner, R. (1988). *Metacognition and Reading Comprehension*. Norwood, N.J.: Ablex Publishing.

Garrett, A. J., Mazzocco, M. M. M., & Baker, L. (2006). Development of the metacognitive skills of prediction and evaluation in children with or without math disability. *Learning Disabilities Research & Practice, 21*(2), 77–88.

Garrod, S., & Clark, A. (1993). The development of dialogue co-ordination skills in school-children. *Language and Cognitive Processes, 8*(1), 101–126.

Gaultney, J. F. (1998). Utilization deficiencies among children with learning disabilities. *Learning and Individual Differences, 10*(1), 13–29.

Glaubman, R., Ofir, L., & Glaubman, H. (1997). Effects of self-directed learning, story comprehension, and self-questioning in kindergarten. *The Journal of Educational Research, 90*(6), 361–373.

Gombert, J. E. (1993). Metacognition, metalanguage and metapragmatics. *International Journal of Psychology, 28*(5), 571–580.

Goswami, U., & Bryant, P. (2007). *Children's Cognitive Development and Learning (Primary Review Research Survey 2/1a)*. Cambridge: University of Cambridge Faculty of Education.

Gowin, B. (1981). *Educating*. Ithaca: Cornell University.

Grigorenko, E. L. (2007). How can geonomics inform education? *Mind, Brain, and Education, 1*(1), 20–27.

Grimmitt, M. (1989). *Religious Education and Human Development*. Great Wakering, UK: McCrimmon Publishing Co. Ltd.

Gussow, Z. (1964). The observer–observed relationship as information about structures in small group research. *Psychiatry, 27*, 236–247.

Hallam, R. N. (1970). Piaget and thinking in history. In M. Ballard (Ed.), *New Movements in the Study and Teaching of History* (pp. 162–178). London: Temple Smith.

Hallam, S. (2001). The development of metacognition in musicians: Implications for education. *British Journal of Music Education, 18*(1), 27–39.

Hamel, S., Leclerc, G., & Lefrançois, R. (2003). A psychological outlook on the concept of transcendent actualization. *The International Journal for the Psychology of Religion, 13*(1), 3–15.

Hardman, F., & Beverton, S. (1993). Co-operative group work and the development of metadiscoursal skills. *Support for Learning, 8*(4), 146–150.

Hayes, J. R. (1981). *The Complete Problem Solver*. Hillsdale, N.J.: Lawrence Erlbaum Associates.

Hayes, J. R., & Flower, L. S. (1980). Identifying the organisation of writing processes. In L. W. Gregg, & E. R. Steinberg (Eds.), *Cognitive Processes in Writing* (pp. 3–30). Hillsdale, N.J.: Lawrence Erlbaum Associates.

Hennessey, M. G. (1999). *Probing the Dimensions of Metacognition: Implications for Conceptual Change Teaching-Learning*. Paper presented at the National Association for Research in Science Technology (NARST), Boston, MA.

Higgins, S., Hall, E., Baumfield, V., & David Moseley (2005). A meta-analysis of the impact of the implementation of thinking skills approaches on pupils. Retrieved June 2007 from http://www.eppi.ioe.ac.uk

Hockaday, F. (1984). Collaborative learning with young children. *Educational Studies, 10*(3), 237–242.

Hoffmann Davis, J. (2000). Metacognition and multiplicity: The arts as models and agents. *Educational Psychology Review, 12*(3), 339–359.

Huffaker, D. A., & Calvert, S. L. (2003). The new science of learning: Active learning, metacognition, and transfer of knowledge in e-learning applications. *Journal of Educational Computing Research, 29*(3), 325–334.

Hurme, T.-R., Palonen, T., & Järvelä, S. (2006). Metacognition in joint discussions: An analysis of the patterns of interaction and the metacognitive content of the networked discussions in mathematics. *Metacognition Learning, 1*(1), 181–200.

Illich, I. (1973). *Deschooling Society*. Harmondsworth: Penguin.

Israel, S. E., & Massey, D. (2005). Metacognitive think-alouds: Using a gradual release model with middle school students. In S. E. Israel, C. C. Block, K. L. Bauserman, & K. Kinnucan-Welsch (Eds.), *Metacognition in Literacy Learning Theory, Assessment, Instruction and Professional Development* (pp. 183–198). Mahwah, N.J.: Lawrence Erlbaum Associates.

Jacobs, G. M. (2004). A classroom investigation of the growth of metacognitive awareness in kindergarten children through the writing process. *Early Childhood Education Journal, 32*(1), 17–23.

Johnson, C. (2002). Drama and metacognition. *Early Child Development and Care, 172*, 595–602.

Jost, J. T., Kruglanski, A. W., & Nelson, T. O. (1998). Social metacognition: An expansionist review. *Personality and Social Psychology Review, 2*(2), 137–154.

Joyce, B. R. (1991). The doors to school improvement. *Educational Leadership, 48*(8), 59–62.

Kafai, Y. (1996). Gender differences in children's constructions of video games. In P. M. Greenfield, & R. R. Cocking (Eds.), *Interacting with Video Games* (pp. 39–66). Norwood, N.J.: Erlbaum.

Karmiloff-Smith, A. (1992). *Beyond Modularity: A Developmental Perspective on Cognitive Science*. Cambridge, MA: Massachusetts Institute of Technology.

Kellner, D. (2003). Toward a critical theory of education. *Democracy & Nature, 9*(1), 51–64.

Kellogg, R. T. (1994). *The Psychology of Writing*. Oxford: Oxford University Press.

Kincheloe, J. L., & Steinberg, S. R. (1999). A tentative description of post-formal thinking: The critical confrontation with cognitive theory. In J. L. Kincheloe, S. R. Steinberg, & P. H. Hinchey (Eds.), *The Post-formal Reader: Cognition and Education* (pp. 55–90). New York: Falmer.

Kirkwood, M. (2000). Infusing higher-order thinking and learning to learn into content instruction: A case study of secondary computing studies in Scotland. *Journal of Curriculum Studies, 32*(4), 509–535.

Kivinen, O., & Ristelä, P. (2003). From constructivism to a pragmatist conception of learning. *Oxford Review of Education, 29*(3), 363–375.

Kluwe, R. H. (1987). Executive decisions and regulation of problem solving behaviour. In F. Weinert, & R. Kluwe (Eds.), *Metacognition, Motivation and Understanding* (pp. 31–63). Hillsdale, N.J.: LEA.

Kontos, S. (1983). Adult-child interaction and the origins of metacognition. *Journal of Educational Research, 77*, 43–64.

Kornell, N., Son, L. K., & Terrace, H. S. (2007). Transfer of metacognitive skills and hint seeking in monkeys. *Psychological Science, 18*(1), 64–71.

Kreutzer, M. A., Leonard, C., & Flavell, J. H. (1975). An interview study of children's knowledge about memory. *Monographs of the Society for Research in Child Development, 40*(159), 60.

Kriewaldt, J. (2006). The key role of metacognition in an inquiry-based geography curriculum. *Geographical Education, 2006, 19*, 24–30.

Kuhn, D. (2000). Theory of mind, metacognition and reasoning: A life-span perspective. In P. Mitchell, & K. J. Riggs (Eds.), *Children's Reasoning and the Mind* (pp. 301–326). Hove: Psychology Press Ltd.

Kuhn, D., & Dean, D. J. (2004). Metacognition: A bridge between cognitive psychology and educational practice. *Theory into Practice, 43*(4), 268–273.

Kutnick, P., & Rogers, C. (1994). Groups in classrooms. In P. Kutnick, & C. Rogers (Eds.), *Groups in Schools* (pp. 1–33). London: Cassell.

Lang, S. (2003). Narrative: the under-rated skill. *Teaching History, 110,* 8–13.

Langer, E. (1997). *The Power of Mindful Learning.* Reading, MA.: Addison-Wesley.

Larkin, S. (2007a). A phenomenological analysis of the metamemory of 5–6-year-old children. *Qualitative Research in Psychology, 4*(4), 281–293.

Larkin, S. (2007b, September). *Researching the Role of Metacognition in Young Writers.* Paper presented at the European Education Research Association Conference (ECER), Ghent, Belgium.

Larkin, S. (2008, March). *The Development of Metacognition within the Context of Learning to Write.* Paper presented at the American Educational Research Association Annual Conference, New York.

Le Fevre, D. M., Moore, D. W., & Wilkinson, I. A. G. (2003). Tape-assisted reciprocal teaching: Cognitive bootstrapping for poor decoders. *British Journal of Educational Psychology, 73,* 37–58.

Learning and Teaching Scotland (2002). *ICT in Pre-School: A "Benign Addiction"? A Review of the Literature on ICT in Pre-School Settings.* Dundee: Learning and Teaching Scotland.

Leat, D. J. K. (1993). Competence, teaching, thinking and feeling. *Oxford Review of Education, 19*(4), 499–510.

Lerch, C. (2004). Control decisions and personal beliefs: Their effect on solving mathematical problems. *Journal of Mathematical Behavior, 23,* 21–36.

Lester, F. K., & Garofalo, J. (1982, March). *Metacognitive Aspects of Elementary School Children's Performance on Arithmetic Tasks.* Paper presented at the Annual Meeting of the American Educational Research Association, San Francisco.

Lin, X., Schwartz, D. L., & Hatano, G. (2005). Toward teachers' adaptive metacognition. *Educational Psychologist, 40*(4), 245–255.

Lockl, K., & Schneider, W. (2006). Precursors of metamemory in young children: The role of theory of mind and metacognitive vocabulary. *Metacognition and Learning, 1,* 15–31.

Luke, I. (1999). Appreciating the complexity of learning in physical education: The utilization of a metacognitive ability conceptual framework. *Sport, Education & Society, 4*(2), 175–191.

McGuinness, C. (1999). *From Thinking Skills to Thinking Classrooms: A Review and Evaluation of Approaches for Developing Students' Thinking (No. 115).* Norwich: Department for Education and Employment.

McGuinness, C. (2006). Building thinking skills in thinking classrooms: ACTS (Activating Children's Thinking Skills) in Northern Ireland. Retrieved June 2008 from http://www.tlrp.org

McPherson, S. L. (2000). Expert–novice differences in planning strategies during collegiate singles tennis competition. *Journal of Sport & Exercise Psychology, 22,* 39–62.

Markman, E. M. (1977). Realising that you don't understand: A preliminary investigation. *Child Development, 46,* 986–992.

Meloth, M., & Deering, P. (1994). Task talk and task awareness under different cooperative conditions. *American Educational Research Journal, 31,* 138–165.

Mercer, N., Wegerif, R., & Dawes, L. (1999). Children's talk and the development of reasoning in the classroom. *British Educational Research Journal, 25*(1), 95–111.

Merleau-Ponty, M. (1962). *Phenomenology of Perception* (C. Smith, Trans.). London: Routledge.

Mevarech, Z., & Fridkin, S. (2006). The effects of IMPROVE on mathematical knowledge, mathematical reasoning and meta-cognition. *Metacognition Learning, 1,* 85–97.

Miller, A. (2007). Rhetoric, paideia and the old idea of a liberal education. *Journal of Philosophy of Education, 41*(2), 183–206.

Ministry of Education (2007). The school curriculum: Design and review. From New Zealand Curriculum to school curriculum. Retrieved 9 December 2008 from http://www.newzealand.govt.nz

Morgan, A. (2006). Developing geographical wisdom: Post-formal thinking about, and relating to, the world. *International Research in Geographical and Environmental Education, 15*(4), 336–352.

Moseley, D., Baumfield, V., Elliott, J., Higgins, S., Miller, J., Newton, D. P., *et al.* (2005). *Frameworks for Thinking: A Handbook for Teaching and Learning.* Cambridge, UK: Cambridge University Press.

NAGC – National Association for Gifted Children [website]. Accessed 1 October 2008 at http://www.nagcbritain.org.uk/

Nelson, T. O., & Narens, L. (1990). Metamemory: A theoretical framework and new findings. In G. H. Bower (Ed.), *The Psychology of Learning and Motivation: Advances in Research and Theory* (Vol. 26, pp. 125–173). San Diego, CA: Academic Press.

Nespor, J. (1987). The role of beliefs in the practice of teaching. *Journal of Curriculum Studies, 19*, 317–328.

Nichol, J. (2007). Learning styles and CACHE (Cognitive Acceleration in History Education): Children as thinkers. Retrieved 30 November 2008 from http://www.history.org.uk/resources

Nichol, J., & Watson, K. (2003). Editorial: Rhetoric and reality – the present and future of ICT in education. *British Journal of Educational Technology, 34*(2), 131–136.

Nietfield, J. L. (2003). An examination of metacognitive strategy use and monitoring skills by competitive middle distance runners. *Journal of Applied Sport Psychology, 15*, 307–320.

Ofsted – Office for Standards in Education (2007). *History in the Balance.* Retrieved 30 November 2007 from http://www.ofsted.gov.uk

Ofsted (2008). *Schools and Sustainability.* Retrieved 1 December 2008 from http://www.ofsted.gov.uk

Okagaki, L., & Sternberg, R. J. (1990). Teaching thinking skills: We're getting the context wrong. In D. Kuhn (Ed.), *Developmental Perspectives on Teaching and Learning Thinking Skills* (Vol. 21, pp. 63–78). Basel: Karger.

Open EYE Steering Group (2008). Memorandum submitted by the Open EYE Early Years Campaign to Select Committee on Children, Schools and Families Minutes of Evidence. Retrieved 30 November 2008 from http://www.parliament.uk

Palinscar, A. M., & Brown, A. L. (1984). Reciprocal teaching of comprehension-monitoring activities. *Cognition and Instruction, 1*, 117–175.

Palinscar, A. S. (1982). Improving the reading comprehension of junior high school students through the reciprocal teaching of comprehension-monitoring strategies. Unpublished Doctoral Dissertation, University of Illinois at Urbana–Champaign.

Panaoura, A., & Philippou, G. (2007). The developmental change of young pupils' metacognitive ability in mathematics in relation to their cognitive abilities. *Cognitive Development, 22*(2), 149–164.

Papaioannou, A., Marsh, H. W., & Theodorakis, Y. (2004). A multilevel approach to motivational climate in physical education and sport settings: An individual or a group level construct. *Journal of Sport and Exercise Psychology, 26*(1), 90–118.

Pappas, S., Ginsburg, H. P., & Jiang, M. (2003). SES differences in young children's metacognition in the context of mathematical problem solving. *Cognitive Development, 18*(3), 431–451.

Perry, N. (1998). Young children's self-regulated learning and contexts that support it. *Journal of Educational Psychology, 90*, 715–729.

Perry, N. E., Nordby, C. J., & VandeKamp, K. O. (2003). Promoting self-regulated reading and writing at home and school. *The Elementary School Journal, 103*(4), 317–338.

Perry, N. E., & Vandekamp, K. J. O. (2000). Creating classroom contexts that support young children's development of self-regulated learning. *International Journal of Education al Research, 33,* 821–843.

Piaget, J., & Inhelder, B. (1969). *The Psychology of the Child* (H. Weaver, Trans.). London: Routledge & Kegan Paul.

Piaget, J., & Inhelder, B. (1976). *The Child's Conception of Space.* London: Routledge and Kegan Paul.

Piaget, J., Inhelder, B., & Sinclair-de-Zwart, H. (1968). *Memoire et Intelligence.* Paris: Universitaires de France.

Pintrich, P. R. (1995). Understanding self-regulated learning. In P. R. Pintrich (Ed.), *Understanding Self-Regulated Learning* (Vol. 63, pp. 3–12). San Francisco: Jossey-Bass.

Post, Y., Boyer, W., & Brett1, L. (2006). A historical examination of self-regulation: Helping children now and in the future. *Early Childhood Education Journal, 34*(1), 5–10.

Pramling, I. (1988). Developing children's thinking about their own learning. *British Journal of Educational Psychology, 58,* 266–278.

Premack, D., & Woodruff, G. (1978). Does the chimpanzee have a theory of mind? *Behavioural and Brain Sciences, 1,* 515–526.

Pressley, M. (2000). Development of grounded theories of complex cognitive processing: Exhaustive within – and between – study analyses of think-aloud data. In G. Schraw & J. C. Impara (Eds.), *Issues in the Measurement of Metacognition* (pp. 260–295). Nebraska: Buros Institute of Mental Measurements.

Pressley, M., & Gaskins, I. W. (2006). Metacognitvely competent reading comprehension is constructively responsive reading: How can such reading be developed in students? *Metacognition Learning, 1,* 99–113.

Pui-wah, D. C. (2008). Meta-learning ability – a crucial component for the professional development of teachers in a changing context. *Teacher Development, 12*(1), 85–95.

QCA – Qualifications and Curriculum Authority (2001). *Analysis of Evidence from an International Study on Early Years Education.* London: QCA.

QCA (2004). *Religious Education: The Non-Statutory National Framework.* London: QCA.

QCA (2008). *Early Years Foundation Stage.* London: QCA.

Reder, L. M., & Ritter, F. E. (1992). What determines initial feeling of knowing? Familiarity with question terms, not with the answer. *Journal of Experimental Psychology: Learning, Memory and Cognition, 18,* 435–451.

Resnick, L. B. (1987). *Education and Learning to Think.* Washington, D.C.: National Academy Press.

Robinson, C., & Fielding, M. (2007). *Children and Their Primary Schools: Pupils' Voices. Primary Review Research Survey 5/3.* Cambridge: University of Cambridge, Faculty of Education.

Roebers, C. M., & Howie, P. (2003). Confidence judgments in event recall: Developmental progression in the impact of question format. *Journal of Experimental Child Psychology, 85*(4), 352–371.

Rose, J. (2008). *The Independent Review of the Primary Curriculum.* Retrieved 8 December 2008 from http://publications.teachernet.gov.uk

Rosenblatt, L. M. (1969). Towards a transactional theory of reading. *Journal of Reading Behavior, 1*(1), 31–49.

Rosenshine, B., & Meister, C. (1994). Reciprocal teaching: A review of the research. *Review of Educational Research, 64,* 479–530.

Salonen, P., Vauras, M., & Efklides, A. (2005). Social interaction – what can it tell us about metacognition and coregulation in learning? *European Psychologist 10*(3), 199–208.

Sanchez, J. M. (1998). Nature and modes of metacognition. In J. M. Martinez, J. Lebeer, & R. Garbo (Eds.), *Is Intelligence Modifiable* (pp. 23–48). Spain: Bruno.

Schneider, W. (1985). Developmental trends in the metamemory–memory behavior relationship: An integrative review. In D. L. Forrest-Pressley, G. E. MacKinnon, & T. G. Waller (Eds.), *Metacognition, Cognition and Human Performance* (Vol. 1, pp. 57–109). Orlando: Academic Press.

Schneider, W. (1998). Performance prediction in young children: Effects of skill, metacognition and wishful thinking. *Developmental Science, 1*, 291–297.

Schoenfeld, A. H. (1987). What's all the fuss about metacognition? In A. H. Schoenfeld (Ed.), *Cognitive Science and Mathematics Education* (pp. 189–215). Hillsdale, N.J.: Lawrence Erlbaum Associates.

Schraw, G. (1998). Promoting general metacognitive awareness. *Instructional Science, 26*, 113–125.

Schraw, G., & Moshman, D. (1995). Metacognitive theories. *Educational Psychological Review, 7*, 351–371.

Schraw, G., Wise, S. L., & Roos, L. L. (2000). Metacognition and computer-based testing. In G. Schraw, & J. C. Impara (Eds.), *Issues in the Measurement of Metacognition* (pp. 222–260). Nebraska: Buros Institute of Mental Measurements.

Schwanenflugel, P. J., Stevens, T. P., Moore, & Carr, M. (1997). Metacognitive knowledge of gifted children and nonidentified children in early elementary school. *Gifted Child Quarterly, 41*(2), 25–35.

Sebba, J., Crick, R. D., Yu, G., Lawson, H., Harlen, W., & Durant, K. (2008, October). *Systematic Review of Research Evidence of the Impact on Students in Secondary Schools of Self and Peer Assessment (Report No. 1614)*. London: EPPI-Centre.

Seligman, M. E. P., & Maier, S. F. (1967). Failure to escape traumatic shock. *Journal of Experimental Psychology: Learning, Memory and Cognition, 74*, 1–9.

Shakespeare, W. (1593–1600). Sonnet 55. In W. H. Auden (1964) (Ed.), *Shakespeare, The Sonnets* (p. 95): Signet Classic.

Shakespeare, W. (1600). *Hamlet, Prince of Denmark*. In W. J. Craig (1974) (Ed.), *Shakespeare: Complete Works* (pp. 870–907). London: Oxford University Press.

Sharples, M. (1999). *How We Write*. London: Routledge.

Shore, B. (1997). Keeping the conversation going: An interview with Jerome Bruner. *Ethos, 25*(1), 7–62.

Smith, J. D., Shields, W. E., & Washburn, D. A. (2003). The comparative psychology of uncertainty monitoring and metacognition. *Behavioral and Brain Sciences, 26*(3), 317–373.

Sonnenschein, S., Baker, L., & Cerro, L. C. (1992). Mothers' views on teaching their preschoolers. *Early Education and Development, 3*, 1–22.

Stanovich, K. (1986). Matthew effects in reading: Some consequences of individual differences in the acquisition of literacy. *Reading Research Quarterly, 21*, 360–407.

Steiner, H. H., & Carr, M. (2003). Cognitive development in gifted children: Toward a more precise understanding of emerging differences in intelligence. *Educational Psychology Review, 15*(3), 215–246.

Sternberg, R. J. (1985). *Beyond IQ: A Triarchic Theory of Human Intelligence*. New York: Cambridge University Press.

Sternberg, R. J. (2004). What is wisdom and how can we develop it? *The Annals of the American Academy of Political and Social Science, 591*, 164–174.

Swanson, H. L. (1990). Influence of metacognitive knowledge and aptitude on problem solving. *Educational Psychology, 82*(2), 306–314.

Theodosiou, A., & Papaioannou, A. (2006). Motivational climate, achievement goals and metacognitive activity in physical education and exercise involvement in out-of-school settings. *Psychology of Sport and Exercise, 7*, 361–379.

Thomas, G. P. (2002). The social mediation of metacognition. In D. McInery, & S. Van Etten (Eds.), *Research on Sociocultural Influences on Motivation and Learning*. (Vol. 2, pp. 225–247). Greenwich, CT: Information Age Publishing.

Thomas, G. P. (2003). *Investigating Variations between Confucian-Heritage Culture and Non-Confucian-Heritage Culture Science Classroom Learning Environments: Initial Findings*. Paper presented at the EARLI conference, Padova, Italy.

Thomas, G. P., & McRobbie, C. J. (2001). Using a metaphor for learning to improve students' metacognition in the chemistry classroom. *Journal of Research in Science Teaching, 38*(2), 222–259.

Thomas, G. P., & Mee, D. A. K. (2005). Changing the learning environment to enhance students' metacognition in Hong Kong primary school classrooms. *Learning Environments Research, 8*, 221–243.

Thorpe, K. J., & Satterly, D. J. H. (1990). The development and inter-relationship of metacognitive components among primary school children. *Educational Psychology, 10*(1), 5–21.

Tiedens, L. Z., & Linton, S. (2001). Judgment under emotional certainty and uncertainty: The effects of specific emotions on information processing. *Journal of Personality and Social Psychology, 81*, 973–988.

Tobin, J. (2004). The disappearance of the body in early childhood education. In L. Bresler (Ed.), *Knowing Bodies, Moving Minds. Towards Embodied Teaching and Learning* (pp. 111–125). Dordrecht: Kluwer Academic Publishers.

Togerson, J., & Houck, G. (1980). Processing deficiencies in learning disabled children who perform poorly on the digit span task. *Journal of Educational Psychology, 72*, 141–160.

Tunmer, W. E., & Bowey, J. A. (1984). Metalinguistic awareness and reading acquisition. In W. E. Tunmer, C. Pratt, & M. L. Herriman (Eds.), *Metalinguistic Awareness in Children* (pp. 144–168). New York: Springer-Verlag.

Van der Zee, T., Hermans, C., & Aarnoutse, C. (2006). Primary school students' metacognitive beliefs about religious education. *Educational Research and Evaluation, 12*(3), 271–293.

Varela, F., & Shear, J. (Eds.) (1999). *The View From Within: First-Person Approaches to the Study of Consciousness*. Lawrence: Allen Press.

Veenman, M. V. J., Prins, F. J., & Elshout, J. J. (2002). Initial inductive learning in a complex computer simulated environment: The role of metacognitive skills and intellectual ability. *Computers in Human Behavior, 18*(3), 327–341.

Veenman, M. V. J., Wilhelm, P., & Beishuizen, J. J. (2004). The relation between intellectual and metacognitive skills from a developmental perspective. *Learning and Instruction, 14*, 89–109.

Velmans, M. (1991). Is human information processing conscious? *Behavioral and Brain Sciences, 14*, 651–726.

Vygotsky, L. S. (1978). *Mind in Society*. Cambridge, MA: Harvard University Press.

Wall, K. (2002). Pupils' communication and perceptions of group work in cognitive intervention activities. In M. Shayer, & P. Adey (Eds.), *Learning Intelligence. Cognitive Acceleration Across the Curriculum from 5 to 15 Years* (pp. 80–97). Buckingham: Open University Press.

Wall, K., Higgins, S., & Smith, H. (2005). "The visual helps me understand the complicated things": Pupil views of teaching and learning with interactive whiteboards. *British Journal of Educational Technology, 36*(5), 851–867.

Watson, J. S., & Wilcox, S. (2000). Reading for understanding: Methods of reflecting on practice. *Reflective Practice, 1*(1), 57–67.

Webb, N. (1991). Task-related verbal instruction and mathematics learning in small groups. *Journal for Research in Mathematics Education, 22*, 366–389.

Wellman, H. M., & Johnson, C. N. (1979). Understanding of mental processes: A developmental study of "remember" and "forget". *Child Development, 50*, 79–88.

Wertsch, J., McNamee, G., McLane, J., & Budwig, N. (1980). The adult-child dyad as a problem solving system. *Child Development, 51*, 1215–1221.

Wertsch, J. V. (1978). Adult-child interaction and the roots of metacognition. *Quarterly Newsletter of the Institute for Comparative Human Development, 2*, 15–18.

White, B., & Frederiksen, J. (2005). A theoretical framework and approach for fostering metacognitive development. *Educational Psychologist, 40*(4), 211–223.

Whitebread, D., Bingham, S., Grau, V., Pasternak, D. P., & Sangster, C. (2007). Development of metacognition and self-regulated learning in young children: The role of collaborative and peer-assisted learning. *Journal of Cognitive Education and Psychology, 3*, 433–455.

Whitebread, D., Coltman, P., Anderson, H., Mehta, S., & Pasternak, D. P. (2005). *Metacognition in Young Children: Evidence from a Naturalistic Study of 3–5 Year Olds.* Paper presented at the EARLI conference, Nicosia, Cyprus, August 2005.

Wimmer, H., & Perner, J. (1983). Beliefs about beliefs: Representation and constraining function of wrong beliefs in young children's understanding of deception. *Cognition, 13*, 103–128.

Wordsworth, W. (1801). To a butterfly. In M. V. Doren (Ed.) (2002) *Selected Poetry of William Wordsworth* (Vol. 22). New York: Modern Library.

Wright, P. (2002). Marketplace metacognition and social intelligence. *Journal of Consumer Research 28*(4), 677–682.

Yaden, D. B., & McGee, L. (1984). Reading as a meaning seeking activity: What children's questions reveal. In J. A. Niles, & L. A. Harris (Eds.), *Changing Perspectives on Research in Reading/Language Processing and Instruction* (pp. 101–109). Rochester, NY: National Reading Conference.

Yussen, S. R. (1985). The role of metacognition in contemporary theories of cognitive development. In D. L. Forrest-Pressley, G. E. MacKinnon, & T. G. Waller (Eds.), *Metacognition, Cognition and Human Performance* (Vol. 1, pp. 253–281). Orlando: Academic Press.

Zimmerman, B. J. (2000). Attaining self-regulation: A social cognitive perspective. In M. Boekaerts, P. Pintrinch, & M. Zeidner (Eds.), *Handbook of Self-Regulation* (pp. 13–39). New York: Academic.

Zimmerman, B. J., & Schunk, D. H. (Eds.) (1989). *Self-Regulated Learning and Academic Achievement.* New York: Springer-Verlag.

Index

Routledge Education and EARLI

New Perspectives
on Learning and Instruction

Series Editor: Mien Segers

New Perspectives on Learning and Instruction is published by Routledge in conjunction with EARLI (European Association for Research on Learning and Instruction). The series publishes cutting edge international research focusing on all aspects of learning and instruction in both traditional and non-traditional educational settings. Titles published within the series take a broad and innovative approach to topical areas of research, are written by leading international researchers and are aimed at a research and post-graduate student audience.

NEW

Transformation of Knowledge Through Classroom Interaction
Baruch Schwarz, Tommy Dreyfus and **Rina Hershkowitz**

Transformation of Knowledge Through Classroom Interaction examines and evaluates different methods of supporting student learning in classrooms.

April 2009: 234x156: 328pp
Hb: 978-0-415-49224-9: **£80.00**
Pb: 978-0-415-49225-6: **£24.99**

NEW

Contemporary Perspectives on Reading and Spelling
Clare Wood and **Vincent Connolly**

With contributions from leading international researchers, *Contemporary Perspectives on Reading and Spelling* offers a critique of current thinking and research on reading, reading comprehension and writing.

July 2009: 234x156: 292pp
Hb: 978-0-415-49716-9: **£80.00**
Pb: 978-0-415-49717-6: **£24.99**

NEW IN 2010:

Use of External Representations in Reasoning and Problem Solving
Lieven Verschaffel, Erik de Corte, Ton de Jong and **Jan Elen**

For more information on the books in this series, please visit:
www.routledge.com/education